A MUSKET FOR THE KING

L S Ives

Thank you for a wonderful programme about the Malaya we knew – all those years ago !

Les Ives

THE TRIALS AND TRIBULATIONS

OF A

NATIONAL SERVICEMAN

1949 TO 1951

(1999) Published By Leslie Ives Books, (0-9536813)

7, Elm Close, Bishopsmead, Tavistock, PL19 9AP

ISBN: 0-9536813-0-0

DEDICATIONS

This book is dedicated to my Father – who served on the Western Front in World War One. He fought in many of the major battles and was awarded The Military Medal for Gallantry. He was wounded and gassed but survived to take part in the British Army of Occupation afterwards. Any small adventures I may have had were minuscule in comparison with his!

Also

John Lancashire

1931 – 1997

The Green Howards

1949/1951

Leslie Ives, although born in London was brought up by kindly grandparents in Sheffield. After their deaths, family friends stepped in and cared for him until his marriage in 1955.

Leaving school at fourteen was commonplace in those days and Leslie joined the staff at a large department store as a trainee.

Here he stayed until 'call-up' for National Service at 18. Leslie chose the army – despite at that time there being the opportunity to choose which service was preferred – i.e Army, Navy or RAF. (Later on, choice became much more difficult.)

Training was as for a European conflict – even the extra period – when it was known that the cadre were destined for Malaya!

The author describes with some humour his time with a famous Yorkshire regiment The Green Howards – during the early days of the Malayan campaign – when the elusive enemy were known as 'Bandits' – rather than what they really were, Communist guerrillas. Six months extra service was added to National Service time during 1950 – which was another hardship – together with the leeches, mosquitoes and an elusive enemy! After many adventures with 'D' Coy. and No 11 Platoon, Leslie returned home to a much changed England in 1951.

It was not the end of a military life however, for three and a half years in the T.A awaited returning N/S men. Leslie spent his with the Hallamshires – where amongst other things he learned to drive a half track. Romance blossomed back at the department store with the girl on the shoe polish counter!

Later, a career in advertising took Les and his family – first to Reading and then to Tavistock in Devon.

Retired now Leslie reads, gardens and fishes with equal enthusiasm – but can never forget those days of hardship, danger and comradeship spent in a far off land with the Green Howards of Yorkshire!

Printed in Great Britain by
Peter Howell & Co.,
The Printing Press,
21 Clare Place,
Coxside,
Plymouth PL4 0JW.
Tel: 01752 250580   Fax: 01752 223855
Email:Peterhowellco@btinternet.com

FOREWORD

In 1973, aged just over forty - I journeyed to Barnard Castle for a business meeting. On the day following I had no more duties other than to make my way homewards to Reading. A chance sighting of a signpost to Richmond caused me to turn off the major road and head for Richmond - the ancestral home of The Green Howards Regiment with whom I had served from 1949 to 1951.

I could remember little of the town having had only a few weeks there at the end of my service. As intended I sought out the Regimental Museum and gazed again at the fortress like barracks. The Museum was open and because I was the only one in there at the time - the curator had some time to spend with me. He unearthed many photographs of my era, including some faces I had known well - even my own. He also brought me up to date on many personalities known to my mates and I from our time in the regiment. We had a really good yarn - and I was sorry to have to go. As I drove away I was seized by a sweeping nostalgia for my lost youth - when in the company of many fine guys I had worn the Green Howards cap badge and found great comradeship in often unpleasant surroundings.

National Service was the University of our youth - Malaya our particular campus. I shall never forget it.

One or two names in this narrative have been changed to avoid possible embarrassment.

Fifty years is a long time for the memory process.
The author apologises for any inaccuracies in
dates or sequence of events.

CHAPTER ONE

It is approaching fifty years ago now since I was called up for National Service - but sometimes it seems like yesterday!

On the nineteenth of May, 1949 - aged eighteen - I relinquished the courtesy title of 'Mr.' - and became No. 22139844, Private Leslie Ives, York & Lancaster Regiment.

This was not an unexpected event as National Service had been in operation since 1947. Short of leaving the country, (not an option in those days unless you were possessed of considerable wealth!) or a coalminer, University student - or in some highly reserved category of employment - you had to go and do your bit for King and Country. Call up followed your 'registration' at your local employment office strangely enough, some six or so months before.

Next came your medical - held in my case at premises in Eccleshall Road, Sheffield - next door to a nationally famous meat paste factory. If you were passed as fit (and you certainly knew before you left the premises what your fate was) you were asked to nominate the service of your choice, i.e. Army Navy or Air Force.

In those early days of National Service you really had a choice! Later I believe the Navy and RAF got the cream - and even later, am I right in thinking you had to sign on for 3 years to get in either of these? Anyway I have this vague memory of an elderly retired major interviewing me after the medical and assuring me what a fine adventurous time I was going to have etc. etc. I chose the Army because of personal preference - most of my family had done their bit in various wars in the Army. Several medical officers examined and probed you pretty thoroughly during your 'medical' - and were I guess well aware of the various dodges used by some to avoid being called up for service.

For instance an acquaintance of mine had heard that large quantities of aspirin tablets, taken for a period before the medical would simulate a possible heart condition! It didn't work entirely as he would have wished as he finished up doing his National Service down the mines as a 'Bevin boy' - not a career move that I would have fancied thank you very much - nor I suspect would most of the blokes I served with.

Colour blindness and flat feet were pretty much the main reasons for failing the medical - although obviously there were people who were completely unfit and were weeded out pretty quickly. I'm not sure whether the family Doctor had to pass on any medical history problems - but it would seem quite likely that he might. Strangely enough the flat feet problem often only showed up when you had actually been inducted - and you then had a very swift demob.

In my case, I was quite surprised to find myself classed medically fit and in the A1 category. For a start I was as thin as a rail (being about 9 stones) and was referred to by my granny as one of Pharaoh's 'lean kind' - this being a Biblical quotation often used in those days. Indeed my nickname at school was 'sparrow' partly because of my skinniness and partly because I was brought up by my grandparents in Sheffield - whose name incidently was Starling!

Years before, strange to relate this perennial thinness secured me a place at an open air school in Sheffield during World War Two. Needless to say it was not my idea. I certainly didn't want to leave all my mates behind and change to a regime of 'open air' education - which might be regarded as a somewhat sissified carry on! The one good thing about the system was that they fed you like fighting cocks! Wartime rationing was a fact of life then, but whatever you might have started off the day with at home (food-wise) you arrived at school courtesy of free transport (tram token) - clad, if wet in an all embracing waterproof garment - and were stuffed full of a not inconsiderable breakfast, then later a mid morning snack followed by a hearty lunch. A compulsory 'nap' followed on your own numbered camp bed and unless I'm mistaken there was cocoa and a bun before leaving! Cod liver oil and other 'tonic' items were administered at prescribed intervals subject to your considered needs.

Sounds ideal doesn't it? But I couldn't wait to get away. Fresh air lessons in classrooms minus one wall in all weathers wasn't too appealing - although come summer it had its moments. However despite our supposed weaknesses, medically speaking there was a high level of bullying going on, and some of the staff were more than handy with canes and some very hard slaps which rather defeated the object in my humble view. Anyway I must have appeared to have benefited from the regime and some accidental damage to one of the ruling Mafia boys got me back to my old school once more. Did I put any extra weight on? Doubtful! Anyway, I digress.

Another reason I was surprised at my A1 medical classification was that I had had surgery at about ten or eleven requiring the removal of a somewhat dodgy appendix. Peritonitis had set in after the operation - and I had been on my back for a whole month and had to learn to walk again. Also at around fifteen or sixteen, a lump was discovered in my lower abdomen - (which turned out to be an undescended testicle). Shock, horror! This had to be removed of course and needless to say was a most embarrassing medical problem. To all visitors to my hospital bed (including some very attractive young ladies from the department store where I worked) I lied to one and all and claimed to have had a hernia operation! In those days the Health Service ran to two weeks convalescence for post operative trauma (?) - and so I had a lovely holiday for two weeks in Bridlington.

From time to time during my service life I had to visit an M.O. (Medical Officer) and if I were new to him these two abdominal scars of mine proved to be something of a talking point and you found you were treated more like a human being!

However, this surgery was felt by my relatives to be a considerable drain on my general medical condition and likely to disallow me from active participation in National Service which I have to say at this point I was quite looking forward to. I personally didn't think my eyesight was all that clever either, although at that time I had no requirement for glasses.

Therefore one and all were surprised at the result of this medical, not least my employer, who having heard my assumptions on the matter felt that he would be retaining my services for the foreseeable future! At this point it might be fair to mention that, in terms of career prospects - National Service was not conducive to job mobility in those days. Employers knew darned well that you were (barring a failed medical) going to be lost to them for 18 months - or two years as it turned out to be from 1950 onwards, thanks to the Korean War. Therefore any career moves you might wish to contemplate were doomed from the start.

It might also be fair to mention that during this period there was no shortage of jobs. Schools told their pupils who were about to leave to avoid 'dead end' jobs with no prospects! I guess you could say there was something of a labour shortage on - so the loss of several workers or staff members from a firm could well be quite a blow to them - particularly if they had been in training for a while. Bear in mind also that many pupils had left school at fourteen - including me! So you might just about be becoming effective as a staff member by 18! You got your full pay in those days when, and usually only when you had reached twenty one.

So, the great day dawned when I joined the York train from Sheffield Midland Station to make my way to No.23 (I think it was) ABTU (Army Basic Training Unit) at Strensall Camp - a few miles out of York. I have since gathered that this camp has been in existence since

3

the days of the Crimea and a goodly amount of the British Army had been trained here at one time or another. For some reason I must have been at the front of the train, and was one of the first off. Coming towards me on the platform at York station was a very smart orderly sergeant, complete with red sash and a large swagger stick. I enquired rather diffidently if he was looking for me? "You and a trainload of other buggers" he replied. Looking round I saw behind me a large number of worried looking young men clutching suitcases hurrying towards this authority figure.

Well versed in this routine he had us sorted out pretty pronto - following our first roll call. Soon we were aboard Bedford 3 tonners and speeding out of the city towards Strensall Camp. We waved excitedly at any passing females - who, having seen it all before were less than enthusiastic about another load of conscripts being delivered to their fair city. As we found out later, York was somewhat saturated with military men - there being other barracks, camps and various establishments scattered around the city.

On arrival we were sorted out eventually into training platoons, allocated a barrack room and began to draw kit. This latter was a bit of a lottery as very few of us knew our sizes - apart from footwear that is. I mean - as anybody knows that's what Mums are for isn't it - and who wore a hat previously? Needless to say the exasperated quartermasters & assistants dished out what they thought would be just about right for us - knowing that there would be a good deal of swopping around for a reasonable fit later. Once back in our barrack rooms - we commenced the onerous task of marking each and every item with our army number. Memory fails me here! Did we each get a stamp? Or - was there something like a large library date stamp that we borrowed in turn? This sounds likely as there was an enormous amount of kit to be stamped and we probably did it in alphabetical order - which is the army way of doing things - and I have to say is not a bad way either.

This frenzied numbering went even as far as boot brushes and 'eating irons' - (knife, fork and spoon.) On these latter items, numbers were embossed like hallmarks. Most of this kit stayed with you until demob - and its owners identity was thus for ever established. Not incidently a completely foolproof way of protecting your gear against determined assaults upon it usually by those who had lost an item of their own.

Blessed were they whose names came early in the alphabet - for their queuing and waiting time was minimal! Pay parade being a particular example. The 'As' could have spent theirs in the NAAFI before the tail enders got a penny! As 'I' is just a modest way into the said alphabet, overall I didn't fare too badly

Needless to say we couldn't wait to see ourselves in uniform and any mirrors available were inundated with very raw recruits posing and hoping they looked like budding Errol Flynn's - (he being at that time at the height of his Hollywood acting fame.). 'Twas not so, obviously and the big test eventually came when we were allowed to 'walk out' and had to get past the eagle eyed scrutiny of the guard commander or Regimental Police NCO who had a more jaundiced idea on how we should look whilst dressed in the Kings uniform. However I'm well ahead of myself here.

The amount of kit issued was staggering. Many items came in two's like battledress uniforms, boots, berets, (khaki and blue) denim overalls, shirts, underclothes. Packs large and small and seemingly unending amounts of webbing straps for connecting the packs together. Would we ever learn where it all fitted - and what about this 'Blanco' stuff we'd heard about? Well we did learn - the hard way - and pretty tout-suite too!

The barrack block my platoon was allocated was fairly modern being like a large bungalow - divided into two halves - with a training platoon in each. Ablutions - the army word for washing and toilet facilities - were centrally placed and used by both platoons. I might add that hot water was definitely not an option! You shaved washed and showered in very cold water. Try it, it's very invigorating.

Most of us had some sort of 'bum-fluff' on our chins - but hadn't started shaving regularly, but by gum! We soon did after close examination of our virgin cheeks on the morning's first parade, with names been taken and 'jankers' (punishment) being dished out for the slightest hint of stubble or whisker! The army likes it's guys to be smooth of cheek and they made quite an issue out of it. Just off the 'ablutions' area was a room set aside for the blancoing of belts gaiters and webbing. I seem to remember it being slate lined, for blancoing is a very messy business!

There would be about 26 bed spaces per barrack room with a reserved area at the end of each room for an NCO. He was there to keep discipline in the barrack and ensure we leaped out of bed sharpish each morning after reveille. Likewise quiet etc. after the last post bugle call for lights out - signalling the end of the day. This frequently came all too soon as you might be frantically 'bulling' your boots, or, trying desperately to get a sharp crease into your reluctant new garments. Quietly you carried on as long as possible - your immediate future welfare might depend on it.

Your barrack room was home for about ten weeks. At the end of this you knew it pretty intimately as you had scrubbed, polished, buffed and cleaned it - every inch of it over and over again. Germs do not thrive in army barracks! An iron stove stood centrally on a cement plinth. This was designed to provide any heating that might be required - but mostly its innards were painted white to give a good impression (and brownie points) during the all too frequent room inspections. Beds were pretty basic iron frames. The mattress was three 'biscuits' of a very hard material plus three blankets a pillow, and two sheets.

These items and the biscuits had to be laid out in a particular order each morning, with an almost mathematical precision with the folded sheets sandwiched between the blankets and the pillow I think on top, all enclosed in another blanket folded and tightly wrapped around. Heaven help you if it didn't come up to scratch display and precision-wise, the whole lot would be tipped up and you had to start again with the vital seconds ticking away before room inspection.

As if this wasn't all - outside, at the side of your block was a small grassed area. This needed cutting from time to time and it is surprising the cut you can get - using lots of guys and a few pairs of scissors. Anything to get extra brownie points over a rival platoon! I seem to recall some sort of ongoing competition between platoons - with a league table published regularly. Was there a challenge shield - or similar? Needless to say your platoon sergeant was a happy sergeant if his lads were doing well in the points area. So, after a day or two you became familiar with your new great clunking ammunition boots, a strange tightness around your head due to your beret's snug fit and an equally tight waist embrace due to a webbing belt.

CHAPTER TWO

If our leaders were concerned about the hair on our chins they were besotted with the hair on our heads! We were sheared at frequent intervals to a sort of uniform scalping. Two languid individuals ran the camp barbers shop. They must have made a fortune as obviously they were never short of work. They gossiped to each other, and discussed their social and private lives - whilst hacking great chunks off our already denuded locks.

The scenario on parade might go something like this. NCO facing private with perhaps a hint of a sideburn. "Do you think you are in the Spanish 'effing' army you horrible little man or from behind this time, to one whose hair was a millimetre or two longer than the standard. "Am I hurting you private X?" "No Sergeant" - "then I should be 'cos I'm standing on your back hair." Names would then be taken and checks would be made later to see these haircutting directives had been carried out. Boy if they didn't like you, you saw a great deal of the barbers shop - in your own time too!

Recently I was on holiday in Fuerteventura. There was a Spanish Army training camp there and soldiers abounded. Needless to say these troops had very, very short hair. Had one known this in those pre - package holiday days - it would have been unwise to have made a comment. The company office and summary justice awaited those whose lip became unbuttoned in a rash moment. In primary training the NCO is a God. An officer is a demigod and as for the C.O - he walked the earth in the company of the Saints!

Our own platoon sergeant, Sgt. Reeves, was a grizzled wartime veteran. He was short in stature, brusque on parade but I think had a kind heart behind the facade. The only time I ever saw him lose his temper was when, fairly advanced in drill, we were marching purposefully around the barrack square under his command. (Strutting our stuff you might say.) Suddenly the Regimental band, no doubt practising for the next passing out parade, struck up a brisk military march. This caught us in mid stride and our precision went all to pieces. He cursed us up hill and down dale as we attempted to change step and march in unison to the band. Not a pretty sight! The air was blue and we may have learned some interesting expletives - and a few extra fatigues!

Our full corporal (two stripes) was in a similar ex-wartime mode, and was fairly patient with us. However the lance corporal (one stripe) was a totally different animal! He breathed fire and smoke. His religion was regimentalism and there were no shades of grey as far as he was concerned. After training - and out with your battalion, a lance corporal's whims were not taken too seriously - but in basic training he was a very superior being. Cross him at your peril and life could become very difficult.

In training life is troublesome enough - with so much to try and absorb - personal appearance - mounds of kit to watch over and keep in pristine condition, trying to get on with your fellow squaddies and a million other worries. Getting the wrong side of an NCO was not conducive to happy soldiering!

I have read somewhere that whatever your background or profession might have been, a slice of army basic training shuts out everything else. Your milieu has been changed completely and nothing of your past life has any importance compared to your current existence. Your main aim is to survive this period, which for the foreseeable future has to be endured. There are lighter moments of course. Each platoon produces its own comedian who, even in moments of dire stress, can produce a highly topical quip that lifts everyone's morale. Such a guy was our Pte. England. A rough diamond he with a penchant for opening crown cork bottles with his teeth. Current songs would be murdered by his voice - but his comments and wit were irrepressible.

Even at this early stage you begin to understand why the British Army had won so many of their battles over the centuries! It is not - "the voice of a schoolboy that rallies the ranks" - it's more likely a totally irreverent quip from a natural born humorist.

Much is made of by the press these days about the bullying that goes on in the barrack room - with ethnic minorities perhaps suffering the worst. Nothing has changed. Any foible you might have had that could raise a laugh was exploited. God help you if you had an odd name or mannerism - or if you had any sort of physical abnormality - you suffered but survived and often became a character because of your tolerance to such ribbing. From time to time when tempers became really frayed and violence ensued, the powers-that-be had you appear in the gym boxing ring with your antagonist - where you fought with the gloves on for three supervised rounds or a capitulation. These contests usually ended in new friendships being formed.

You soon realised too what your big, new, (very stiff) ammunition boots were for. Marching! Everywhere you went as a platoon you marched. You marched to the cookhouse. You marched to physical training - pay parade, lectures - the assault course - just about everywhere you went as a group, you marched. Sometime for a change you doubled! This marching soon became second nature and after a while a cohesion developed and dare I say it? You almost began to enjoy it.

You marched to the medical centre for your inoculations of which there were many. Strong men quailed. Some fainted but strangely enough this was not a cause for ribbing! We were pleased to have it over and done with. Next day we were in considerable discomfort - most of us - with swollen painful bruised arms. However the show needed to go on, arms were swung - and salutes punctiliously delivered as ever, etc. etc.

However I seem to be getting ahead of myself. The first night in a barrack room - with a load of complete strangers is an ordeal for most people. For a start you strip off to get into bed (pyjamas not an option.) Previously only your mother had seen you in this state! You slept usually in your shirt or your underclothes. I think the odd dressing gown made a brief appearance - but definitely not for long. Lights out revealed that one of our number was extremely well endowed in a certain area! He had a tough life for a while at bed time as ribald comments and crude jokes flew about - as well as requests for viewings of this quite exceptional anatomical specimen!

You do not sleep too well during this first night. There is much snoring from those who are sleeping. Groans, occasional sobs from those already homesick, and the general night noises from twenty six blokes keep you wide awake - but eventually you succumb, to be blasted awake, seemingly just a few minutes later by a strident bugle call (which appears to be from just outside your billet window.) The strains of this devil music has just died down when storming into your room comes an equally strident NCO who orders you out of bed with immediate effect, uttering a mixture of oaths, threats and witticisms! Such as - 'hands off cocks, get into your socks' and 'wakey wakey - the sun's hot enough to scorch your eyeballs!' You stagger from your bed, and hasten to the ablutions area in an effort to find a vacant wash basin. Here you then wallow in the luxury of a cold water wash and shave. You scrape your tender cheeks - cursing the inevitable cuts and rush back to don the dress of the hour - as declared in company orders.

I say dress of the hour because during any given day during basic training you might change your attire (and sometimes equipment) several times. It is vital to read, learn and inwardly digest company orders. By this typed piece of paper pinned to the notice board, is your daily life regulated and controlled. You know exactly where you will be and what you will be wearing at any given hour on the morrow. I believe it was a chargeable offence not to have consulted this daily orders sheet!

The change over from one dress to another (say from P.T kit to second best battledress for drill) had to be done at the double. Only a few minutes were allowed for the change over and you learned to get outside pretty smartish because the last man out had a special chore to do - usually to polish the fire bucket. This gleaming receptacle had never seen a fire in its life, but remained pristine and glistening and appeared to have been chrome plated! Needless to say the speediness of change-over from dress to dress - and from subject to subject was part of the 'obeying orders promptly syndrome'. In the training curriculum it probably held an important place in the transformation of civilians to soldiers.

It very soon emerged that a great deal of time (your time) was going to be spent in the care, polishing, pressing and 'preening' the kit that the kind government had seen fit to entrust to you! Boots came very high on the list. Both pairs issued were soon expected to be miracles of gleaming leather. However your best pair were to be in a class of their own with toe caps and the rear portions gleaming like patent leather. This was achieved after hours and hours of work. First you anointed the areas concerned with liberal quantities of boot polish. You then set fire to these parts and after the flames died down you attacked the leather with a piece of bone - or a toothbrush handle very vigorously - which resulted in the heavy grain of the leather being smoothed out - allowing you then to sit, and with much spit and polish produce the desired effect. The process I believe is not unlike the french polishing of furniture. You endeavour to protect your 'best' boots from being scratched or damaged in any way - just like grandma might protect her treasured piano! Hours of re-working would be involved in the repair if heavy scratching or scraping occurred.

These boots are almost a passport to happiness - if your sergeant or even sergeant major thinks you have put a lot of effort into them they may overlook some of your other shortcomings. So you sit with your new found comrades (not unlike a sewing circle) and it is in these moments you find kindred spirits and likely as not your long time mates are discovered as you yarn about the events of the day - like how sergeant 'X' gripped private 'Y' etc. etc. Male bonding I suppose the psychologists would call it these days. In our barrack room we had quite a few old soldiers (of which more later.) They were always ready with advice on how to make your kit 'inspection worthy' and the quickest way to achieve maximum results.

Singsongs would develop as someone perhaps sang a few bars or hummed a tune from a hit of the day. Al Jolson songs were the ones we mainly all joined in. The hit film starring Larry Parks as Jolson had swept the country and his famous songs had a new life with the young people of the time. Doris Day was extremely popular but the main hit song of that time was "Nickel Odeon" by Teresa Brewer. The old hands were keen on some revised songs from really way back. There were several of these but the one that springs instantly to mind (and takes me back all those years when I hear it) is something called "Abdul the Bull-bull Emir." Strangely enough these songs (and Abdul) were featured in some television advertising in the late eighties or early nineties - promoting beer I think!

My emerging mates at this time were Richard Smith and 'Buffalo' Lingard - we did everything together - and went everywhere together. We shared our meagre spending money, and when (rarely) one was flush, we all celebrated at the NAAFI. Needless to say there are many many Smiths and also Browns in the army - each platoon may have two or three Smiths and Browns. To avoid mix-ups, common names like these were referred to by surname - suffixed by their last two army numbers.

'My' Richard Smith was Smith '69. I think our other Smith was Smith '11. About this time a group of us had pooled together to buy an electric iron. Use of an iron was essential to keep our two battledress uniforms in well pressed order. Of my two, one had straight pleats at the back - the other had had curving pleats - three each side as I recall. All had to be carefully pressed. Brown paper saved you from scorching from time to time - and half crowns or two bob pieces when rubbed face down across scorch marks, generally did remove them. Again advice from the old sweats. Damage to uniforms was greatly feared since young Smailes was put on a charge for defacing the Kings uniform. Proud owner he, of one of the new fangled Biro pens, had suffered a leak and an irremovable stain of ink had defaced a pocket on his best battledress blouse. I cannot remember the punishment handed out, but it certainly scared the living daylights out of the rest of us! Plus his having to buy a new tunic at a then seemingly enormous cost. You can see why we lived in a somewhat high degree of tension during our training period!

Whilst on the subject of kit - I mentioned blanco and the blanco room earlier. For the uninitiated blanco is a sort of coloured emulsion type of paste which is spread evenly over all your webbing equipment. Your belt, gaiters and rifle sling were the daily items done, but small pack, side pouches and even large packs were anointed at frequent intervals. Each regiment had its own blanco colour which might change at any time on the C.O's whim. The process was a messy one, and needed to be repeated on a daily basis - as it was pretty obvious whether you had blancoed or not. The process also needed several hours drying time! You will have gathered from all this that our spare time after a hectic day, would be eaten away by this constant and never ending 'bull'. The climax of which was of course the weekly kit inspection by your platoon commander (2nd. Lieut.) with an entourage of NCOs clasping notebooks eager to note down the names of transgressors. Every item of your kit was put on display in a precise order - being laid out on your bed. Other items not able to be laid out were in your locker - which also was inspected keenly - and again was laid out in a set pattern. You waited tensely as the entourage slowly progressed towards you - noting the comments made to each ramrod straight recruit. You were not to gaze directly into the eyes of your officer - instead you were to fix your gaze at a spot just above his head. You dare not speak until addressed by this demigod - who might if displeased, have your whole kit tipped on the floor with injunction to do a lot better next time - or else!

I have not mentioned your rifle yet! This obvious *raison d'etre* for your entire existence was a holy piece of work. A dirty rifle got you into more trouble probably than anything else. I think it came into the provenance of the kit inspection sometimes - but more often than not it was inspected like a microscopic specimen on at least one parade of the day. By the way 'parade' was army-speak for doing virtually anything outside the barrack room connected with a body of men - small or large. So, when your rifle was being examined by way of a special drill movement - the bolt was drawn back and your thumbnail inserted at the bottom of the barrel. This reflected light up the barrel enabling the rifling to be scrutinised. The rest of the weapon was then checked over minutely whilst you prayed that last nights cleaning process had been thorough!

CHAPTER THREE

Having mentioned weaponry, it's perhaps appropriate to mention the stuff we handled was straight out of WW2! Having said that - my father and uncles - who fought in WW1! - would have been quite familiar with the Lee-Enfield rifle and the Mills bomb, (or no.36 hand grenade.) The 2 inch mortar would have been new to them also the Bren gun - although there was the Stokes mortar later in WW1 - also the Lewis light machine gun - operated in similar circumstances as our Bren gun, and being a highly accurate, highly mobile platoon weapon. What they would not have known was the PIAT (or, projectile infantry anti-tank) - which had been developed in WW2 to give the infantry something to defend themselves with against tanks. More on this later.

The first firing of our Lee-Enfields took place very shortly after induction. Just off-camp was a small range for this purpose, and where the targets were approx. 30 yards away. As we marched towards this range, firing parties were already at work. We were amazed at the loud crack as each shot was fired and also how far back the shoulder of the person firing was jolted! However, on getting down to it - you do not particularly hear the shot you are firing particularly clearly - nor is the recoil as fearsome as you might imagine. You are concentrating on your aim and the target - and like many things it looks worse than it is! Following this first firing you are introduced to the 'boiling-out' procedure. When a weapon is fired the barrel becomes hot and absorbs some of the explosive gases from the cartridges. These have to be flushed out of the rifling with boiling water so that the barrel does not become pitted and useless over time - which is what would happen without the boiling out procedure. What, you may ask do you do on active service, where it is unlikely you would find the special vats and equipment all lined up ready for you after an action? Well what you do is suck a piece of 4"x2" cleaning felt - and as soon as possible after firing pull it through your barrel to remove the worst of the pollutant. That's the theory anyway.

Back to real life. The procedure for boiling requires you to pour boiling water down your rifle barrel by means of a funnel - in sufficient quantities and temperature to remove all pollutants. It's then back to the barrack room for some concentrated further drying, cleaning, pulling through and oiling ready for inspection. A pullthrough cord and small oil container are kept in a special orifice accessed through a cover in the butt plate of your rifle. Same goes for the Bren gun. However this weapon is complicated by the working parts which are known by various groups, i.e. butt group, barrel group, piston group etc. After a heavy day on the range the amount of pitting and polluting from the explosive gases calls for a great deal of cleaning. It is usual to have several people involved in the cleaning of each gun. A hell of a lot of elbow grease is required to get the Bren to inspection standard. When we were first involved in such work, we had our first real close encounter with our platoon officer. He was hypercritical and we loathed his appearances after Bren firing.

After a while he began to mellow a bit when he saw we were putting our backs into it - and on one unbelievable day started to joke and talk with us. He was, it appeared, trying to live on his pay - which in those days was very difficult for an under resourced officer, mess bills and all that! He told us of how he had gone to a very posh reception locally - and not having a car, had borrowed the company bike and had to hide it in the shrubbery! The baronial door was apparently opened by a butler of tremendous presence. So much so that our officer had nearly saluted him!

We quite began to warm to this bloke and as our training continued began to see that there was another sort of leadership, brought about by mutual respect - and other than screaming and shouting and constant threats. I have sadly forgotten this young officers name, but he was with the Duke of Wellington's Regiment - they being the holding regiment of the Strensall camp. We were saddened to hear later that he had been killed in Korea, where The Duke of Wellington's distinguished themselves apparently. He was the one officer we got to know in training - others are now faceless - but all without doubt in those days came from similar, upper class, well educated backgrounds. My mates and I had about as much chance of becoming officers as becoming King. In the eighties and nineties I guess it all changed. Social background didn't matter so much - ability and education is the thing that counts. Many young sergeants of my day would have made the grade to officer without difficulty were now - then!

There are so many ranks in the British army. The reason is obvious. In war in serious battles, sometimes all officers are killed or become casualties. The NCOs then take over - right down to your humble lance-jack. If he bites the dust the senior private takes over! So, beware the film or T.V play folks, where the highly personable star (who happens to be a private) is called upon to lead the lads to glorious victory. He might just, if all other commanders were deceased!

This brings me to the oath of allegiance. Somewhere along the line we must have sworn allegiance to His Majesty, King George the Sixth, his heirs and successors! For the life of me I cannot remember where or when we did this! We didn't mind swearing allegiance to The King - he seemed a decent enough cove - it was some of those 'placed in authority over us' we were not too keen on! Particularly the PTI's (physical training instructors) - we loathed them to a man! In fairness I guess they had a difficult job - turning a host of unfit young men into useful physical specimens - able to take up the challenges of maintaining an empire, large chunks of which still existed in 1949!

The PTI's were all superbly fit and looked with disdain on our poor physical condition - which they set about righting forthwith. If you look back to your schooldays chums - you will recall that nobody really liked PT very much did they? I'm constantly amazed these days that people will pay extravagant fees to join and 'pump' iron in health clubs. Our PTI's seemed to exist in a special world, where their word was law. Who their leaders were and who assessed their success rate we knew not! All we knew was that for 45 minutes or so each day (usually in a morning) they harried and verbally abused us and were saved from physical violence by one or two NCO's stripes on their muscular arms. Woe betide any man not putting his back into his exercises or letting slip a caustic comment on PTI's in general. Huge numbers of press ups were awarded to nonconformists! Doubling around the PT area till your legs felt like jelly was a favourite punishment, keeping your arms up an added refinement. Doubling around the camp water tower - about a mile distant in the early morning mist was another favourite that could knacker you for the rest of the day!

It was a wise soldier who appeared to be giving his all at these sessions. When wet of course PT took place in the camp gym. You are divided into sections, your instructor screams like a banshee! Touch four walls and back in front of my striped jersey in 20 seconds - now wait for it, move! (Last man does 20 press-ups!) There would be much whistle blowing too, nobody really knowing who or what was being whistled at or what for. When in the gym we did work on the vaulting horse, parallel bars climbing ropes etc. So like I say we hated these guys. If you were sluggish or unresponsive they had a huge range of professional insults which could make you feel deeply embarrassed. Your parentage and sexual prowess were frequently called into question.

One glorious day (for us) was when, after a five mile run to an outer suburb of York, we were in a state of collapse by the roadside, and Cpl. loathsome was giving one of our number a tongue lashing in the usual mode. He was in full flight and facing us, was not aware of a delicious damsel - tripping daintily along behind him to the nearby bus stop. Pausing for full effect, and still unaware of the passing girl - he said "and as for Private Bloggs - he hasn't reached the wanking stage yet!" Exit blushing female - who we prayed might be an officers daughter (preferably the C.O's!) Hasty exit too for PTI and us - he was remarkably quiet on the run back!

Another of the hated ones was 'stroked' on the head with a Sten gun magazine one dark night due to a 'romantic' situation and rendered U.S for a bit, and later, when out east, we heard that yet another had been up before the C.O for some serious reason or other. Not a situation for the squeamish. The result was not known, but we remained broadly unsympathetic!. It has to be said in all honesty though - that these tender ministrations from the fitness boys probably helped us survive some pretty awful terrain in our future posting.

It might be felt that there was a chip on our shoulders regarding leadership. Later in our service we saw leadership of the very highest order - but perhaps in training it was not considered important? Most of our NCOs were wartime veterans - with many medal ribbons to prove it. Brave they may have been - but many were just not cut out for training young recruits and were reliant upon bully boy tactics and fear to keep people in line. Broadly speaking, many NCOs of that time were not overly intelligent - but the winds of change were beginning to blow even then, as, coming in were the new educational requirements for NCOs - who had to achieve certificated ratings to move up through the ranks.

Various 'rackets' were perpetrated by some. One involved selling small padlocks to new entrants to secure their lockers. (We were all advised to obtain these.) At the end of the ten weeks, this particular NCO begged them back from his squad who were moving on - to sell on to the next intake. We heard that he had been busted (reduced to the ranks) for this but after a short period reinstated. It has to be said of course that pay in those days was pretty abysmal. We, as new privates got around a pound a week. A full corporal would be on about three and a sergeant perhaps about four pounds ten shillings. (£4.50) per week. Many NCOs had wives and families to support on this - although married quarters were provided.

A mysterious deduction to our pay called ostensibly 'barrack room damages' was levied each week. This amounted to around a shilling and threepence (I think) - but certainly a significant percentage of what we earned - when you think back to what a few pence would buy for that amount.

Nobody knew exactly what happened to this money - it went to a mysterious thing called the PRI - which we labelled 'the privates' robbery institution'. Despite the comparatively cheap cost of living in those days - (best bitter beer about six old pence a pint) we had difficulty in making ends meet. Once our reserves of cash from our former lives had gone we had a problem. Some perhaps had an allowance from home. However most of us were from homes where budgets were pretty strained anyway - so nothing from that source!

When we were allowed weekend leave home - York/Sheffield - for me, the train fare was around ten shillings (50p) return. This left not a lot if you saved a bit through the Post Office, or as some lads did - sent money home to help Mums in strained circumstances. If you smoked and drank then - well your burden was increased. I didn't smoke or drink at that time - although I have to admit making up for it later! We rushed off home whenever possible - longing to get our teeth into some good home cooking! Financially your weekend could wipe you out. My then girlfriend - Lorna had a family who were kindness itself - but they loved to play Newmarket (a card game) on Sunday afternoon. The stakes were very small - but a bad run could deplete the already depleted - and you could be without NAAFI money for the rest of the week. Calamity! So it would be borrowing time and hopefully time for calling in a few favours.

Now - nobody reading this would believe that most wartime rationing was still in existence in 1949. Sweets were still on your ration book points system and cigarettes were in very short supply - and the best brands still under the counter. You got your fags from your regular supplier - anywhere else didn't stand much of a chance of picking any up casually. Now one advantage in the army was that your ration book had been handed in on your induction. Therefore you could get fags and sweets 'off the ration' in the Naafi. I was still friendly with a blonde lassie from my old youth club back in Sheffield, and because I didn't smoke I would take a few packs home to pass on to her (Marjorie's) dad. This also put my finances in a parlous state till I got my money back! I would also have to contend with 'broke' smokers who came to borrow a pack till payday! Can't quite remember the price of cigarettes - not a lot - probably two bob for twenty (20p.)

This brings me to another big problem we had in those days - we were always ravenously hungry. Army food was substantial (albeit uniformly awful) but it did not assuage our constant appetites. The

NAAFI was our lifeline in some respects but didn't always fill the gap. The transition to an active outdoor life with constant exercise was the culprit - and transformed us into ravening wolves. A word about army food here. The portions were adequate but the food badly cooked and served. Now I had been brought up - first by my grandparents, and gran was a lovely (if plain) Yorkshire cook. Upon granny's death I was 'adopted' by my Aunty and Uncle Jones. Aunty, who too was a superb producer of food - also, managing somehow to do this on a very tight budget. Therefore having been very well catered for, my first army meal came as something of a shock. No choices in those days - you took it or left it! You queued at a self-servery and the guys behind dumped your meat and two veg. on top of each other plus a flood of gravy at the end. I was appalled - it looked awful! The sweet looked like a inedible island in a sea of very, very yellow lumpy custard. I gazed at this and took a few unbelieving mouthfuls - not wishing to proceed much further. My neighbour - who told me he'd been 'in' for a few weeks enquired if I was going to eat any more. On being told no, he wolfed down my meal like a ravenous wolf, saying that I too would feel this way very soon! He was right. After a few days of frenzied activity we would all have eaten a horse given the chance! As time went on we recognised that the food wasn't too bad really - just mangled in the cooking process a little. There were never any seconds alas! Modern servicemen it would appear have 'proper' menus and multiple choice dishes, they should be so lucky.

As previously mentioned in training you march down to the dining hall - your eating irons and pint mug tucked in the small of the back. You halted and queued in an orderly fashion before passing through the servery where a few insults would be traded by the braver 'old soldiers' amongst us. Although issued with mess tins I believe we had plates in the dining halls. Any unfortunate who dropped his pot mug (which would reverberate around the dining hall like a cannon shot) would be cheered to the echo by two or three hundred voices. After your meal you would find at the outside rear of the hall three huge cauldrons of steaming water. They would be marked in order as 'wash, rinse and sterilise' So you washed rinsed and sterilised your plates or mess tins. At the end of a busy meal session there wasn't much to choose in clarity between any of the water containers! During our training days a cartoon appeared in *The Soldier Magazine* it depicted a senior officers function where guests emerging from their formal dinner were also asked to 'wash, rinse and sterilise' - some hopes!

On cookhouse fatigues from time to time we peeled mountains of spuds and carrots etc. We always assumed the meals would taste better after our efforts - alas! They never did. During one period on fatigue duty I was cleaning what I think was a potato 'rumbler'. Why we had to peel spuds when they had equipment like this I don't know. Inside the drum I found a neatly wrapped chunk of what Yorkshire people call 'best butter' weighing about a pound. What should I do? To report it might bring suspicion on myself or another member of the fatigue squad - as it had obviously been purloined. I questioned the lads - no, none of them. Take it home tomorrow they said, as the weekend was almost upon us. So I did and Aunty was very grateful - butter being still a highly rationed commodity. Later on, when with your battalion - food was much better prepared and cooked. The difference being that the cooks knew the blokes they were cooking for - an excellent arrangement. When we were in the final stages of our extended training period, we were if possible even hungrier. One night we put into practice our 'stealth and infiltration' techniques and infiltrated the cookhouse store, relieving it of some bread loaves which we consumed dry as they were, with great gusto!

CHAPTER FOUR

Our training continued apace. We were getting the hang of things more after a couple of weeks or so. No longer did we have to shout "one, two three - one," between each drill movement (this helps to generate a uniform timing throughout the squad.) We were beginning to look more like soldiers too I guess. Our berets had been shrunken to the desired size, again with assistance of the old sweats. We had made, borrowed or acquired the necklace type weights which lay in your trouser leg bottoms giving them a more professional 'hang' - relative to your boots and gaiters. I don't know if they were officially approved - but they did look a great deal better! Otherwise your new stiff trousers would not hang correctly in the desired area.

Our daily routine would probably include PT, two lots of drill - sometimes with and sometimes without rifles. Weapon training, field craft and map reading. Also lectures, training films, short route marches, and maybe a whizz round part of the assault course. You were on the go from 6.0 am until about 4.30 pm - with NAAFI canteen tea breaks, when on the camp site. Off camp it would be more likely just smoking breaks - and haversack rations, so called for your midday meal. I hesitate to call this a 'lunch' break as many northern people class it as dinner. Out east it is known as 'tiffin' - and to the old soldiers, the main meals of the day are known as 'connor' but for what reason I never found out. Dishing up time was known as 'connor-up'. I don't think it was from the Hindustani - or other languages that the old sweats used to quote words and phrases from. These frequently came part of our vocabulary too, words like 'jildi' - get a move on, and 'alakeefic' - to mean you couldn't care less. Also 'bondook' meaning your rifle.

On long days at the ranges haversack rations were again provided (huge doorstep sandwiches) - usually filled with cheese or corned beef. If sufficient numbers of men were involved then you might see a Church Army or Salvation Army tea waggon, which also provided buns and other succulent pastries for those with a few coppers to spare. Incidently, thinking again of food the NAAFI canteen on the camp was our lifeline for extra food when we could afford it. Light meals were served - also buns, cakes and other fancies. Tea, coffee and soft drinks were available plus light beers I think. Important things like razor blades, brasso and blanco could be had there too. What wasn't on offer were the NAAFI girls. The pretty ones particularly. All were probably propositioned dozens of times per night - if not more! Mainly they were spoken for already by regular squaddies on the camp - or boy friends where they lived. Still it must have been interesting for them to know that they were being lusted after by literally hundreds of young men daily!

Having said all that, it is true that we didn't have a great deal of time in our early training days for lustful thoughts. We were so knackered at the end of the day - plus all we had to do in the evenings - that we just didn't have time for them. Needless to say when we got the hang of things better we soon got back to normal! Rumour had it of course that our tea was laced with bromide to concentrate our minds on training. Was our tea so laced? We never knew and officially no-one was saying!

To conclude this brief description of the NAAFI - it was also a haven from bossy NCOs - they had separate rooms in the building. Sergeants of course had their refreshment facilities in their own mess. Officers were never seen in the NAAFI - they would have been as uncomfortable there as we would have been in the officers mess!

However back to training - much weapon training could take place without actually firing. For the all important 'sighting' of your weapon, be it rifle or Bren gun, your instructors had various quite simple implements to check on your sighting accuracy. If you didn't get it right first time - you tried, tried and tried again till you did get it right. This exercise was called 'dry firing'. With the Bren gun there were other special activities involved. As this light machine gun was the mainstay of our armament at that time, it was important that we knew it intimately. A series of 'I.As' (immediate actions) came into play if the gun stopped firing. Any one who has ever done these exercises will never forget them! In battle they would be vital to you and your platoon's survival. A Bren gun team has two members - a No.1 and a No.2 - with No.1 doing the actual firing.

So important were these I.As considered to be - that we quite enthusiastically carried on doing them in our spare time in the barrack room. Forever trying to better our timings for the various drills. Needless to say the guns we used in the barrack area were D.P (drill purposes only.) The intimate 'innards' of this gun were the subject of many lectures. The trigger group area was quite complicated - and you were supposed to be able to sort out problems if ever they arose like a part breaking. During one lecture my concentration had gone completely when the instructor hurled a question at me. "Explain, Ives - what does the part known as the 'sear' do within the trigger group?" Caught completely by surprise, and probably mentally bearing down on the luscious Betty

Grable (film star) at the time, I grasped at straws and hastily replied "it bears down, Sarn't." As this was near enough to the correct answer I just about got away with it, that time.

In map reading I just about got the hang of it and quite understood the build up of a hill or mountain by the contour lines. I could never work out what 'colls and re-entrants' were - despite seeing them in training films etc.

These films were in black and white and were pretty boring with the most drab funereal music as a background. It was hard to stay awake through them - particularly if you had been outside during most of the day. These films had been made during the war and badly needed updating. Later we saw some American training films. These were made in colour and had a better approach. Mind you they did have the Hollywood film industry to help them! For instance when they talked about how easily spotted even one mans footmarks in a field were from the air the camera went up in a plane - and you saw exactly what they meant!

Actually it is quite incredible - how just one man's tracks in a grassy field show up like they were in neon! Also who could ever forget the vital four 'S's we learned - shape, shine, silhouette and shadow! Etc.

Another practical demonstration of most peoples night sight capabilities was seen in a pitch black room. A model small town was laid out and gradually as our eyes adjusted to the darkness we could clearly make out the detailed layout and other features of the model. Later, on night exercises we were amazed how our eyes quickly adjusted to the dark. Buildings, groups of trees, rivers and bridges are clearly visible when you eyes get adjusted - provided there is no mist or fog.

I am not sure when exactly we were allowed to 'walk out' of the camp for the first time in the evenings. Probably after two or three weeks. Similarly with weekend passes for home. As previously stated - you had to get past some pretty sharp eyed scrutiny on the gate before you were let out into the real world, a world you had almost forgotten. Those who had done particularly well at drill or weapon training - (or all round achievement) were awarded different coloured bands of cloth which slid around the epaulettes of your battledress blouse. These marks of distinction were definitely something to brag about when you got home! Secretly we all hoped to get one or more of these marks of glory - but I for one never did!

I was in a great panic when our very first weekend pass was coming up. I had somehow contrived to break a lavatory brush (or some such article) whilst on rota cleaning duty in the ablutions area. Such was our combined terror at breaking anything belonging to H.M Government that I was convinced that my leave would be up the shute. I cannot think what the outcome of this high treason was - probably I had to buy another one out of my shrinking pay! However I did get home on leave - phew! Incidentally for evenings out and leave you were allowed to wear shoes (preferably brown.) Also, because your best battledress blouse had open facings you were permitted to wear a collar and tie. Not long before my service you wore the tunic fastened all the way to the top! You still wore your freshly blancoed belt with brasses highly polished of course.

Your standard of dress dare not slip when strolling around York (our nearest town) as large numbers of Redcaps (military police) were deployed to see you behaved in a soldierly manner and dressed correctly at all times. Caught without your beret on - or hands in your pockets meant being on a charge when you got back.

Back in those days, such were the number of servicemen of all kinds abounding, that most largish towns would have a contingent of military police garrisoned there, so, particularly in town centres you had to watch your step and general turnout.

Your first weekend home is wonderful. Lovely home cooking admiring glances (you hope) from your girl friends, and freedom from that blasted bugle that runs your life from dawn to dusk! It did too. Bugle calls covered every eventuality from cookhouse to 'charge the enemy'. We began to know them all particularly the mail call. Letters from home - even though 'twas not too far away then, were manna from heaven. Telephones were available but hardly used for the simple reason that only the well off possessed a receiver. You would have to have arranged a particular time to call when your mum (say) would be at a friends, or at a shop who might have one. I don't know how you personally might have received a call. Probably at the Company office - if it were meaningful enough?

It was important for your ego and standing with your mates to have frequent letters from your girlfriends - the more perfumed the better. They should also be heavily embossed with the initials of affection on the flap. SWALK, BOLTP and other more intimate ones were the order of the day. My two lasses used to write to me regularly plus some of the delightful females where I had worked so I was frequently in receipt of the right kind of mail.

'Dear John' letters were sometimes received too - these led to   great depression till the recipient found another object of affection. It would be interesting to know the statistics of the survival of romances in progress during National Service. Mine certainly didn't. If one went overseas for a long period, both you and she had changed considerably in attitude when you got back! Letters were the very life blood of morale when you were overseas. Needless to say, regular mail with news from home was desperately important. Meanwhile we were beginning to think of ourselves as soldiers. What 'civvy' things we had brought with us had long since been sent home. In those days we were definitely not encouraged to wear civilian clothes at any time. Officers wore 'mufti' around the camp when off-duty, but you had to salute them just the same. Even if you did not recognise the person it was quite obvious after a while who was an officer - something in the style or bearing I suppose. So, even on home leave wearing your 'civvies' wasn't the done thing - and anyway we fancied ourselves a bit in our uniforms - wearing the regimental badges that our fathers, brothers and uncles had proudly worn throughout various conflicts as I have already said. Lets be honest also - we hoped the uniform would help us make a greater hit with the feminine fraternity, wherever we happened to be.

Talking of badges - we had a motley selection in our barrack room. Because it was a basic training camp many famous regiments were represented - corresponding to our home locality. There were Yorks and Lancs. (like me.) East and West Yorkshires, Northumberland Fusiliers - Green Howards, Duke of Wellingtons etc. After finishing your basic training and passing out you were generally posted to your original regiment. Sometimes if the need arose you could be transferred to another outfit, but the original always remained your parent regiment. If you lost your cap-badge whilst jumping or crawling around - you felt quite naked till you acquired another one. Sometimes when on parade, if you had transgressed, you could be asked questions about your regimental history and other military lore. So a little bit of knowledge - like, say, when your regiment was formed, or a major battle honour could save you from a punishment like jankers - meaning endless fatigues in your own time, and being confined to barracks to boot. The other form of regimental identification was on a shoulder flash - white letters on red, spelling out your regiment.

Being completely naive specimens - most of us were completely confused when any body of men wearing the Duke of Wellingtons distinctive cap-badge (impressively backed with a red triangle) - received bleating noises whilst passing or being passed by men of other regiments. Our enquiries revealed that a member of the regiment had allegedly been caught 'in-flagrante' at sometime or other with a sheep. If true it was probably back in Napoleonic times - the army has a long memory! This stretched our credulity to the limits - and we figured it was just a way of antagonising members of this regiment - who supplied the officers and NCOs for our basic training unit. We also noticed that the bleatings were always when members of the Duke's regiment were not in a position to retaliate - from regimental pride - as they would be on the march perhaps, or in transit on trucks! Regimental pride could be quite lively sometimes!

CHAPTER FIVE

Now that our barrack room was seemingly getting more like home - and living with some 26 other blokes quite the norm, we began to learn something about one another's past lives and activities. Looking out at me from a platoon photograph of that era are young, eager, smiling faces. But amongst these are a number of slightly older faces. These faces belong to men who having served in WW2 have found civilian life too tame - and missing the camaraderie they have known, have been seemingly compelled to join up again! I found this quite astonishing at the time - but at the end of my service I could comprehend why. There is great comradeship in the forces - and unless you are a recluse you need never be alone. Your mates will go through thick and thin to stick by you in times of trouble, and most would happily perjure themselves before any court in the land on your behalf! Often these older men including some who joined our draft (overseas bound echelon) - later were married men with families!

In our midst we had an ex-guardsman, an ex-Palestinian policemen and two men who had been in a naval formation. When these 'veterans' were able to put up their medal ribbons later in our training - the latter two both had the Atlantic Star decorations. Sometimes when we were all engaged in our evening 'bull' sessions, these two would talk about various ships they had known and served in, how many funnels this and that vessel had had and the places they had visited during the war. Of these two men I can only recall the name of one - Peter Johns, who hailed from West Yorkshire. The other's name completely escapes me now - but his home town was South Shields. How these two came to be in the army at this time I do not know, except that Peter was re-training after a spell in the glasshouse (military prison.) It may not be well known, but after serving whatever sentence is handed down to you for your offence - you then return to your regiment to complete your service. Peter was a very tough hombre. He was of medium height and extremely well muscled. You did not mess with him! We heard that at one time he had been a professional middleweight boxer. He always represented the company in camp boxing tournaments. I can remember our platoon sergeant asking him to go easy on his opponents to lengthen the bouts he was boxing in - as usually just one punch was enough to put the opposition to sleep - or give up! He scared the living daylights out of us rookies and we treated him with great respect - he could have eaten any of us for breakfast - one handed.

There is a sequel to this story. He was with us through our ten weeks training - which he sailed through - dealing with anything requiring strenuous effort with ease. After our passing out ceremony he was recruited into the Parachute Regiment and disappeared to Aldershot. I never expected to hear anything ever again of this man - but just a couple of years ago I was reading the autobiography of Col. 'Mad' Mike Hoare - the distinguished soldier of WW2 fame. Some years ago now the Belgian Congo erupted into a fierce and tragic civil war. Horrendous atrocities were committed against black and white members of the populace and a strong force of European mercenaries was formed by Col. Hoare to go to the aid of the beleaguered government forces. The Colonel speaks of recruiting a Peter Johns one time middleweight boxer from West Yorkshire. A man who had served in both the Paras and the SAS with distinction, and a soldier par-excellence.

He goes on to say how, as the civil war intensified, Peter Johns was always in the thick of things - and became a legend for bravery. He was wounded several times apparently - and on one or more occasions - rescued groups of Nuns and Priests from a grisly fate. He was subsequently decorated and commissioned in the field for his outstanding conduct! As I read this story I began to wonder if this was the Peter Johns we had trained with all those years ago? An illustration later in the book confirmed that indeed it was. There was no mistaking the stocky figure and smiling features of 'our man'. According to the book, he became a right hand man to the Colonel to the end of the campaign.

At about week four of our training it was announced that Princess Elizabeth (as she was then) and the Duke of Edinburgh would be visiting York. They would be attending a special service at York Minster during this visit - and a guard of honour would be drawn up outside the Minster to greet them and be inspected by them. Obviously our platoon drill must have been pretty good as we provided a good percent of those chosen. My mate Smithy and I were picked for guard reserves - in case anyone fainted prior to the main event. This happened quite frequently, as standing around for long periods, particularly in the hot sun, can have people fainting like flies. On an event of this nature the guard of honour would be paraded 30 to 40 minutes in advance at least! So, we had to do all the extra bull - plus attend all the rehearsals.

On the great day itself we were not required as it happened so we had a ringside view of the whole event - which was pretty impressive. It was a beautiful day and all went off very smoothly. Our two platoon members with the Atlantic Star decoration were strategically placed on the front row and needless to say the Duke spotted the medals and spoke at length to each one - for he too had had a distinguished naval career as is well known. I suspect these conversations added a few brownie points to our platoon's accumulator!

CHAPTER SIX

I see from my old paybook, that at about four weeks we had TOET - tests on elementary training. This included an early qualifying session on the rifle, Bren and Sten guns. We also primed and threw No. 36 grenades which exploded with a satisfactory bang. The throwing of these grenades was very carefully monitored because of the risk of accident and so you were supervised very thoroughly. Definitely a head below the parapet job - as the fragmentation is quite widespread! I believe you were supposed to watch until the grenade smoked slightly before ducking down. 'Chuck and duck' was the order of the day for most of us. Obviously there is a short delay in the fusing so in real life you would pull the pin and hold it for a moment or two before throwing - lest your enemy throw it back at you. During this exercise - and also with the 2 inch mortar firing - an officer is always in the wings. You begin to see how the guy does perhaps earn his pay because, he's the chappie that has to crawl out to the thing if it fails to explode, and blow it up in a controlled explosion using guncotton.

On the rifle and Bren I didn't seem too hot at that stage - but with a Sten I would have found a place in 'Al Capone's gang'. The Sten was a small automatic piece - with a metal butt and a very short barrel. It had the look of something knocked up by the local plumber, but had been developed urgently in WW2 and could be made very cheaply. Its short barrel precluded it from long range use - but at close quarters it was very effective. The Americans apparently called it 'the burp gun'. It had many drawbacks as we found when we were carrying them around for real. The working parts were very sensitive and the slightest banging down of the butt on to a hard object, however accidental - could set the thing off if your safety catch wasn't securely on that is! The magazine springs were too weak as well, so, if you did not remove the bullets at the end of the day, it might well let you down in a tight spot. The spring hadn't the strength to push up the bullets to the breech.

I duly qualified as a first class shot on rifle and Bren at a later stage. This was a reasonable standard but the one below marksman. Being a marksman got you more pay - and a cross rifles badge on the bottom of your sleeve. Imagine my horror when, many many years later I joined our company rifle club to find young secretaries licking the pants off me on the 25 yard .22 ranges! I just couldn't get the hang of the sights on the .22. They are so small. On a service rifle you have this very simple sighting system - a large backsight plus a pretty prominent foresight designed for quick action. That's my story anyway. Using ear mufflers or 'defenders' as they are now called would have had you classed as a wimp or a pansy - had they been around then!

Talking of weaponry - should it be thought that our platoon had more than its fair share of characters - a neighbouring one (and rivals) from the same intake had a firearms expert in its ranks. This man I believe was with the wartime Royal Ordinance Corps. He too had re-enlisted and at the time of our training was carrying on a heated argument through the pages of *Soldier* magazine - with another expert on the merits of automatic weapons. The other party had accused successive Governments of parsimony in this area and he had quoted the American Winchester rifle as an example of a very early successful automatic weapon as far back as 1873 - when the Brits were still using single shot rifles without magazines!

The main argument over semi or fully automatic weapons was the amount of ammunition used and possible supply problems in the field. These two guys argued for weeks about accuracy and ruggedness versus fire power and effectiveness on a charging enemy. Effective killing ranges etc. etc. Academic stuff really - but it interested us as we had both automatic and single shot weapons - and after all were we, or were we not, half way to being professionals? Anyway the argument was ended by the magazine calling the debate a draw and refusing to print any more arguments!

We also had so called 'trade tests' at around this four week appraisal session. The idea was to identify anyone who was competent in say engineering skills - and who might be more usefully employed in the REME or Royal Engineers or perhaps even as an armourer. All I can recall of these tests was one particular one, where you were expected to replace the ball bearings in a cycle hub without the benefit of grease to hold them in place (whilst you slid the axle back in situ!) I don't think any of us were considered competent enough to escape a career in the infantry. We also sat exams to assess our academic standing - which wasn't very high in my case I have to say, as my education then was only of elementary standard. However I was well versed in the three 'R's' and obviously got through this O.K.

Now if you were found to be below a certain educational standard - plus perhaps a bad showing in other areas, you were packed off to the Pioneer Corps - which was a fate worse than death in our eyes then! No doubt the Pioneer Corps was a very useful formation - doing first class work - but not quite carrying the macho image we considered ourselves to have. Again, if you were seen as requiring more training time - you could be put back to a newer intake to go over the same ground once again.

This also happened if you were injured in training (a not infrequent event) so you were put back to a new intake at the level you had been at before your injury. I once saw one of our number break his ankle like a stick whilst running the assault course. We never saw him again.

Most people these days are familiar with assault courses as such - having seen them on film or television. The Strensall one lacked none of the usual refinements! The climbing wall was very high, the pool crossed by the swinging rope method was both deep and muddy. I cannot remember whether or not it was at this stage we had to get through the physical programme with the required number of marks - or whether it came before passing-out? It probably did come around at 4 weeks with our initial tests because it was probably part of the weeding out process mentioned already - that might have you 'put back' - or sent to the Pioneers.

Many of us, including myself had trouble on three counts. Rope climbing - scaling the high wall on the assault course - and carrying a comrade, fireman's lift style for a hundred yards at least, to simulate carrying a wounded man to safety. Fortunately you did get another go at the ones you failed first time round! Incidently for those not aware of it - climbing up a rope, say to 25 feet - is not easy till you know the technique. Our ancient platoon sergeant (probably all of 35) to our complete amazement, went up hand over hand like a monkey - very impressive. Much as we wanted to emulate him some of us just couldn't - until that is, we were taught to use our feet to grip the rope and virtually push ourselves upwards using our leg power. Eventually too we conquered the high wall by grim determination and scraped limbs.

In the session requiring you to carry a man for a hundred yards or so, you could not choose your own partner alas! The guy I got first time, seemingly weighed twice as much as me - so we collapsed about half way through the run - to some ribald comments and laughter. Firstly, and by no means least, you had to get the bloke over your shoulder - not as easy as you might think if he should be a heavy individual! Anyway second time around, I got a lighter subject to carry, and I finally made the necessary physical grades. My paybook also tells me that I got my first star after these initial tests. Your star rating determined your pay as a private - and like all the rest of the platoon who had made it - we probably got another two or three bob a week! The equivalent now of

20/30p. But a lot of money in those days! The highest star rating a private could attain was five. Very few national servicemen reached these dizzy heights, only regular squaddies were in the frame for this!

Talking about physical endeavour - the army is very pro-active in the field of sport. Despite busy training sessions there were sports periods which you were encouraged to participate in. Soccer was the number one sport for which it was soon confirmed I had absolutely no talent. However in our platoon we had a man that was superbly talented. Ken Sanderson, Sheffield United trialist and a joy to watch with the ball. Even I, a dodo at the game could see his skill and fluency with the ball - which seemed to be glued to his feet at all times. I suspect National Service may have ruined his prospects for a career in the game as those two vital years were missed and at 20 it might be considered that you were too old for apprenticeships etc. The story doesn't quite end there. He was obviously spotted early on - and could have had an easy life playing for a senior army team - but he chose to stay with his mates in a rifle platoon. He could have also avoided the far east draft had he so wished, but to his great credit he stayed one of us!

If you were gifted at sport the army was a fine career prospect for you. You were excused most parades and drills - even guard duty (once you had done your basic training.) Not only did they pay you to do what you enjoyed doing most, you spent much of your time in sports training! As well as having great prestige - you would in all probability be put in charge of the sports equipment store - or some other sinecure. Needless to say you had to be pretty good at it to get this sort of treatment

However, much to my personal surprise I found that I was quite good at the high jump - and after doing reasonably well in a five mile run in full battle order found myself a reserve runner in the company mile team at the forthcoming sports day. I took my legs to a sports meeting - but no-one asked me to run!

But getting thus far was the equivalent of an Olympic medal for non-sporting me. I did just have one moment of glory however probably about half way through basic training. I was told to report to company office forthwith. You do not hang about when so called - as the company office is not noted for its welfare and kindness of thought to private soldiers - particularly rookies. I was addressed tersely by the CSM (company sergeant major) who informed me that from my original registration records I appeared to have played cricket for my place of work. This was true but I was obviously not in Len Hutton's class - just an occasional member of our department team, and generally batting round about No.9. I did once score a memorable 12 off some very mediocre bowling! As I stood to attention in front of the great man he informed me that I would be playing that very afternoon in a match 'officers *v* other ranks'. No arguments like - "well 'er I'm a bit out of practice sir" - it was, "get to it man, dismiss!"

With some trepidation I reported to the cricket pitch at the appointed hour. There I found myself billed as going in to bat as last man (phew!) I can't recall much of the match except that it was a lovely hot day. The sun reflecting off the officers' whites - whilst most other ranks were in khaki. Now earlier in this book I have quoted from the famous poem by Sir Henry Newbolt *Vitiei Lampada* - now here was the famous line come to life - just for me. "A bumping pitch and a blinding light - four to make and the match to win - an hour to play and the last man's in etc." Except the last man is little old me!

Terror struck as I faced the demon bowler. They say that in moments of stress you automatically remember any training you might have had in the subject - and I remembered back to my schooldays! The bowler was a hazy figure fronting a bright golden light - but I saw his arm come up and I struck out and struck home. The ball went for a neat four runs - we'd only gone and won! I wasn't exactly chaired off the field - but the tea and sandwiches tasted good in the pavilion afterwards.

Pride goeth before a fall doth it not. My army career prospects probably foundered after the next match. I went in at No.6 and did not even see the ball which spread-eagled my wicket and so was promptly out for a duck! No other sporting moments touched me for the rest of my service - sadly.

The 'powers that be' were frequently on the prowl looking for suitable talent for the camp boxing tournaments. Most of us tried to escape when the press gang was afoot. I had a keen interest in boxing at one time and had read up on all the old time champions including the bare knuckle boys. However sparring about at my youth club had been fine - till the day I took on a visitor to the club who apparently was profoundly deaf. All was going well till I happened to catch him on the nose. He then hit me with the proverbial sledgehammer and I was out for the count! I lost interest in personal participation after that! Even though it emerged he was something of a champion in an amateur league.

After the halfway stage, our training progressed at a rapid rate. We did night schemes (for instance) which had us marching like zombies to meet particular target points. Three day exercises on the Yorkshire moors - with overnight bivouacking and lots of attacking and defending. "Bren gunner (me) can't you move any faster?" - as we charge up a blooming great hill for the fourth time. As the thing weighed a ton -

plus all its bits and pieces I was completely knackered! We arrived back to camp and ate the NAAFI dry as our exertions had left us starving.

You also know you are scaling the training ladder when your name comes up for guard duty. Everyone has heard the old army maxim I'm sure - which goes something like - 'If it moves salute it.' 'If it's stationary - whitewash it.' 'If it's big and immovable - guard it.' To acclimatise you for this heady responsibility you are first required to be guard orderly one night. This means you are available to fetch and carry for the blokes on guard - who are not officially allowed to leave the guard room whilst on duty. So until lights out you are running back and forth to the NAAFI on a variety of missions.

This does give you an insight into procedure and guard changing for when your time comes. When it does, your turn-out must be spot on as you are inspected by the guard commander and the orderly officer and the ceremony of guard mounting takes place. Two hours on and four off is the routine and you pace up and down outside the guardroom with rifle and bayonet, checking traffic in and out of the barracks. Not that there was much traffic during the evening period. During the night's long hours it paid you to keep an eye opened for the orderly officer who might well sneak up on you to check your wakefulness. If he was in that sort of mood he might turn out the guard - which meant that those asleep in their 'four off' period - plus guard commander, had to appear in drill order outside pretty smartish, to be inspected and harangued.

Whilst on guard duty you come across one of the army's many little whims. Above all else it does not care for bed-wetters. Now some people try to 'work their ticket' by constant bed-wetting. Being aware of this a crafty ploy takes place. To wean those in the habit of bed-wetting off their problem - they are required to sleep in the guard room and are awakened on the hour, every hour by the guard to ensure their bladders are emptied frequently! This is kill or cure chums and many choice phrases are used in the waking up process - the favourite being "Ayup! Chum - wanna buy a battleship?" (Don't ask me why.) No sympathy at all was extended to the victim. Why should he work his ticket when we're going to be stuck in this lot for the foreseeable future? There would be a guard dismounting ceremony again about reveille time I think - and then the daytime contingent of regimental police took over for the day.

Depending on the guard commander - your guard duty could be a fairly relaxed night or a 'I do it by the book' - routine sort of night - but whichever, you were pretty zombified next day! Off guard you could play cards - read or chat and later snooze your four hours off but generally you were supposed to adopt a soldier like pose at all times. Nothing exciting ever happened on my guard nights - but later on - another platoon's guards let a prisoner escape. Shock horror - and a swift demotion to the rank of private for the guard commander. (He came out east with us and soon got his stripes back!) The other type of guard duty you found yourself on during training, and after was 'fire picket guard'. On this duty you strolled around in pairs armed with pick axe handles. I suppose you worked in conjunction with the fixed guards at the gate - in that you patrolled the camp - ostensibly looking out for fires. Did we mount guard with the others ? I cannot recall.

When returning from a weekend or 48 hour pass you needed to check in at the guardroom before 23.59 (or one minute to 12). It was always said that your only real free time in the army was between 23.59 and midnight. Exactly one minute! On one occasion I missed my train returning from a weekend home. The next one got me into York about midnight and I cannot recall how I got to the camp - but I must have had lifts or a very long walk. Suffice to say I rolled up about 1.30 a.m. expecting a rocket but the guard commander knew more than I did and let me through without a problem. I crept into the barrack room quietly to avoid waking the rest - to find them all lying fully dressed with full marching order kit in readiness. They were on 15 mins notice to embus (lovely word that) and join a fire fighting team on Fylingdales Moors, which were being ravaged by extensive fires. Had I been much later in returning they would have gone, and I would have been for the chop! Virtually just as I'd got my kit together we were off, and spent three or four days battling a hairy old moor fire. On returning it took days to get the smell from our clothes and bodies. Again we consumed all the extra food we could lay our hands on as we were famished - having lived mainly on sandwiches during our fire-fighting activities.

The guard room incidents previously related, remind me of two interesting episodes towards the end of our ten weeks training. On the first parade of the day we were asked if anyone lived near Leeds. Not being sure exactly where Leeds lay in relation to Sheffield I thought it sounded fairly near and hoping for an unexpected hour or two at home I put up my hand. I was the only one that did as we had learned never to volunteer! For once though I had done the right thing. Report to the company office in best bib and tucker was the next thing. Here close scrutiny by a three striped person led to an interesting briefing. We are proceeding to Leeds he said dramatically - to bring back a soldier prisoner from Leeds jail. So we were, and so we did! Can't remember much of the journey there - except we had a sojourn in the station buffet on expenses.

I was mildly interested in the handcuffs the sergeant had - but didn't pay too much attention to them. On arrival at Leeds we must have taken a taxi from station to clink - which to my surprise was under Leeds Town Hall. We wandered around and down many dingy corridors till we reached a desk containing a police sergeant. We formally identified ourselves and explained our business. Documents were exchanged and severe unease gripped me when the desk sergeant indicated the prisoner might be violent.

We collected him from the cell and I found myself handcuffed to a person a great deal larger than me! We escaped the portals of the jail and the prisoner said something like - "O.K, - now if you want me to come quietly you had better take the cuffs off or I shall wrap him (me) around every obstacle I can see." Not quite what I had in mind chums! Sergeant weighed it all up in his mind and decided to take the prisoner's word that he wouldn't do a bunk on us! He kept his word and our journey back was most affable. Was army transport awaiting us or did we take a taxi back to camp? I cannot recall. The handcuffs were ceremonially replaced just outside the camp gates for appearances sake - and we duly handed over our prisoner to the guard room! What he had done or why he was in clink I cannot remember.

For whatever reason I was detailed to do this again shortly afterwards. This time to Middlesboro' - a much further distance. I think this chap had had a 'Dear John' letter from his wife and he had deserted to sort things out. The M.P's had picked him up and we went to collect him. From where I cannot remember - but I think we had a private compartment on the train coming back. He was I think a little guy and the handcuffs didn't seem appropriate. We had a pretty convivial journey back with food and drink in the station buffets. My 'almost' mother-in-law - Ethel was most impressed by these expeditions, and saw me promoted to dizzy heights!

CHAPTER SEVEN

Exciting though these extra-curricular activities were for me, they paled into insignificance compared to those of a bunch of the lads who, being taller than most, were obviously considered to have a more soldier like bearing. They were chosen to be the military representatives at the funerals of two 'old' soldiers who had recently passed on. I do not know what the criteria is for the attendance of a military 'honour guard' but it must be in recognition of many, many years of service. The two funerals our lads attended had the full works - gun carriages and the graveside volley! This entailed some special drills - slow marching with rifle reversed - reversing of arms at the graveside, and perfect volleys over the grave. An imperfect volley would sound a bit like the gunfight at the O.K corral! A bugler is also involved to sound the last post!

At least one of these funerals was of a publican and the 'spread' apparently was terrific. Both events went off well and we were green with envy at the descriptions of the food and drink our mates were plied with afterwards. Not only all this but young ladies were allegedly present at these ceremonies! As previously mentioned our contact with the opposite sex in our first ten weeks was minimal - but our libido's were recovering, so we were doubly green on this score.

There was the 'passion wagon' into York each evening (a 3 ton truck) - which returned about 10.30 I believe. I don't think many of us availed ourselves of this service at this stage as usually we had no money to spend and too much to do in the evenings. I have vague recollections of the odd summer evening walking around York - which is the most picturesque and historic place imaginable. Much of the city is still surrounded by its ancient city walls and you can stroll around the top of these walls taking in the centuries old views of the River Ouse and the medieval buildings. However with our training heading towards its climax I think we had too much on our hands for expeditions to York. On camp the powers that be did their best to provide some sort of entertainment. There were frequent boxing tournaments - amateur talent nights, but I cannot remember any camp dances at that stage or film shows - although probably there were such happenings. Some large camps had a cinema - but I'm pretty certain ours didn't. Was there table tennis and snooker in the NAAFI - probably.

On talent nights the platoon had a star in Brian Norrie - who had a very good voice. He sang modern songs and usually brought the house down - plus winning the half-crown 1st prize. He had a big advantage over most as he actually knew the words! Brian came from Hull. Later in life I spent a lot of time in Hull but never caught a glimpse of him. Before being called up, he like many others from the city, had worked on fishing trawlers. Might just be that army life was a little bit more agreeable than fishing trips up around the Arctic fringes! However the major moan of the ex-trawler lads was money. When the catch had been good they made a lot of money, far more than we had ever dreamed of, even if you were a lowly deckhand. Just over a quid a week army pay (which was all we got) was hardly what they were used to. My own pay had been about £3 p.w in civvy street.

I'd like to think that Brian might have gone into showbiz afterwards, although I never heard of him in that context. However the north of England has a very well developed club circuit and I could imagine Brian earning a good living touring the clubs. He was very much like the well known T/V entertainer of today, Les Dennis, in looks. Whenever I see Les on the box I immediately think of Brian Norrie and the pleasure his voice gave us in those pre-television days. Towards the end of our first ten weeks I think the platoon might have rented a 'steam' radio. Transistors and portables just weren't around then.

As we neared the end of our training period we began to think of ourselves as soldiers. 'Civvies' were spoken of slightly disdainfully - as if we'd been at it for years. You summed up a man by his medal ribbons and learned to recognise where he had spent the wartime years. Remember this was only just over four years since the war had finished. Naturally you were highly conversant with badges of rank - it didn't pay to get those wrong. RSM's (Regimental Sergeant Majors) wore virtually officers dress and it didn't do to salute them - although they'd probably come up the hard way and deserved your salute. It didn't do not to salute an officer - with or without uniform. You always knew - as said before - something in the bearing tells you, and generally the only people around camp in 'civvies' were officers in mufti.

We had got to grips with our uniforms and kit. Our brasses gleamed even down to our rifle slings. We knew where all the packs and webbing went, having paraded and marched in FSMO (full service marching order.) Normally these packs were 'squared off' with cardboard or ply - to look good when laid out for the dreaded kit inspections. As you got your gear shipshape they were less and less onerous. Our uniforms had lost that coarse new look and were smoother and much more professional after scores of pressings. With the three distinct pleats either side of the back centre seam - plus one or two horizontal creases across between the shoulder blades.

We hadn't learned too much about tactics at this stage but our weapon training was good, and by this time had included the firing of a couple of 2 inch mortar bombs each. For the uninitiated the mortar is rather like a short length of drainpipe mounted on a base plate. The bomb - which has small guidance fins is dropped fin end first down the metal tube. A tug on the trigger mechanism fires the projectile cartridge and up she goes - hopefully where you've aimed it. Can't remember the range but it was a comfortable distance away. The trick was to judge the arc and bring it down near the target marker. The bombs were marked by a raised symbol - rather like braille - so you could tell in the dark which were smoke bombs and which high explosive - as we learned on yet more night schemes.

We were now pretty cohesive on the square. We had long mastered the fixing of bayonets - a difficult manoeuvre - turning on the march and marching in three's in extended line - also changing step on the march - and the slow march. All equally difficult without a lot of practice. Your drill instructor needed to know what he was about too! Give a command on the wrong foot such as the halt - and turning on the march for instance, and you had a disaster. We had mastered the art of hearing and reacting to only our own instructor on the square - which might well have had other squads upon it in various stages of training. As mentioned before the band too might strike up in a practice session - but we were now wise to that one! So, as they say in the navy we were to all intents and purposes ready and able to go to sea! Except that in our case it was more like go defend the Empire - as there was still a fair bit of it left.

CHAPTER EIGHT

These days I believe, passing out parades of young servicemen are given the full video and photographic treatment. Much is made of the ceremony. Very senior officers are frequently present etc. We did of course have the full drill ceremonial and a band. I believe the CO from the Duke of Wellingtons Regiment took the salute. However because of the huge numbers of national servicemen going through the training system all over the country at that time, our passing out parade was nothing special - except for we, the participants - and any relations able to get to York for our great day. So a box Brownie coverage of the event was the most we could expect.

There would have been four or five platoons of us in training together and passing out together. So, a goodly number of relatives could be expected. We had rehearsed the parade several times so our drill would be pretty good and our major worry at this point was who would be coming from home for our rites of passage into the world of trained soldiers! Many guys had a whole family of relatives expected - including girl friends.

The social aspect of this event gave me a small problem. My folks lived in Abergavenny at the time. There were many others in the brood - which is why I had been brought up by grandparents and latterly granny only. So my parents certainly didn't have the time or the funds to journey to York! Because I had never lived with them we weren't close in any way either so their presence wasn't expected really, or an option. Granny had died when I was about 14, and my Aunty and Uncle Jones had taken me into their home and shown me great kindness. They weren't really my aunt and uncle - just family friends. Uncle had recently died (he'd had a terrible time in WW1) and they had lost their only son in Burma in WW2. I guess aunty would have come if I'd pressed the point - but she certainly wasn't too keen on the army at that time, and who can blame her.

Most of the young guys in our room had mums and being slightly embarrassed by not having a normal family relationship, I had kept pretty quiet about my upbringing, away from a mum and dad. I therefore needed a mother figure urgently. As the event came really close another blow came in that my very pretty girlfriend, Lorna, couldn't come either because of a new job. It looked like I might be the only guy without any family representative at all! Lorna's mum Ethel (Effie) stepped into the breach. She would come and pretend to be my 'mum' for the day. We had always got on well and so I went along with the idea - with great pleasure.

Come the day, all went well. The drill was highly polished the weather fine after overnight rain - and even in line abreast we did look pretty professional. After the address by the CO we marched off as soldiers of the King, ready in all respects to serve where he decided we should go. After the parade we met up with our guests and I assume there must have been some sort of refreshment provided - but where it was served I cannot remember. Then we were encouraged to tour the camp with our guests - displaying the Spartan conditions of our barrack room - the gym and assault courses - plus any other interesting parts we felt they might like to see. Also a great many explanations. Why do you have to keep saluting all the time? (The officers were very much in evidence on passing out day.) Well, er! We're acknowledging a senior colleague you see! Or, why can't we walk across the barrack square? Well er! It's sort of sacred see. A bit like saluting the quarter deck where Nelson fell at Trafalgar - it represents the battlefields where many soldiers fell, so you only go on it on duty! etc. etc.

Now my supposed mother was a great success. It was easy to see where my girlfriend's looks came from - Effie was a real cracker! She made her own smart clothes and had a svelte figure. At that time she would have only been in her late thirties I guess. She took a good few wolf whistles as we walked around the camp and squaddies rushed to their barrack block windows to get a closer look! She took it all in good part and was highly amused. It was interesting too to meet our mates parents, sisters and girl friends. One or two introductions to sisters bore fruit for some of the lads afterwards. The rest of the day was free so I took Effie for a tour of York where we had afternoon tea somewhere (no doubt at her expense) before I put her on the Sheffield train some time later. Back at the camp I was quizzed somewhat about this glamourous mum and how could a specimen like myself have been produced by such an attractive person etc.? But I stuck to my guns - after all she was going to be my mother (in law) one day wasn't she. In the event it didn't happen - but that's another story.

So my record of that passing out ceremony is a long distance shot - taken with Effie's box-Brownie camera of some tiny figures which were of our platoon before being inspected. Surprisingly enough, no group photo was taken that day either! Everyone knows that the night before or the night after passing-out there is a monumental party where the lads reveal how much they really liked their NCOs and vice versa! There probably was some sort of party - but I can remember little of it. A sing song round the NAAFI piano was the most likely I would think. As for a monumental booze-up, it certainly didn't happen to us! Most of us didn't really drink at that stage. I doubt if I'd had any alcohol at all before being called up mainly because it was never in the house. Granny and aunty were both strictly TT! I have made up for lost time since!

At the weekend we left camp on 10 days passing out leave. We had no idea what the future had in store for us - all we knew was that a whole ten day period of leave had been granted us, and we meant to enjoy every minute of it!

I can recall nothing of this leave either - although I'm sure it was pretty joyous. I would certainly have spent a lot of time at my girl friends house, for amongst many other things my 'almost mother-in-law' was a pretty good cook! I did come clean with the lads eventually about my little subterfuge - they thought it was a pretty good wheeze - and were there any more at home like that!

When we returned from leave we found ourselves billeted in a much older part of the camp called 'The Spider'. This was a large complex of wooden barrack rooms interconnected with corridors and store rooms. The whole thing looked like it had been built for WW1 - which it probably had - and it did really resemble a giant black wooden spider. Here we were joined by the other platoons of our intake and for the first week we were busily engaged in fatigue duties to keep us occupied. All this was to change dramatically one fine morning at muster parade. We were addressed by a very elegant major who must have been an advertising executive at some time - going on the superb selling presentation he gave us! He told us of an opportunity to serve in the far east. Malaya in particular. "Do some real soldiering eh! Chaps." He painted a picture of a tropical life - with cool white barracks and of sarong clad dusky maidens - Palm trees with blue skies and sea. All most of us knew about Malaya was that the Japs had captured it during the war (WW2) and most of Gt. Britain's rubber and tin came from the area. He went on to explain that the current 'fly in the ointment' out there were gangs of semi-organised bandits who were bumping off rather too many people and rather upsetting the rubber planters and tin traders. He went on to say that troops on anti-bandit patrols tended to swan about on trains, returning to their nice barracks for tea after duffing up a few of these undesirables and teaching them that they couldn't muck about with the Raj.

This was the gist of what he said to us - and when asking for volunteers to step forward he must have been very gratified that 90% of us did take the traditional 'one pace forward'. What he didn't tell us - and what a great many people in the country didn't know either - was that there was a serious attempt afoot to completely destabilise Malaya, ready for a Communist take over. Historians think that this was decided upon at a very high level meeting of world communist leaders held in Moscow in 1947. The British trained and armed (Malayan People's Anti-Japanese Army) had been reactivated, they had dug up their weapons, built a network of jungle camps and were carrying out a programme of assassinations and terror attacks all across the country - including the murder of the British High Commissioner - Sir Henry Gurney! So there was a much more serious situation out there than most people knew about - including us. But even if we had known I don't think it would have put most of us off. Our elegant major had spun far too good a story for us to change our minds over minor political matters.

Another thing we were not aware of was that the extra six weeks training we were to undergo came about by the intervention of an MP - via a constituent, who complained about 'our boys' (and I believe including her own son) - being sent off to fight wily enemies with insufficient training. Normally your extra training is received when you joined your battalion - but here there was a clear need of a more advanced programme than we had so far received! It seemed right and proper to us that our training should be beefed up in the appropriate areas.

So, I suppose all this added a bit of swagger to our step. We were amused to see that the new intake platoon (in our old barrack room) were being organised in the absence of any NCO by a recruit in the shape of an ex-Royal Marine, who looked (and sounded about 50) we felt. What was the army coming to!

CHAPTER NINE

Three things happened in our new pre-draft situation. One was that we got a lot more free time. When in camp our training seemed to end around the four o'clock mark - giving us plenty of time to get spruced up and more often than not, head for the bright lights of York. We certainly didn't have a lot of extra pay to blow - apart from the small amount our extra 'star' had brought us. I guess we were finding that Strensall camp was a little bit limited in scope for a social life - and in those days a couple of bob (20p) went a long long way! For instance a cinema ticket would have been about one shilling (5p) admission to a dance roughly the same. The passion wagon truck into York each evening was helpful in that it was free! I suppose dances were the favourite social activity as there were girls to be found there in goodly numbers. Like I said we were beginning to recover our seemingly lost libidos'

I soon discovered that my mate Richard Smith was a magnet to young ladies. He was a very good looking lad - and emanated a sort of charm that girls found irresistible. He certainly raised a flutter in a few feminine hearts. My only claim to fame was that I was a reasonable ballroom dancer. I had spent a lot of time at so called tea dances in Sheffield - these being held on midweek afternoons to cater for the many 'shop' people who had a Thursday half day off. The day of half day closing varied from town to town obviously. However many of the girls and women who attended these tea dances were interested in one thing only and that was dancing. Proper dancing of the slow, slow - quick, quick, slow variety - where not only did you have to know the steps - but you also were expected to converse with your partner as well! Anyway following many many excursions to Sheffield City Hall - dancing to Bernard Taylor and his band I could trip the light fantastic with the best!

I cannot recall anything like the trail of smitten females a la my friend Richard - but somewhere I encountered a young lady called Anne. She was pretty and a very nice lassie - but more important still, she worked (like so many other girls from York) in the huge chocolate industry that was, and still is based in and around York! She worked at Terry's factory and joy of joys had a perk involving large quantities of chocolate 'mis-shapes'. I may not at that time have been either a drinker or smoker - but boy! Did I like chocolate. So, many an evening sitting in a York cinema - I would chomp my way through large quantities of Terry's chocolate. Although not necessarily good for my teeth - this was manna from heaven as the strict rationing of sweets was still in force. She like many people in the industry hardly touched the stuff! Apparently any new girl on the production line is allowed to eat her fill - whenever she wishes. This soon means they become completely sick of the sight and taste and smell of chocolate. Our 'brief encounter' romance only lasted a few weeks. There was no future in a boy friend who was about to take off to the other side of the world. It was pleasant while it lasted - we no doubt kissed and cuddled - and in those days chum, that was as far as it went. I still had my main girl friend in Sheffield but things were beginning to cool off in that direction. I had lots of competition from the guys at her work - who had a distinct advantage, they were there and I was not! We still went home all of us on as many weekend passes as we could get - and we all still enjoyed the home cooking delights that came our way. We had got used to army cuisine - rough that it was, but were still always eternally, fiercely hungry.

The second part of our new existence saw us being transferred to The Green Howards Regiment. We knew nothing about them and were a bit sorry to say farewell to our familiar cap-badges and shoulder flashes. However the Green Howards badge was displayed on a square of green material and the shoulder flashes were white lettering on a green background. A brief history lesson showed us that there weren't many conflicts that the Green Howards hadn't been in since 1688 and they had acquitted themselves well on most occasions! Their battle honours were on a par with the greatest and of course they were still a proud Yorkshire Regiment! So - under our new badging and regimental status - we went forth to finalise our training in readiness for the tropics and the Palm trees - and not forgetting dusky maidens. We also found ourselves merged with some much older servicemen - most of whom had been in WW2 and who were also joining our far-east draft. Many of these men were very tough indeed. Some had been let out of the glasshouse (military prison) early - by volunteering for far-east service. Not one of these men that I can think of were anything but good comrades and their tales of derring-do were well worth listening to. To hear the old sweats talking about the respective merits (?) of different army prisons was quite an eye-opener, and one thing was for sure we didn't want to experience it for ourselves. Many years later I got my son-in-law to take me to see 'The Mallet' - an army prison at Shepton Mallet - near to where we were staying. Of all the ones we heard discussed - this one was the most feared. When I saw it, it was a joint services/civilian prison - but emanated an air of menace still! Apparently the idea behind these fearsome regimes was to put you off ever entering one again!

So we learned all about 'the screws' (guards) - how you learned how to speak out of the corner of your mouth, and how 'snout' (tobacco) was the *raison d'etre* of your existence! Fascinating stuff - and we immediately adopted 'snout' into our own vocabulary! I think speaking out of the corner of your mouth was also practised - as it came in handy when silence had been ordered in the ranks on parade. All this was brought back to me later, and many others I'll bet - by the famous film *The Hill* starring Sean Connery - featuring, and about an army 'nick'. The few kit inspections we had at this stage were child's play to these lads, who, when inside had had to go to tremendous lengths of bull to just get through a daily kit inspection.

One of our favourite 'old soldier' storytellers was George, his was a very interesting tale. Bit of a lad was our George, who was a Geordie, through and through! Always just one step ahead of the law in his youth apparently - he had swum the Tyne on more than one occasion to escape the clutches of the law. He been in WW2 and had fetched up in Germany at the end of the conflict. Here he became part of the BAOR - (British Army of the Rhine) - or the Army of Occupation as it was sometimes known. He had been billeted on a German family whose man had not come back from the war. The lady of the house observing his teenage acne had apparently said something on the lines of, "George - what you need is a good woman - who will rid you of these terrible spots!" As she had a nice looking daughter George proceeded to engage in a little local therapy to test out the theory!

He and some of his mates kept a cache of ex-Wermacht weapons up in some nearby woods, where they would utilise them to shoot game - like rabbits hares and pheasants - to augment their rations in the billets. Their favourite amongst these illegal weapons was the Schmeisser sub-machine gun.

However, being somewhat bored eventually with the anti-climax of peace, George embarked on one or two illegal enterprises - including allegedly, the odd armed robbery. With the redcaps breathing down his neck he had deserted and was holed up somewhere till betrayed by a lover, whom he was apparently two-timing. Hell having no fury etc. etc.!

Another wartime 'old timer' comes to my mind - each time I hear mention of the SAS. Having said that we were not encouraged to wear civilian rig when off duty - this particular guy always wore a blazer when free - which sported the SAS badge. I seem to recall that he was ribbed about this at the time by the older hands - who I think had some doubts about his service claims. Much later a bizarre incident occurred involving this man which if I may, will be described later on.

There were two other real characters in our midst - and straight out of Rudyard Kipling. They were Privates Dudley and Cheyney. They had both been true soldiers of the Raj - even before WW2! Both were well built men and in their mid-thirties I would imagine. Their knowledge and experience of military matters obviously was extensive as they rarely accompanied us on any training exercise. Seemingly they were on permanent 'ablutions' cleaning duties. They were present on morning muster parade - complete with their brooms which they sloped and ordered arms with, as we did our rifles. We were completely amazed that this was tolerated by our new Sergeant-major, who was something of a disciplinarian. (We had not seen much of warrant officers in our first ten weeks of training - and had assumed that they were heavily into administrative work.) Now, we were being very closely scrutinised by this slightly portly WO2 gentleman - who breathed fire and smoke at all times!

However to go back to Messrs. Dudley and Cheyney - who seemed to be completely inseparable. Of the two Dudley was the most intriguing. We suspected he was the black sheep of some notable family as he was of quite distinguished appearance - and could burst forth into a cut glass Oxford accent should the need arise. When we were at our first substantial camp out east he developed two highly acclaimed 'cabaret' acts. The first was to hide in the darkness by the camp gate and bawl out some luckless, slightly tipsy returning soldier - in this superb upper crust accent - convincing the victim that he was undoubtedly being addressed, and torn off a strip by, at the very least the CO in person! We in the know found it riveting to watch the discomfiture of the victim!

The second trick was to sneak up on some camp maintenance contractor's workman (usually from the Indian subcontinent) who, suddenly finding himself being addressed fluently from behind in his own language - by an obvious 'pukka sahib' would almost fall off his ladder or whatever he was perched on at the time! Should it be thought there was a racist motive underlying this little game - rest assured this was not so. After the initial shock there would be much laughter - the man's family would be enquired after - where his home village was etc. etc. Obviously 'our' Dudley had spent a considerable time in India during his early service - where apparently you received extra pay for each language or dialect you learned to speak! I don't think this harmed our public relations either!

I lost track of both these characters later when the draft was split up. However in true Hollywood fashion Dudley was 'persuaded' to become an NCO later - when apparently there was an acute shortage of experienced leadership! Wherever Dudley and Cheyney are now, I wish them both well. They injected us all with a special dose of good morale.

Talking of injections - we were shipped off to Catterick Camp during this our second spell of training for 'booster' inoculations - plus the M.O's special in the form of the Yellow Fever jab. This was the worst one we had had and it felt like being injected with molten metal. It affected us all in some way or other. My 'turn' was to faint into my pudding on our return to Strensall. This caused me to be dragged outside by my mates for some fresh air - and returning to find my pudding eaten and my pristine set of 'eating irons' swopped for a much more worn and moth eaten set!

About this time too I became affected by some very painful facial boils. A particularly bad one over an eye caused me to be resplendently bandaged at the Medical Centre (or M.I room.) I couldn't believe it when our fearsome Sarn't-major (the gripper) expressed words of sympathy towards me, and gave me light duties as barrack room orderly for a few days. This was an exceedingly cushy number, which meant just keeping the room tidy in case of a sudden inspection from on high. It meant actually being able to catch up on your reading or letter writing - but having an extended 'kip' was frowned upon. What did we read you may well ask? Comics mainly - perhaps the odd magazine such as *Readers Digest - John Bull* or very occasionally the odd *Men Only* periodical - containing - wait for it - a lady with no clothes on! Not a common event in those heavily censored days! The first of the so called 'top shelf' magazines possibly?

What we really liked to get hold of were the bulky American magazines which had come over via the American forces stationed here. It wasn't the articles contained in these magazines that fascinated us - it was the advertisements depicting a way of life and luxury which we in austerity blanketed Great Britain could barely dream of! Not only all of that - but some of the 'ad's' were in colour too! Even American films to which most people were addicted, somehow didn't quite convey the sheer scale, depth and luxury of the then quite average American family's standard of living. So under each mans pillow (if you looked) would be a range of reading matter from *The Wizard* comic through to *The Soldier* magazine - all of which would be swopped around the barrack room.

The older soldiers played a lot of cards in their free time particularly when they were out of funds. Sometimes they would just sit around and talk - and a favourite gambit might be how would you find your way from the (say) Three Tuns public house to The Dog and Partridge which might be a few miles away? Arguments would develop along the lines of "Surely, a better way would be to go via such and such a road - or pub?" You may think I'm joking - but they would spend many a happy hour discussing routes like this. I doubt I ever saw the inside of a pub in York. Most of the young N/S men around me were pretty much the same. Drinking hadn't (then) had much of an attraction for many of us. Not long after National Service I worked for a Sheffield brewery - where of course a totally different philosophy was the order of the day - naturally.

However our soldiering was about to take a more serious turn so we did get more accustomed to the taste of beer as time went on. (Or the 'Electric Juice' as the old timers would have it!)

CHAPTER TEN

It would be boring to detail our extra six weeks training in detail but here are a few highlights.

We did much more work on the Strensall firing ranges. One noteworthy exercise was to fire several rounds at 600 yards and dropping and firing more rounds each further hundred yards - whilst at the double. The final practice was fired at 100 yards and was followed by a 'bayonets fix' order - and we then charged the target area - lots of heavy breathing by that stage!

We fired two weapons new to us. One was the E.Y rifle - which was a WW1 Lee-Enfield rifle with a specially reinforced barrel - enabling you to project a hand grenade two or three hundred yards, via a special cup mounting at the end of the barrel. The projective power came from a blank cartridge which had enough poke to send the grenade a fair way and give the platoon an extra bit of fire-power. The second was the fearsome PIAT (Projectile Infantry Anti-tank.) This thing really did look fearsome. It also looked a lot like a pneumatic road drill. It was cocked via a huge coil spring which you heaved upwards to lock into place - whilst standing on what did look very much like the handles of a road drill! A huge dart-like projectile was placed in the breach and this was activated by a large cartridge in its base. The feature of the projectile was a spiked projection at the front - which gave it the dart like look. Apparently when fired at a tank - and on hitting the target - the explosive charge was concentrated at the sharp end of the round, which then blasted the entire charge through a small area with astoundingly deadly results. I have since read that it was amazingly effective against a whole range of targets in WW2. My reason for relating all this is because it was yet again another example of what looked very much like a 'lash-up' that was astoundingly successful! Even in 1949 we still hadn't got rocket powered tank killers like the German Panzerfaust.

The kick back (for it was fired in the conventional manner - as with a rifle) - was quite something. When you saw the shoulders of those ahead of you heave backwards you knew it was no toy. Now, you would think perhaps that there would be some old tank hulks to practice on - with a weapon of this sort - way out on the Strensall ranges? Not a bit of it. We fired at a piece of sacking, held by two poles at either end of a small rail trolley that was indeed pulled along a small gauge track (by a very long rope) to simulate a tank in motion! Most of us hit the sacking OK but amongst us was one Private Plows - a big rawboned lad from North Yorkshire. He took to this weird gun like a duck to water. Not only did he shoot off the sacking entirely, he also in a tour-de-force, removed the two supporting poles as well - to much applause! More will be heard of young Plows later. I mentioned German equipment at the end of the last paragraph. We were astonished when engaged in various attack/ defence / ambush exercises, to find some of us kitted out in genuine Wermacht WW2 uniforms - even down to the jackboots. I kid you not. They were stored in a goods wagon out on the exercise grounds - and we were a bit miffed when it always seemed to be the other lot that got to dress-up. Imagine sending a photo home dressed in full German uniform! Mind boggling! However, this was only four years after the war - so much of our exercising was based on WW2 tactics. How much would this waggon load be worth today?

Thinking about it frequently afterwards, it occurred to me many times that there must have been hundreds if not thousands of ex - Chindits or Burma veterans still in the army, and it doesn't take much imagination to consider what jungle lore we could have picked up from one or two of these guys. However, at this time we hadn't any idea we would become fully fledged 'jungle bashers' in a few short weeks. So, our exercising was about conventional warfare mostly - nothing remotely connected with guerilla activity. We were vastly amused when we were the 'enemy' for some officer cadet exercises once or twice. We fired blanks of course and it was found that we could fire reeds through our rifles at them, with these. During the tea breaks on these schemes we would listen to these budding officers having to comment on various moves that had been made by both sides, and the effectiveness thereof. Great humour back in camp with our natural entertainers taking off one or two of the more 'Blimpish' would - be officer's mannerisms.

It would be unfair to state that the extra training we received was of no value whatsoever. It obviously toughened us up and the firing practices were obviously very necessary. I'm sure we must have done schemes where we were fired over by live rounds - but I cannot recall such an event or events. So, sufficed to say that our six extra weeks training passed quickly enough and soon we were ready for the off - and quite keen if the truth were known to get away. One final event caused Smithy and I to think we really had learned something from our training - the art of stillness and complete silence. We had been on guard duty and were totally knackered in the morning afterwards. We were detailed for fatigue duties in the cookhouse, and seeing that there were plenty of others so employed, we very quietly and unobtrusively slunk away. We had discovered an old blanket store in the 'Spider' complex where we were billeted and this room had very conveniently, lots of stout shelving - which we figured would take a recumbent body! Within moments we were asleep - to be awoken suddenly and dramatically as the door crashed open and there in the doorway we could see to our horror, none other than our Sarn't-major (the gripper) and a civilian policeman. Both had torches which they waved about, searching we gathered for a stolen bicycle. We also gathered from the conversation that it was quite common for squaddies to steal a bike if they had missed the passion wagon - or last bus, back to Strensall. Sure enough there was a bike leaning up against the wall. This probably saved us from a fate worse than death at the hands of the gripper, who obviously had not seen us quietly laying-up in the shadows of the blanket store shelving. Satisfied they retreated with the bike, and we with great sang-froid resumed our kip! Moral keep quiet and still when danger threatens!

During our extra training I had seen a great civilian mate, Brian Stevens - come in on a further intake of new recruits. I don't think I saw him socially at all as he was, as we had been during that first ten weeks - almost totally committed! As it happens he stayed in The Yorks. and Lancs. - and did his service in Germany.

Soon we were bulling up for our final passing out parade in front of the Camp CO - who addressed us in patriotic style before dismissing us from his kingdom. We then entrained for Liverpool docks as Draft DAFKT 8-33. By the time we arrived at the Albert Docks we were somewhat creased and very un-bulled.

CHAPTER ELEVEN

After a train journey of some hours - completed by buses or lorried transport to the quayside, we stood in three somewhat creased ranks - the whole draft of us, probably dying for a mug of char and gazing up in some awe at the T.S. *Orbita*. I say gazed up - as this vessel seemed to grow upwards out of the water like a huge block of flats! Not having seen a ship much larger than a seaside pleasure boat - most of us were astonished at the sheer bulk of the thing. She had a black hull, and white superstructure surmounted (somewhere just below the cloud line seemingly) - by two yellow funnels.

We embarked eventually and were allocated our messdecks - and as is the way with boats and sailing, put away our metal shod army boots for the next four weeks. At the time no one had told us how long the voyage might take - and we would have been astounded to hear just how long we would spend on *Orbita*! In later years of course with the world growth in air transport and the increased size of aircraft, troops could be ferried to their destinations by air within a day or so. Mind you we reckoned that our new floating home could accommodate at least 2,000 passengers - which would have taken an awful lot of planes to shift, on reflection!

On the *Orbita*, passengers were accommodated above and below the main deck according to status. The more spacious upper decks were 'verboten' to us - as we were obviously Rudyard Kipling's rough, licentious soldiery! Sentries were posted to discourage any romantic forays aloft! Thus upper decks were for officers, their ladies, and other ranks wives and families, heading out east to join their menfolk. Quite a few unaccompanied nurses and other females were aboard en-route to jobs connected with the armed forces at various ports of call.

Our own 'below stairs' messdecks weren't too cramped really. No more so than our barrack rooms. We slept on 'standees', bunks which let down from the walls or bulkheads. These were quite comfortable. I have a memory though that some blokes were still accommodated in hammocks in a corner of the messdeck. I cannot recall whether we were just above or just below the waterline in our particular area or not. Nor can I recall what date we sailed out of Liverpool - but apparently there was an item on the BBC Radio News indicating our departure. This was a little premature - as we were stuck in dock still, due to severe gales having blown up in our area of passage. Special customs dispensation had to be sought so that the 'wet' canteen could be opened for beer and cigarettes. I might add that we were amazed at the cheap duty free prices charged. We were also amazed that the beer came in cans - the first we'd seen. The fags were universally hated. Their brand was Black Cat I think - which the old hands reckoned had been aboard ship since wartime' But cheap they certainly were - they came packed in boxes of 50 - again the first we'd seen. Rarely at home were cigarettes ever handed around - because of their scarcity and for the times, expense. Here with fags being so cheap it was 'be my guest old boy!'

Eventually, sail we did, to a new life and to new experiences awaiting us. We were beginning to find our way around the ship - marvelling at the cafeteria system (with the trays pressed out to form containers for a complete meal) and at our new freedom from a training regime - when two things happened. The first was that most of us were allocated a job to do on board (for a portion of the day at any rate) - and secondly we began to feel a bit queasy as the ship began to be tossed around a little. Going up and down the companion ways sort of started it all off. If you were descending and the ship was on an 'up' wave you were slowed almost to a stop - and conversely, if ascending in a down trough - you found yourself moving very quickly! This, and a few nice wallowing rolls brought most of the ship to its knees over a few days. Some held out for a while but by the time we hit the worst gales for years in the Bay of Biscay - we all felt we were dying!

It was awful. As I say, the whole ship was affected - apart from the crew. Lifeboat drill took place as we lay comatose at our stations wishing we might die. The only people not allowed to be seasick were a contingent of Guardsman, whose NCOs had them doing P.T exercises and drills - as we lay or slumped down in our misery. I had been allocated a job with the ship's carrying party - which was a team of blokes fetching and carrying for the ship's canteens manager - and somehow retching and heaving - this job had to be carried out - ugh! The smell of oil as you neared the engine room was enough to turn your stomach over. This black period lasted three or four days at least - until our sea legs arrived. Then we could marvel at the size of the waves and start enjoying solid food again. Until this voyage very few of us had experienced seasickness. No 'Quells', 'Sea-Legs' or other travel pills available in those days!

The ship's carrying party moved about the whole ship above and below, and gave us an idea of the large size of the vessel. Deep in the holds we had to go for various supplies and it was hard to believe how far below the waterline we were sometimes. Not too many perks came our way until a bright soul suggested that the empty spirit bottles from the 'posh' upstairs accommodation had quite sizeable dregs left in them. So we mixed many a lethal cocktail whilst listening to the swish of water past the hull. Still not quite my scene - but soft drinks could be collected too. As we neared Spain the weather improved and we began to really feel human again. Gibraltar was passed in the night and I think at this point we changed into our tropical kit - which was olive green in colour. We spent a lot of time letter writing in anticipation of our letters being despatched from our first port of call - and hoping to receive significant amounts too!

We all reminisced about our 14 days embarkation leave - which had passed all too quickly. Many (allegedly) had 'made it' with their girlfriends on this leave - and made much of being men of the world. In my case, although the leave was more than welcome - it was pretty obvious my own romantic relationship wasn't going anywhere. However she wrote to me frequently during my time out east - and I was very grateful for that. So did my 'pretend' mother Ethel. The lassie that I got cigarettes for had also been snapped up - so I was pretty forlorn in the love life department.

Our first port of call was Port Said. We awoke to the sound of 'foreign' dockside noises and a babble of unintelligible voices. 'Twas a revelation I can tell you that! Bright, bright sun, natives in fez hats and long nightgownish garments and ultra bright buildings reflecting the sun - interposed with our first ever Palm trees! The 'bumboats' offering all manner of goods were already in the offing. However most of us had applied for shore leave and were taken off by lighters to the quayside. Here we changed our money into piastres and hit the town. Complete novices, we were conned left right and centre, one of life's rich experiences I guess - which stood us in good stead during our time abroad. All too soon we were back on board and heading for our next port of call, Aden. As we were about to pull away we watched the skill of the bumboat men as they closed their last deals and sent the goods up by lines to the waiting hands aboard. Again no austerity seemingly in this part of the world.

From now on we saw the full range of 'Rudyard Kipling' effects. Glorious sunsets - flying fish - porpoises swimming in escort by the bows and seas as calm as glass, quite unbelievable after our Bay of Biscay experiences! I have often wondered incidently what a skilled advertising copywriter could have created for an 'ad' incorporating the whole saga to-date. Something along the lines of - 'welcome your time in the army peace corps boys!' And - 'cruise the tropic seas to exotic far eastern shores

- in a fabulous floating world - with gastronomic delights and all entertainment provided.' 'Don't forget boys you'll be paid generously as well!' To complete the picture, a handsome 'tommy' would be seen leaning over a ship's rail with a ravishing ATS girl at his side! Not quite the true picture sadly.

The people running the ship certainly did do their best to help us avoid boredom. There were feature film shows, boxing tournaments, talent nights and I do recall the occasional dance. This latter being the only time we were allowed 'upstairs' - to the best of my recollection. There was a library aboard which I made good use of - and a writing room where you could compose your letters home in comfort and privacy. Our light tenor, Brian Norrie did well in the amateur talent nights - but as mentioned earlier our champion boxer had left us long ago to join the Paras. If you fancied a flutter you could join a bingo (or housey-housey) session - held regularly and you could gamble on the ships daily mileage sweep. I got it right just the once, and found myself £8 the richer. There must have been some sort of shop on board - as I bought myself a handsome automatic cigarette lighter, rather than fritter all the money away. Needless to say I had succumbed to the delights of nicotine on the voyage! Later, out east, this lighter was about the only personal possession that I had pinched in my entire two year service. The culprit was found eventually as I was not the only victim, but I never saw my lighter again - neither was any other property recovered.

The man in question was transferred swiftly after being up before the company commander. Had he not been so removed, I think the old sweats would have sorted him out - as stealing from comrades is a pastime fraught with extreme physical hazard. Perhaps where the odd item of equipment was concerned a blind eye might be taken - but personal items were generally sacrosanct.

There may have been two or three film shows per week but I cannot recall what we saw. The films were fairly up to date which was noticeable at a time when cinema going was the major pastime of most people in those pre - T.V days! All the major Hollywood stars were still going strong - your Clark Gables, your Robert Taylors - Humphrey Bogarts and your Gary Coopers etc. etc. Feminine wise - the legendary glamour and acting queens like Betty Grable, Rita Hayworth, Rosalind Russell, Hedy Lamarr and my own all time favourite - Ingrid Bergman - were in their prime. The likes of Sophia Loren and Marilyn Monroe had not yet burst onto the silver screen then! As I recall we watched the films somewhere on the main deck - probably with the 'upper deck' passengers watching from the balcony seats! Most people find almost total recall from a bygone tune or piece of music. I am certainly no exception - so sometimes on the radio, even today, a particular rhumba tune from the Edmundo Ros orchestra takes me back in a flash to a warm starry night on board the old *Orbita* - waiting for the film to roll!

I say old correctly - because she was an old ship! A plaque was displayed on the main deck advising everyone that she had been torpedoed in WW1 - salvaged, and still living to sail yet many another day! No serviceman or woman will ever forget the name of the boat they sailed on - both out from, and back to home. I have chatted to many people who travelled on troopships in the early fifties. None had heard of *Orbita*. I began to think she was a figment of my imagination - until, only recently, when I read the autobiographies of two servicemen who sailed in her in WW2 - where the old girl had an exciting career! I suspect she disappeared to the breakers yard in the early fifties as she was very slow. Her average speed would have been only 12 or 13 knots per hour. Much less in bad weather. Not that we saw any more bad weather after our Bay of Biscay trauma - it was a luxury cruise in that respect.

Our next port of call was Aden - then a British Protectorate. I went ashore with my mates and recall very little except it was extremely hot and dusty - and without much architectural merit. We were joined by an older squaddie - who said he would show us how to find - for want of a better phrase 'a lady of the night'. Not that we had the slightest wish for the services of such a lady! However he decided to demonstrate. Hailing a passing youth he said something along the lines of "you have beautiful sister yes?" "You take me to her for jig-a-jig, yes?" The youth, contrary to expectations - fled! Not to be outdone our friend then hailed a passing cab. "Take me to nearest brothel for jig-a-jig he commanded." The cabbie just accelerated away like Fangio! Can't understand it said the old soldier - last time I was here they all had beautiful sisters!!

My two abiding memories of Aden are watching from our main deck vantage point a lone soldier from the Argyles I think, being slowly forced back to the ship by local police - as he swung his service belt in an arc in their direction. The brass clasp was a lethal weapon if it caught you unawares. Slowly and patiently he was eased back - and all the time drinking from a half bottle of brandy, available ashore at the unbelievable price of 3/6d (roughly 15p today.) If beer was a new taste to some of us - then brandy was really out of this world! And the idea of a half bottle costing so little was unbelievable. Our Argyll friend finally made the gangplank and we sailed. He went straight to the cells to sleep it off. We lined the decks as the ship departed. The setting sun was out of this world as it slid behind ranges of mountain peaks - the like of which we imagined you would only encounter on the moon - so stark and razor edged they seemed to be.

On then to Colombo next stop. I cannot recall many incidents worthy of note from around this period - except that we had three lectures - with two I suppose being of particular interest. The first (still a puzzle - in terms of what it was supposed to impart to us) seemed to imply that we were leaving good old England at exactly the right time, as general conditions and austerity measures were going to worsen there. A great deal of political unrest was forecast and the prophecy made that we might never recover our pre-war influence and standing in the world. Much of this went over our heads as we were anything but political animals at the time. What it was all about still baffles me - I can but think it had a party political slant somewhere - as the current Labour government had been elected in 1945 by a landslide and was certainly not popular at home at this point due to its austerity measures. Newly eighteen, perhaps we were seen as potential voters?

The second lecture was the usual one to which troops going abroad were subjected to. It concerned personal hygiene and the dreaded VD! To our astonishment it appeared there was in most bases, special 'aid posts' you could visit after indulging in sex with a prostitute. Here an injection might be given - but certainly prophylactic measures could and would be taken. So, if you stuck by these rules and still caught a dose then you would avoid the 28 days field punishment you got if you went down with 'the pox' - which was considered then to be a self inflicted wound. Then a film was shown which showed various rotting 'willies' in quite appalling condition due to VD. Now I have always been a sucker for visual aids and later made a career in producing health education films and videos. This film made a deep impression on me and I thought I really ain't going to take that sort of risk with my prize possession! So, believe it or not I came home probably the one and only original, real life 'Virgin Soldier'. This despite the many temptations out east - where the ladies are exceedingly attractive and very sexy. Combine all this with a hot, lush tropical climate and you certainly know your libido exists!

I suppose the most important lecture as far as we were concerned was a briefing on the situation in Malaya - but who gave it and what his status was I cannot recall. From what he said, I assume he was speaking from a military point of view, so I guess he was an officer returning from leave perhaps? Or maybe an officer en-route like we were - and passing on the briefing he had received. At any rate the 'sitrep' (situation report) he gave us was woefully inadequate. For the first time we heard that we might have to pursue our enemy into the jungle. Not to worry - they were abysmal shots because they couldn't practice much for shortages of 'ammo' - and the chance that their firing might be heard and pinpointed! This turned out to be a load of tosh. 'They' practised by shooting at real people and were quite good at it as events showed. The terrorists were still referred to as 'bandits' and I think it took some time still to admit that they were highly organised Communists, hell bent on taking over the country!

Being highly respectful still at this stage (don't speak to the officer till spoken to) any questions were tendered by our NCOs who we had brought with us from the U.K. I don't recall we brought any officers - but we had a full contingent of striped persons. Some of these were 'made up' just for the journey and didn't keep their stripes long after arrival.

We learned from our lecturer that we might spend time on rubber estates, where apparently a few determined terrorists could wreck production in a night's sabotage - plus scaring off the rubber tappers for a few weeks. This element of the talk came perfectly true as most of our service was spent in encampments adjacent to, or on rubber estates, and jungle patrols set off from these encampments. I seem to recall that it was also admitted that a lot of prominent people were being bumped-off by these so called bandits - usually in road ambushes. Finally I think we learned that the majority of terrorists were of Chinese origin with very few Malays or Indians amongst them.

No doubt we talked about what we had heard amongst ourselves. I don't think we felt any particular alarm at what we'd been told - and even back in those early days of soldiering, did not necessarily believe all we were told!

Back then to shipboard life - which followed the same pattern as in previous weeks. Despite the difficulties of getting 'upstairs' on the ship - some romances did take place. One of our number achieved great fame by equipping his beloved with a spare uniform - so she slipped down at dusk to join him with her hair up under a beret!

CHAPTER TWELVE

Four of us had become inseparable on the voyage out - Dick Smith, 'Buffalo' Lingard, Frank Salf and myself. Despite the complete lack of feminine company we enjoyed being together as young men - bound for adventure obviously do. We went ashore together naturally and shared our meagre pay, 'all for one and one for all', 20th century musketeers were we! We howled at stupid schoolboy jokes and family anecdotes, tried to learn a particular card game from Frank who was very keen. What was the game? I recall one of the gambits was to 'go misere' - we never mastered it although it was a great favourite with the old soldiers. I don't think all four of us were on the ship's carrying party - but at least two of us were. So the days passed - hot and sunny - so we soaked it all up and generally lived the life of 'old Riley'. Reading, writing, chatting and doing not a lot seemed a far cry from our hectic training days - not that we were allowed ever to forget we were soldiers! I have a feeling that beer was rationed to about two cans a day certainly there was no drunkenness that I can recall. Spirits were not obtainable whatsoever to us then. Our last port of call was Colombo - now part of Sri-Lanka I believe. This was our first taste of the east and we liked it a lot. We saw our first sari clad 'dusky maidens' and the tropical luxuriant greenness was a foretaste of things to come! I do recall seeing some fine colonial buildings in Colombo town too. As we strolled around we gazed at the locals - and they back at us. A great deal of mutual smiling took place. We were not 'conned' from our money in any way shape or form, and I think we would have been happy to be stationed there. Sadly the country is riven by civil strife as I write - which is such a shame for so beautiful a country! One footnote of our brief stay in Ceylon. The huge French liner *Ille de France* moored alongside us in Colombo harbour. It was loaded to the gills with French Legionnaires heading for Vietnam (then French Indo-China) and later on Dien Bien Phu! They were not allowed ashore, but our abiding memory was the sheer bulk of the *Ille de France*. We thought we were on a big boat - but this thing dwarfed us!

And so the old S.S *Orbita* steamed her weary way the last thousand miles or so to Singapore. The time cooped up on a ship was proving a little too much for some of the war time veterans amongst us. The odd scuffle was now taking place and even we were beginning to think that we'd had enough of shipboard life - sunshine or no. We began to get our kit in order and think more of what might be ahead of us.

Did we arrive in Singapore during the night? I cannot recall but whenever - we crowded the decks to see what we could of this most famous of far eastern landfalls. To our complete amazement we were then 'buzzed' by a Spitfire - which flew very low over us. Was this a welcome to the east we asked? Or - did the pilot have a girlfriend - or even wife amongst the passengers? Later we were to see many famous wartime aircraft, Lancasters, Halifaxes, Mosquitos etc. All in action, and the familiar shape of the Douglas Dakota was to play a large part in the lives of most infantrymen of the period in Malaya. All this lay before us as we awaited our turn to disembark and leave our floating home of the last four weeks behind us. Looking back I'm quite sorry now that I haven't a photo of the *Orbita*. If I'd had a camera then no doubt there would have been several in my album to remember her by!

What happened next is a bit of a blur. We struggled ashore with our kit bags which proudly displayed our draft number. I recall our passing down a long 'arrivals' tunnel at the port. At the end of this was a beautiful piece of decorative tiled walling, dressed around with ferns and other species. The wall tiles were emblazoned - 'Welcome to Malaya - Land of Tropical Verdure.' The warmth of this welcome was somewhat spoiled somewhere along the way as we were each issued with the new 'Jungle Carbine' Lee-Enfield rifle, 50 rounds of ammo, and two hand grenades! Cripes, we all thought as one! Alas, no white, air conditioned barracks awaited us - we were soon at Singapore railway station, where we embarked on a steam train whose engine and coaches were somehow familiar in design - and yet totally different to the ones at home! Then came the stern stuff. "If fired upon while in motion, fire back at the flashes." "If the train is stopped by enemy action get off quickly and take up defensive positions." If my memory is correct experienced people were on hand to take command in an emergency - including a train commander. We soon learned we were bound for Kuala Lumpur, well up-country, but firstly over the very famous 'causeway' between Singapore and Malaya. The Japanese had poured over this to capture the greatest city in the east during their invasion - not all that long ago. From Kuala Lumpur it would then be by lorry to our regiment. Distance wise between Singapore and K.L would be about 250 miles and during the journey we saw many aspects of normal life and habitation of the country - from quite large towns to picture book Malay villages and kampongs. These with thatched houses were seemingly perched precariously on stilts! What we assumed to be fishing villages were again also perched on stilts - this time over water. Later, on closer inspection, there was nothing precarious about a Malay house on stilts. They were extremely well built and were kept cool inside by the space beneath - which also protected against unwelcome visitors such as snakes and other undesirable callers! The livestock of the family lived beneath in many cases, and found shelter and security from predators and the elements.

I and my mates have slept beneath such houses on several occasions - grateful for shelter from the heavy rain which swept down on a good many nights each month. As we journeyed northwards during daylight we saw several locomotives overturned and rolling stock scattered around as if by a giant hand. These had been blown up by terrorist mines and the sight certainly gave us cause for thought! Two platoon mates - Joe Slater and Harry Wragg were almost speechless. They worked for the railway back home - and had never seen a loco other than the right way up and on the track! On a lighter note as dusk fell and night overtook us, we noticed that some buildings in towns appeared to have red lights at their entrances. Could these be the legendary 'red lamp shops' we had heard old soldiers talking about? I don't think we ever really found out!

Our overnight journey wasn't disturbed and eventually we arrived at Kuala Lumpur . The station here is of the most elaborate eastern architecture imaginable. Built by the Victorian Raj, it was so grand that one would imagine it to be the government building at least. Here trucks awaited us and we embussed for the quite hair raising ride to our destination Bentong. The road rises and falls over very steep jungle clad hills and passes - with many many hairpin bends. Wartime footage of the famous Burma Road had much in common with what we were seeing. The tortuous switchback route - combined with exhaust fumes made many of us travel sick and perhaps not as vigilant against ambush as we should have been. We were constantly being exhorted by the convoy commander to be on the alert as he dashed up and down the route in his jeep - carrying a drawn revolver! Very reassuring!

We arrived at the town of Bentong somewhere in the late afternoon I would guess. The actual date eludes me - although it must have been getting on towards the back end of 1949. I'm pretty certain we were the first National Servicemen to reinforce what had been until then an all regular battalion. Needless to say we were entirely expected and tented accommodation awaited us as we were 'processed' (as the Americans say) and issued with mosquito netting and other essential items. Bentong - in the state of Pahang, was at that time battalion headquarters for the 1st. Green Howards - who had already been involved in contact with the terrorists on several occasions.

I can recall little of that first evening in our new milieu except that we turned in early, hung our mosquito nets in what we hoped was the regulation manner and were to a man, asleep within seconds! Needless to say we must have been fed and watered too - but I can recall nothing of this. We awoke naturally enough to the sound of the bugle and found that the dress of the day when in camp was shorts (bare torso) standard belts, boots and gaiters over hose tops - with green regimental stocking tabs protruding neatly from beneath the turnover. Our U.K. berets completed the picture. For those who had them, stripes and badges of rank were on wrist bands. Officers if I recollect correctly were not seen without olive green shirt/tunics at all times. Our U.K. blanco was incorrect here and we were given time to change to the standard white - which was achieved and maintained by toothpaste - believe it or not! A stranger would probably not have noticed any difference between us and the troops we were joining as we too were well 'browned' from the sunbathing we had done on the *Orbita*.

Apprehension preceded our 'debut' on first parade - which was akin to a pack of wolf cubs joining the King's Scouts! What sort of scrutiny would we be under we asked ourselves? However the powers that be were not seemingly too interested in us but were certainly on the ball when it came to minor infringements by the old hands we were joining - as we were all together on muster parade. The drill was the same we noticed from our training days - at least something was familiar!

We then discovered two things. One we were to do a further three weeks extensive training - culminating in a short jungle patrol (including a night or two) - to wean us into the general way of life that would soon become standard procedure for most of us. The second was that we would take Paludrin tablets on a daily basis from then on. Paludrin was an anti-Malarial drug that had recently replaced Mepacrin. This had been an effective preventative for Malaria during WW2 - but its chief side effect was to turn users an unfortunate yellow colour - not a particular pleasing aspect - and it is said that many people avoided taking it if they could! Paludrin had no such side effects and I did not hear of anyone catching Malaria in our company of something like 200 men. If you did catch it, it was considered to be a self-inflicted wound - with a 28 days in the 'glasshouse' reward! I read that nowadays you need Paludrin plus something else to be sure of keeping far from the clutches of Malaria - so virulent is the disease. We further learned that we were allowed into the town in off duty periods without a problem. However here it was civilian clothes only when off duty! The standard dress for this - and it was also popular with the locals - was a well laundered open necked white shirt and (generally) lightweight grey long trousers. Sports or lightweight shoes completed the picture. In the case of the locals wearing similar gear - their ensemble would be finished off entirely by wearing at least two pens in the shirt breast pocket. I have been subsequently amused from time to time to see pictures of senior Malaysian politicians adopting the same dress even today. The more senior - the grander and more numerous the pens. Malay locals generally kept to their national dress which was very colourful and topped off with a black 'fez' type hat!

This town of Bentong was well lit at night and the cafes, shops and bazaars stayed open late. I believe it was considered a fairly 'safe' town although there had been many terrorist incidents in the general area - including the town - so we were generally exhorted to keep alert - and have our eyes peeled at all times. We were rarely on our own as more often than not two or three mates would go out together. I was completely amazed when we were issued with a condom when leaving the camp of an evening. First one I think I'd ever seen! Bars there were in the town - but I'm pretty sure that we were not allowed to be served spirits? Tiger beer was the local (and national) brew. Imported lagers like Carlsberg and Tennents were around - but they were considered pretty pricey. I couldn't have told the difference between cheaper and more expensive beers or lagers in those days, so little was my experience. Talking of shops - my first pay parade was a bit of a pleasant shock - something like £4 was handed over to me. A fortune! Seems that there was this thing called local overseas allowance involved which 'bunced up' your pay no end. LOA was granted so that forces pay was subsidised to some extent in areas considered to be more expensive than the U.K. This first weeks pay enabled me to buy my first ever wrist watch - and still have a few dollars left for the canteen. At the time there were four Malayan dollars to the pound. I would say that the local businesses did very well out of the army base - for you could buy most things in the town. I suppose Bentong came more alive in the evenings. Pavement food stalls would be in operation - much patronised by the locals and giving off an unforgettable aroma as the spicy food was stirred briskly around the large cast iron woks - the first we'd ever seen.

CHAPTER THIRTEEN

Exploring the town a day or two after arrival a group of us came across the local Police Station. My memory tells me that it was well fortified and guarded as I think were all such locations. Being possessed of modest arsenals - they were tempting targets for our terrorist friends! The reason I mention this is because, parked outside the Police Station was a Dodge truck similar to the ones the army used. It had been ex-army judging by its colour - and had been ambushed and shot up in mistake for one of ours. So much for the alleged lack of marksmanship! This truck was proof enough these guys knew what they were about. We took due notice.

It would be boring to go into great detail about the further three weeks training we now embarked upon. Needless to say this special cadre was to teach us the skills we would need to be effective jungle warriors - and I suppose to stay alive. Great emphasis on shooting skills saw us blasting away on the ranges zeroing our new rifles and firing Brens from the hip and at various angles for, as the man says, here people may live in trees! Most NCOs carried Stens as a personal weapon, and I have mentioned before that they needed to be handled with great care. I seem to recall we re-qualified on the Bentong ranges and I think I just made first class shot on rifle and Bren. We enjoyed (if that's the right word) a special quick shooting close action range - a type which many people will have seen on their T.V screens. Targets that pop up in front, to the side and behind you. Were there some representing civilians - not to be fired at, and some with hostages in front as a shield? I can't remember - but it would seem likely. Very difficult to guess where a target might appear as they were cleverly sited in thick undergrowth - as would the real life situation be out there.

We were taught the rudiments of jungle cooking using the small, issue tommy cookers - which were lightweight metal pan supports holding a pellet of material - the sort you would light your barbecue with today. These little cookers were very effective and were practically smoke and odour free. If several men were messing together four of these cookers could support, say, a square biscuit tin containing a palatable stew. Needless to say most food eaten on patrols was tinned and taken from composite ration packs. Generally speaking this food was excellent - and had been developed during WW2. We were amused to see tinned cake on the menu and even more surprising, tinned bacon! It seemed we would be carrying at least four days supply of these 'compo' rations on our backs - and would be re-supplied by air drops. This sounded a little unlikely - who would find us in thick jungle we asked ourselves? We were soon to find out - and they always did find us!

The art of 'basha' building was explained and demonstrated to us. A 'basha' could mean anything from a small, one or two man shelter - to a much larger structure with a 'thatched' roof made from jungle materials and able to accommodate a larger number of people. Our terrorist friends were adept at the building of these larger structures and we were often amazed at the skills used to create these weather proof comfortable and long lasting shelters. However the ones we built were made up from a simple frame cut from nearby trees or undergrowth - and covered by a standard issue 'poncho' waterproof cape, with a groundsheet acting as flooring. One of these could be thrown up in a short space of time - once you had got the hang of it. Or if time permitted and you were in one place, jungle wise, for a few days - a more solid structure could be built with a raised floor to keep you away from things that crawled by night.

'Basha' was then a term to cover most temporary buildings including the splendidly engineered structures built by the Sakai - who were nomadic tribes-people living in remote jungle areas. They knew, and as we found out - there is a right and wrong way to chop down a tree - even a small one.

Laid on by our instructors for humour, and I guess our edification (still relative to basha building) - one of our training number was asked to demonstrate the art of tree felling - after what we had been shown. It was a smallish tree as they go and our friend advanced upon it with his newly issued, cutlass sized machete, and proceeded to hack away at it. All he succeeded in doing was dislodging every creepy crawly, biting, stinging thing therein - and he departed for a nearby stream desperately brushing himself down in an effort to rid himself of some of his tormentors. Point well and truly taken.

As we all found out later - ants of the red variety were about the worst culprits in the stinging/biting charts! Leeches were not too bad - they didn't sting or hurt, just sucked up a few teaspoons of your blood - and were easily dislodged at the end of the day by a lighted cigarette tip. First aid on patrols was looked after by trained medics who carried amongst all their other gear a pretty extensive medical kit. Really serious injuries had to be stretchered out. Reputedly there were only three early helicopters throughout the entire country at the time I was there and your priority had to be pretty high to get one. For instance on a particular patrol some months later our Dyak tracker was badly stung - or bitten by a poisonous centipede on his private parts - which swelled up to around the size of a football. No way could the company commander get him flown out. In the end he had to make his own way 'out'- with an escort of course - who helped him all they could! He emerged safely as it happens - to be met by an ambulance and thence to hospital.

Anyway we learned a great deal from this jungle training including the hope that we would not be chosen too often for ambush laying activities. Here you might be in position for days - unable to smoke or cook hot food - plus keeping deathly silent at all times! It was impressed on us that our terrorist friends could smell tobacco smoke - or cooking smells from a long distance away - plus, with their hearing being somewhat acute - any noise could compromise your position. We all took our turn in this activity as time passed. It was a boring yet potentially hazardous scenario.

After the extended training period the powers that be obviously thought we were ready for the real thing and we prepared for our first jungle incursion. For a start we couldn't believe what we had to carry on our backs. Four days tinned compo rations. Spare dry clothing - rifle, Sten - or if unlucky a Bren gun. Fifty rounds of ammunition, two grenades (one a No. 36, one a smoke/ phosphorous bomb) the latter being used mainly to indicate your position during an air drop. On top of all this there would be your poncho cape, groundsheet, a couple of Bren gun magazines, water bottle and possibly a roll of canvas in a 'dayglo' colour to indicate your presence to aircraft! All this and various other bits and bobs - totalled about 60-70lbs I would guess. On the credit side we had been issued with some new lighter weight, airborne style webbing and packs. The big pack was built around a tubular aluminium frame which helped to keep the load comfortably distributed. Jungle boots, laced almost to the knee, helped to support the ankle over rough terrain - and to top it all off, a jungle hat with a wide brim to keep the face in constant shadow. As time passed these hats assumed strange shapes to suit their owners whims. Some were turned up at the sides like cowboy hats - some had just one side turned up - a la Chindit style, others wore theirs floppy, but after a few days all had a very used look about them. Their other uses were legion - like a cowboys stetson they carried water from streams, they helped pick up hot utensils from camp fires or tommy cookers, they were used to mop sweaty brows and had many other practical benefits. Our other main jungle attire was a long sleeved, olive green shirt/tunic with long trousers in the same durable material.

We were also introduced to insect repellent and were encouraged to anoint our clothing with lashings of it. Get any of it near your more sensitive bits and you danced, literally! It was said that the company commander had a thing about the debilitating tropical disease - Scrub Typhus, hence this command to 'splash it all over!' Strange to relate the only person recorded as contracting this disease was the company commander himself - and his batman virtually dipped his clothes in the solution! So we were then ready for the off, and our baptism of fire!

The area for these first 'shakedown' patrols was generally in a supposed safe zone, probably just a few miles (if that) from base. It turned out that our enemies were well aware of this and had their own small camps in these areas too! Do I jest? No - the next cadre after ours stumbled on such a camp and despatched at least one terrorist. An old schoolmate of mine Dennis Bullivant, was on this patrol and his souvenir was a small tin box holding some British issue war medals - and the picture of a smiling 'bandit' at the WW2 Victory Parade in London! So onward we went unaware of this of course and proceeded on our stumbling, sweating, slipping, and sliding progress - putting into practice that which we had learned. You walk warily in single file eying all around you. You cannot see far to the side of you due to thick undergrowth and your view to the front is the man in front's back - or his pack and his hat. When you stop you know not why and wait for whispers to pass down the line. When in dangerous territory hand signals only are used. These were simple - for instance the two hands forming an inverted 'v' would mean Basha ahead. There were many others. Some official - some not! There certainly wasn't one in the manual to cover eventualities like 'the Major is chasing a rare butterfly for his collection!' When this whisper came down the line we shook our heads - but were much amused!

CHAPTER FOURTEEN

Your patrol usually enters the jungle from a point reasonably secure from observation. Generally you advance through lightly forrested areas (or rubber) before encountering real jungle. You do not usually (big surprise this) have to hack and slash every inch of the way forward. Generally the patrol will find tracks made by animals (possibly humans) and by following these you are generally able to move in the direction you wish to go. Sometimes these tracks are quite broad - sometimes very narrow and your equipment snags on every protruding branch or thorn. Roots, vines and other creepers do their best to trip you as you stumble along - trying to be alert and soldier like! Nothing really prepares you for the jungle as an environment it is quite unique. Many people have written about it. Probably the finest book on the subject is *The Jungle is Neutral* - by J. Spencer-Chapman. He was a Force 136 operative - that is a British officer working behind the lines (as it were) during the Japanese occupation of Malaya. He moved about the jungles of Malaya liaising with the communist guerillas and helping train them in their fight against the Japanese. We all read this book - which if anything emphasised the durability of the people we were up against!

I am amazed to read that tourists will pay good money to be taken into the Malayan jungle by guides - sometimes to see wildlife, but mainly to see a fast disappearing entity - the tropical rainforest. Rain it certainly did. Torrential downpours several times a day - and night. This helped to create a foetid, clammy, hothouse atmosphere which meant you were soaking wet most of the time whether raining or not. The sun took a holiday whilst you were jungle bound. Only in occasional clearings did you catch a glimpse of it. Light filtered down through the mighty trees - normally leaving you in a sort of half light. Before going on a patrol we dreaded what might lie ahead. A half day into the jungle (or Ulu) after some months of experience and - believe it or not, we felt quite at home.

Like many other tropical places - the light goes very quickly in the early evening - emphasised by the dark of the forest around you. Unless in hot pursuit - or keeping a rendezvous, it would be normal to call a halt - whilst enough light remained to build a camp - start the evening meal process, plus sending out a recce party and a water party if necessary. 'Stand-to' would be observed in the falling light after booby traps had been set around the camp perimeter. So, by 7.30 - ish you and your mate would be tucked up in your little basha - hoping the rain wouldn't flood you out if it deluged down and that the 'mossies' wouldn't be too aggressive in their nightly rampage.

Inside each of us as we proceeded like pack animals entering the twilight kingdom of the rain forest was a very scared and tense individual. Each one of us no doubt wished to be judged manly, and seen to be pulling our weight - as did our fathers as they marched up to the trenches in WW1. Our situation was not nearly so desperate and dangerous as theirs was - but there was this unknown quantity about it as we gazed up at the tall trees surrounding us - many heavily buttressed like medieval cathedrals to prevent their roots eroding in the constant downpours of tropical rain. We were entering the abode of wild creatures both insect and animal - calls from the latter being frequently heard, but seldom if ever seen! Insects these we saw in their thousands - from giant ants and bloodsucking leeches to huge butterflies, their wings undulating like the gentle flapping of old white fivers! Snakes too were frequently observed - although no-one to my knowledge was ever bitten by one - they slid away pretty pronto when we came across one (apart from a massive cobra) - which I shall describe later in context.

We became aware of the all pervading smell of decay around us which we soon became accustomed to - frequently brought back to me in a flash sometimes even now, when turning earth over in the garden at home! So gradually on this first expedition we began to see the pattern unfold of how most future patrols would go in terms of sheer physical endeavour.

The weight of our packs and equipment in a hothouse environment (and constant vigilance) - sapped our energy as the march and the day wore on. We longed for the hourly break when we sank gratefully to the floor - our laden packs acting as a back rest. All too soon it was OK guys, we go! At this we would pull each other up and once again continue our weary way along this never ending obstacle course. Brew-ups and meal times came and went and eventually we settled down for the night in our newly constructed bashas - completely and utterly knackered. Some of us already knew that our ordeal was far from over as we had been chosen by the platoon sergeant to do an hours guard (or stag) over our sleeping comrades.

I had hardly (seemingly) been asleep for more than a few minutes when a heavy hand woke me very roughly and told me it was time for my stint. He led me to the sentry post beside the track and pointing, muttered that the Bren gun was there - and disappeared like lightening back to his basha. Thus it was that I had my first ever traumatic patrol experience that no training procedure can envisage! It takes a while for the eyes to accustom themselves to the pitch dark night - although ears have already begun to take in the jungle's night noises, which are many and varied. A particular one which comes to mind, as you sit by the track - is the sound of a particular (large) flying beetle which cruises the tracks by night. It sounds as though a two-stroke motor bike is heading directly for your head. As it nears you, you duck to avoid a blow between the eyes - but its little sensor picks you up and - just in time it puts on full power and lifts above your head. A leaf falling from on high, or a distant branch crashing down sets the adrenalin surging too. You know no-one could get close to you without making a hell of a noise - but it certainly beats a fairground white knuckle ride for tension!

However my own little panic was about to start. It seemed a good idea to position myself behind the solid comfort of the gun. Trouble was I couldn't find the bloody thing. I crawled around the jungle floor in all directions - sweeping it with my hands - to no avail! No Bren could I find. A sweeping tide of horror overtook me. Headlines in *The Daily Mirror* formed before my eyes 'Guard's Neglect - Comrades Slain.' I literally died a thousand deaths during that one hour of guard. A theory exists that when mortal man is in great despair and a time limit exists, then time passes like lightening for that individual! I can attest to the truth of this theory. The hour (or was it two) of my guard seemed to pass like minutes as I wrestled with the problem. When the time came to find the next man on guard I suddenly had a cunning plan. Why not do to the next man as had been done unto me? With this brilliant thought in my mind I set off to find my relief. I had gone seemingly but a step - when I fell over the gun that I had spent most of my time trying to find! Later, experience taught us to use a particular type of rotting twig - which gave off a slight glow in pitch darkness. Just enough to follow its trail to a particular point fairly accurately. You may well ask - how did you ever find the next man on guard? I don't know - but we always did.

The batting order for guard duty was, as I have said, worked out by the platoon sergeant - who also had to calculate a fair roster of nights off when on a long patrol. The key to the relief system between sentries was by the handing on of an army issue G10 wristwatch. This was a large affair with a luminous dial and its possession proved that you had taken post as a sentry. If you happened to fall asleep on the job it also proved that you and you alone were to blame! It so happened that one night I had to hand over the watch - and the guard to my basha mate of that patrol. He decided he would sit it out whilst still inside the shelter, probably because it was raining. The inevitable happened he fell asleep.

Daylight brought a berserk sergeant - we had all overslept and the time for 'stand to' was long gone! Fortunately for me my basha mate had put the watch on - which proved that I had handed over both the watch and the guard! Sleeping on guard is a serious business - and heavy punishment can be handed out. In this case because we had had a gruelling patrol, my 'oppo's' fate was not too severe. A bawling out by the Major back in camp - and some pay stopped. The bawling out was not taken lightly. The whole of a tented camp could hear the invective and career assassination of the culprit as he stood before a very angry CO. We were more terrified of letting him down than of the enemy. A final word on jungle guard duty - the watch system had a problem. Bored, tired out - or scared stiff, squaddies would sometimes advance the watch by perhaps as much as half an hour in a two hour stint. If two or three did this - the last man did considerably more than his fair whack. But nothing could be proved - the watch could not speak!

I cannot recall much else about our 'shakedown' patrol. We obviously learned a great deal and we returned to base exhausted and wiser men. Having I suppose passed our 'O' levels, we were now awaiting word of our postings to the rifle companies. The news when it came sadly split up the four musketeers. I was destined for 'D' company - then situated on an extremely large rubber estate at Pertang - in the State of Negri-Sembilan. I'm not sure where the others went - we saw each other again only very briefly - just on odd occasions.

Those posted to 'D' found their new home was some distance from Bentong - which was just a small place then - but is now a famous University town! Our introduction to the far east took place here you might say - and by and large most of quite liked it. The climate was quite agreeable - about 85 - 90°F daily.

So - OK - it rained quite a lot, and very heavily when it did. But a little while after, so warm was it - you would hardly notice it had rained at all! On the downside we had become acquainted with your unfriendly neighbourhood mosquito. Prickly heat could be uncomfortable and we heard of a strange skin problem called Tinea. This was a condition similar to Ringworm and extremely itchy and irritating. Treatment generally was to shower when possible with rainwater (usually from the run off from a tent roof) - and the application of that good old remedy gentian-violet!

Later in my service and during one of the longest patrols to date in the jungle campaign - I contracted this myself and emerged with some interesting skin-tones. Each re-supply airdrop brought a different coloured treatment solution seemingly, and I was at one time coloured in shades of purple, green and orange! So much so that a squaddie returning home said to me something along the lines of "I shall never forget thee Ives - tha's looked just like a fooking red indian for the last four fookin weeks - cheered us all up no fookin end!"

However, back to Bentong and eastern culture. We soon marvelled at the carriage and deportment of Asian ladies particularly Indian and Malay women ~ both of whom wore a sari like garment. Some Chinese girls wore western style clothes even then - but all carried themselves with considerable grace and elegance. Many times when we found ourselves guarding small villages and kampongs we would watch fascinated as the womenfolk bathed in streams or pools under our gaze - still clad in their saris or sarongs, without showing an inch of forbidden flesh! I have also seen a truck load of lecherous squaddies (including me) struck dumb by the carriage and grace of Indian ladies carrying a water jar or some other load upon their heads. We soon got used to seeing young men walking hand in hand with each other too. There was nothing effeminate about this (although it was strange to our eyes) - it was their Asian way of showing friendship. No doubt there were other eastern ladies in Bentong, equally elegant, who made a good living catering for the more amorous squaddies and their needs. I don't think many of us rookies sought out their services at that stage as we were trying to come to terms with our new existence and circumstances.

Local and world news came via radio broadcasts over the 'Blue Riband' English language service of Radio Malaya. This we heard over the camp's loudspeaker system. *The Straits Times* newspaper was the influential press at the time and I think copies of this were available on the camp. We did get British newsprint - but it was usually a week out of date before we got it. The local news via either the radio or press was usually pretty depressing as the terrorist campaign was at its most vicious in early 1950 - and dreadful incidents of murder and atrocity occurred throughout the peninsula on a daily basis sometimes quite close at hand. Rolling grenades into busy shops or restaurants - or tossing them into crowded dance halls was a favourite pastime of our terrorist friends. Assassination of 'bigwigs' was also a popular sport and a common occurrence, as the terrorists sought to intimidate the local population. Needless to say rubber planters and their families were 'dish of the day' to the guerillas at that time and most of the planters houses and bungalows were turned into mini-fortresses. Their cars and station wagons were also armour plated and many presented strange sights when you saw them on the estate roads!

However as young lads the world over our feet tapped to the beat of whatever pop songs were beamed to us via the camp loudspeakers. From time to time there would be records played over this system. Doris Day was still No.1 in those days. Her voice had a magic sex-appeal for us and we would rush from our tents and gather round the speakers as if she was there in person! One of her great hits concerned what a good girl should and shouldn't do in various romantic circumstances. I doubt if she would have remained a good girl for very long had she surfaced amongst her lusty fans.

Down in Bentong town there was a record shop owned by a Chinese family. Like all record shops they advertised their presence by playing records - well audible to passers by. From time to time a number of us would gather outside the shop to soak up what music we could hear from outside - sitting wherever we could. Obviously top of the Chinese pops was an eastern vocalist whose voice (despite singing oriental songs in Cantonese) - was a great favourite with us. The shop owner was much amused by this - although I doubt he sold a single record to any of us - for the simple reason we had nothing to play records on! For those who think transistor radios, record players and cassette recorders have been around for ever - not in 1950 they weren't!

Those were the days of the mouth organ. Most platoons had someone reasonably proficient on one - someone who could lead a sing-song, keep it in tune and carry a reasonable repertoire. I tried one myself and by the end of my service could knock out a reasonable, recognisable tune. The odd guy had a guitar probably one per company. With these two instruments and players, a can or bottle or two of beer, we would have a really good evening singing the songs that everyone knew in those days! Juke boxes may have been around in some of the major towns - but there were none in our particular locality. So all in all, Bentong quite appealed to us, however 'twas time to move on.

CHAPTER FIFTEEN

Leaving behind then the fleshpots of Battalion HQ at Bentong - those posted to 'D' Company were lorried to our new home on the Pertang Rubber Estate in the State of Negri-Sembilan. As described earlier, Pertang was a vast rubber estate with row upon row and mile upon mile of regimented rubber trees lined up like guardsmen. Lord only knows what the output of the estate was - enough to supply the whole of the U.K. with Wellington Boots we surmised. For the uninitiated - rubber trees (about the size of large apple trees back home) - have a spout inserted into their trunks under a special type of cut. This allows the raw rubber or Latex to run out into little china cups where it collects - and in turn is collected by rubber tapping ladies with containers - at intervals throughout the day. A bit like collecting grapes for the wine harvest - except this was a daily occurrence.

Rubber estates such as this one were tempting targets for terrorists. A nights orgy of tree slashing and terrorising the workforce (by murdering the headman probably) caused havoc with rubber production - as the workforce would flee, leaving the ruined trees behind them. Needless to say - that's why it made good sense to post troops in varying strengths on or near vulnerable rubber plantations. From these bases patrols would set forth to sweep the areas around them - hopefully keeping our red friends away. This policy was pretty successful overall I believe!

One humorous vignette comes to mind reference the rubber tapping females on the Pertang Estate. One of our number - new to the game, found himself quite close to a very pretty young Tamil lady. Wishing to introduce himself and chat her up in the approved manner of young men everywhere he gestured to her to come over by crooking his finger at her. Wrong move chum. Blushing she flees the scene and reports our friend for gravely insulting her honour thus. Result - company on parade to be dressed down by CO (with some humour) and then addressed by chief planter who indicates correct method uniform throughout the east (for both sexes) is to beckon with palm downwards and fingers bending inwards! I seem to remember the planter adding something along the lines of "nice though they may be - don't waste your time lads - they're all betrothed to somebody already." That little story illustrates the respect the Brits had for the locals in general - which included even the hard nosed regulars who had been everywhere and seen everything!

So, to 'D' Company I went and remained with them until the time came to come home in 1951. I found myself allocated to No.11 platoon - where only three of us were national servicemen - the rest were regulars, including one or two who had come out on the draft with us. I have a platoon photograph in front of me as I write. Some names, matching faces - come immediately to mind - despite the passage of time. I would have to hear a roll call once again to remember the rest. Due to the vagaries of the posting system I had 'lost' Dick Smith, Buffalo Lingard and Frank Salf - they having gone elsewhere. We did meet up individually on very odd occasions but were only all together again on the boat home. I then palled up with Joe Slater - from Normanton - who I had known in earlier training obviously. Joe proved to be as fine a mate as it was possible to have, and we are still in touch all these years later! Joe came from a mining family - but had been a railway fireman until call-up.

Out there the choice of a good mate was an important one. You marched, messed and watched each others backs when on patrol. You even slept together in your jointly constructed, hopefully waterproof basha - taking all that the jungle could throw at you, together. Number 11 platoon were lucky with the platoon sergeant too - who was called Grimmer. Sgt. Grimmer was an experienced ex-wartime NCO and frequently called upon to act as platoon commander. A good platoon sergeant was arguably the most important member of the group. He was closer to the men and knew pretty much what they were capable of. Our officer was a Lieut. Pearson (I think) although these changed more frequently than NCOs. Of Corporals only one name comes to mind - that being of Macdonald. He was as tough a customer as I have ever come across - he didn't need to act it - he was! The Company Sergeant-Major was CSM Holloway - who seemed to be quite a fatherly figure as far as we young rookies were concerned. His role generally seemed tied up with camp administration. The company commander at that time was I think a Major Gartside. There was to be a change of both battalion commander and company commander shortly after we arrived. Memory being what it is - although I can recall us being paraded, to say farewell to either the O.C company or the commanding officer of the battalion - I cannot recall which. Whichever it was, he was obviously very emotional about leaving the regiment behind!

Talking of our leadership - we had now moved into a situation where real leadership counted at all levels. The guys who led us in Malaya knew what they were about (apart from some very rare exceptions.) Our lives depended on their skill and judgement - particularly in the field of navigation. I know this is a naval term - but I cannot think of another for finding your way through the jungle when there is nothing to see but trees and even more trees - trees so high that even the sun's rays are obliterated! Just once you might emerge into a clearing on a hillside enabling you to see surrounding terrain but not often. Contour lines on maps weren't much use either as we were constantly surrounded by jungle clad hills (or bukits.) Deep flowing rivers criss-crossed the terrain with currents going in opposite directions - despite the closeness of one to another! All we had were No.19 radio sets - maps, and not much else except for experience intelligence and savvy. (Satellites came along about 40 years later!) We always joked that we were lost as soon as we entered the jungle but I very much doubt that we were!

We had Iban or Dyak trackers with us generally - but their role was to assess signs and tracks that we would not have spotted - leading to hideouts and arms caches and general guerilla movements. On many patrols the platoon would be a separate entity in its own right with its own itinerary and search area. It might be on its own for days or weeks - so the quality of platoon leadership - officer and sergeant were absolutely crucial. I think we all realised we were lucky in our junior commanders. Not that we would have told them this at the time you understand!

Before describing some of the adventures we had jungle-wise, (there is no better descriptive word) it might be of interest to describe camp routine - which must have been pretty general throughout every regiment in Malaya. Back as far as Roman times someone obviously decreed that an idle soldier was a bad soldier. This philosophy was certainly applied to us as we had very few idle moments - apart from official rest times. In some camps there were standing guards throughout the full 24 hours.

Another group at platoon or at least section strength, were on constant standby in case of terrorist incident. (This group probably did any camp fatigues that were required also.) Those not in the jungle and permanently employed such as cooks storemen and clericals, were constantly involved in convoy or vehicle escort duties. No vehicle went anywhere without an escort. As we found out later - the roads were very unsafe places unless proper measures were taken, and even well escorted convoys were frequently ambushed. So much so that in particularly troublesome areas scrub and light forestation encroaching near to the roadside was cut right back. So most of us at one time or another saw many towns and villages throughout the country. Looking at a map now many of these place names are still familiar. Raub, Mentakab, Kuala

Lumpur the capital, (and fleshpot centre - or so we thought) Kuala Kluang, Ipoh, Jelibu and many many others.

Some of these places were overnighters - which made a change, and sometimes you might have met up with an old buddy at one of these stops. You do not need to be a major strategist to understand that without an adequate, reliable road transport network the campaign would have been unsustainable. There were many casualties of drivers and escorts in my time there - so you kept your eyes peeled and your weapon handy when on escort duties. Some time after I came home the new company commander, Major Chadwick, was killed in a road ambush - which illustrates the dangers.

Another aspect of our lives in connection with vehicles was that when engaged in stop and search operations - i.e buses and other road transport at road blocks, or sealing off villages and kampongs for search and I.D checks - or even just patrolling sections of road to 'show our faces' - we travelled, armed to the teeth in 15cwt (weapons carrier) Dodge trucks. These were mainly open to the weather but were instantly ready for action. Thus we preceded by some years the famous Somali 'technicals' which held such sway in the civil wars in Somalia. Ten /twelve squaddies would be crammed in the back as we sped forth on our various missions. I am amused nowadays at the size of some of the Patrol type off-road vehicles currently on our roads. They are not much smaller than those we spent such bumping times in all those years ago!

Road blocks incidently brought us into close contact with the civilian population. When buses were stopped the passengers would be taken off and the bus searched for arms and explosives. Searches tended to be cursory as much livestock would be on board and much of the luggage and packages were up on the roof - held in place by a huge roof rack. One of our most agile would swing up on the roof and attempt a search. The passengers - mainly female, would have their I.D cards checked and would then be 'patted down' discreetly for concealed weapons. They would smile as we did our best to avoid unnecessary contact and it says a lot for the average Brit at that time as I never heard of a complaint emanating from a search of this nature. Perhaps we weren't so gentle on patting down the fellows! You will obviously have gathered that all civilians carried an I.D card complete with photograph.

Civilian lorries were curious looking objects in that they were mainly British manufactured chassis and part of the cab - but the rest of the truck was completed by local firms - much influenced by eastern design and decoration - to our eyes they appeared ready to enter carnival vehicle contests at the seaside at home! These too had to be stopped and searched but nothing was ever found in our searches. Obviously contraband did get through to terrorists who at that time had a very sophisticated supply network - which was dealt a heavy blow by the famous Briggs plan, of which more later.

Whilst on the subject of transport I shall never forget the hairiest ride of my life - nor will the others either. We were on standby (as per my description of camp life) when we were scrambled to a terrorist incident in a nearby township. This time there was no shooting - merely a long harangument on the iniquities of the British and the joys of being a communist etc. etc. We were not to know this as we sped to the incident clinging to the side of a half-filled water truck that was the only transport available. I need not tell you what it's like to cling to a small rail while standing on a narrow ledge around the water tank of a speeding truck. This, whilst clutching your weapon for dear life, as at the same time the truck is trying to turn over on each and every bend as the water sloshes around inside! Harry Wragg (the driver) and most of us were quite green round the gills when we arrived at the scene - to find thankfully that our bandit friends had left the area.

Most private cars on the roads out there at that time were prewar British saloons. Where and how they had survived the war I know not. The number of people we saw crammed into small saloon cars sometimes was unbelievable. Many prosperous Chinese and Indian businessmen however drove large American cars. After the Chinese New Year celebrations the number of temporarily abandoned and crunched up 'gas guzzlers' was amazing! Talking of gas guzzlers incidently, each of our rifle companies had an armoured scout car available to the transport section. These worked overtime and then some. I recall the driver of the 'D' company one being ordered to take a rest by the CO - we all appreciated this as he was the company guitarist! Frequently when patrolling the local railway lines we would see larger armoured cars of the 8th. Hussars actually driving on the rail track - their wheels neatly fitting just over the lines. The sleepers obviously played havoc with the tyres - which would be showering bits of rubber as they roared past! Still I suppose a new set of tyres each trip was cheaper than a train blown up! They would be preceding the train which would be close behind.

CHAPTER SIXTEEN

After being absorbed into camp life under canvas, we became involved in operational activities. There may have been one or two small ones before our first major jungle excursion - which coincided with the arrival of our new company commander. It has to be said that he was not a popular leader as far as the old sweats were concerned - some of whom had served under him before. As far as we rookies were concerned, one major was very much the same as another - not necessarily having your interests at heart - and so we preferred to defer judgement until we knew him better.

This first big operation involved at least two full companies and was designed to locate and destroy a large guerilla camp (plus inhabitants) - located about 20 miles deep in thickly forested terrain. We were to be led to this camp by a new animal as far as we were concerned - an SEP (surrendered enemy personnel.) Time was of the essence apparently so that our first days march ended with us collapsing pretty exhausted with no time for cooking or shelter building before dark. I assume we nibbled something from our packs. As for guards, there must have been sentries posted but we were grateful not to be picked! Mercifully it did not rain that night - otherwise we would have been half drowned by morning. We were off again at first light with no breakfast to speak of for another day of forced marching - to bring us close to our objective. I think we did stop earlier on day two, and a strong recce party was sent out to confirm proximity to our objective.

I found myself on sentry this night and being on the edge of our encampment overheard the two majors discussing the morrow as they paced about - probably unaware of my presence. They were discussing our proposed attack and our major was entirely convinced there would be heavy casualties amongst us. The other commander indicated that it had to be done and with that they moved on. The thought of casualties must have affected our new major, as a little later an incident occurred that convinced us that he had had a nervous breakdown. He left us shortly after our return to base and although nothing was said about the incident, we felt we knew the reason. Who knows what this man endured in WW2? The thought of heavy casualties in what was (allegedly) peacetime was probably more than he could bear!

So, guided to the location of the enemy camp, early in the morning we charged in - in the finest traditions - only to find that the birds had well and truly flown! But what an amazing sight this camp was. It was large and built to last. There was a level parade ground with beautifully constructed bashas all around it. A large stage with a proper facia had been built obviously for entertainment and political speeches and there were various hutments which had been storerooms, and even a sick bay. Many documents were found and newspapers, the dates showing that our friends had not long been gone. Of two big surprises, one was that the camp had running water - piped through bamboo pipes from a waterfall nearby, and the other that there had been children in the camp. We knew this as children's shoes were found with other clothing in one of the bashas! It was assumed the camp would have held at least a couple of hundred people - not necessarily one gang but perhaps a district H/Q, so large was it. The general assumption was that there had been a tip off - hence the empty camp. After this anti-climax patrols were sent off to scour the area, without result - so I think we spent one night at this site and destroyed it thoroughly before we left. We returned to base well impressed by the buildings in the camp and marvelled at what had been achieved from just ordinary jungle materials. Over my period of service I saw several bandit camps - both large and small, but nothing came near to the quality of this one in terms of location and skilful construction.

All in all, I must have done something like twenty or so patrols during my service - and the only way I can remember them is by the sometimes bizarre incidents that took place like the latter one!

Mind you, nothing could have been more bizarre than one that took place not long after. Following the swift departure of the company commander, we were temporarily led by a Major Gillies who had been SAS and heaven knows what in the war. He breathed fire and smoke and aggression was his middle name! He conceived a plan to blast some terrorists who were reputedly using a particular confluence of tracks for supply purposes. He acquired a quantity of land mines and the plan was to build a concealed underground bunker, many feet deep which would be surrounded by the mines - and which would be detonated by trip wires or pull strings - or both even, when terrorists approached. The killing range of these mines was such that anyone within thirty yards or so would be fatally wounded. So off we set, loaded to the gills - some of us carrying these large heavy mines (about the size of a small household pedal bin.) These loads were passed up and down the column to ensure everybody did their fair share - but they were extremely heavy - and were handled with the greatest care I can assure you.

After one or two days on the march we reached the chosen spot - and bunker building began. A deep squarish hole was dug out and roofed with logs and tarpaulin - camouflaged with twigs, leaves etc. - so that it was virtually invisible, and as I recall we all took a hand at this digging. A trench was constructed which led to a latrine area, and all the land mines were laid at a suitable distance. Exhausted by this physical effort we then withdrew - leaving the mad major with a hand-picked team of cohorts to await developments. We were all sure that if the crunch came they would all be blown to bits! In the event, some days later we went in again to fetch the major out. Probably due to a tip off - or unreliable information, our red friends had never showed up. This was not quite the end of the story however - some of the mines were considered to be in a dangerous condition and had to be detonated. We were withdrawn to a safe distance whilst this was done - and the noise of these explosions was unbelievable! Had the terrorists come, there is no doubt that they would have been wiped out.

Whilst on the subject of our new 'mad' major - he led us on several further patrols before our next company commander arrived. The one that sticks in my memory is of the occasion when after a strenuous exhortation to keep a dead silence after stand-to, we retired to our bashas to crash out (as they say nowadays!) I suspect we were considered to be near a terrorist area. Anyway as we were drifting off to sleep we were rapidly awakened by the sound of some (very) loud Scottish oaths and much flashing of torches from the major's shelter. His batman had inadvertently built the shelter on top of a red ants nest! Bites from these insects were like jabs from red hot needles and the major's howls could have been heard in K.L - a good many miles away. So much for security and quiet - we shook with suppressed mirth - ants certainly didn't distinguish between the finer points of rank!

On the subject of night times in jungle situations - we were all pleased to find that on most nights there was a tot of very strong rum issued. Despite being soaking wet - as was our general condition - this tot certainly aided and abetted a swift descent into slumber. On my 19th birthday we were somewhere deep into the forest and I received an extra tot plus more from my mates. I went out like a light, but being unused to strong drink in quantity I woke in the night to feel the ground seemingly heaving. Staggering to my feet and convinced there was an earthquake, I lumbered around the camp area - in great danger of being shot by the sentry! Needless to say, nature took its course and I somehow made it back to the shelter unscathed - to wake with a massive hangover.

Being young and fit, when back at base camp after a patrol we rapidly recovered from our exertions and slipped back into camp life easily. Usually a reception committee lined up as we entered camp to ask if we had met and disposed of any terrorists - which was I guess our primary objective. The officers and senior NCOs were I suppose debriefed, but our main concern was for hot food, a shower and sleep. It could well be asked what amenities could a camp offer when situated miles from anywhere 'midst a huge rubber estate'? The answer is quite a lot really. All these camps had a sort of canteen run by senior NCOs from the quartermasters echelon. Only beer was served and that somewhat rationed. This canteen (usually a large tent) would probably sell chocolate and fags - and be the place where sing-songs took place. I should mention that we received 50 cigarettes free per week from the Malayan civil government. Needless to say round tins of fifty fags were a completely new method of packaging as far as we were concerned. Even those who didn't smoke as such, took their ration. On patrol nothing shifted a leech better than a touch with a burning cigarette tip and puffs of tobacco smoke certainly dispersed squadrons of aggressive mosquitoes!

In terms of snack meals (we were still always hungry) obviously there was no NAAFI available - nor could we pop out and find a cafe close by. Our needs were met by a char-wallah or wallahs - depending on the size of the camp. These gentlemen were always Indians and they produced tea (served in glasses) and tasty snacks like egg and chips, egg sandwiches (called banjos) and the like. They allowed you to build up a tab - and lets face it you certainly couldn't avoid paying at the end of the week or month, for - where could you go? Operating with very little in the way of cooking equipment they produced some tasty snacks and were undoubtedly an asset to the camp as a morale booster. It wasn't as if camp grub wasn't good - all in all it was pretty fair, even when much of it was tinned 'compo' rations. Some fresh foods were supplied though by local contractors who ran the risk of assassination for supplying army bases. At one camp - the char-wallah was a Pathan gentleman of a very tough looking appearance. We were surprised when firing on the range that he was always allowed to shoot off a number of rounds. This he did in a strange firing position as far as we were concerned i.e, sitting with elbows resting on knees! Memory has it he was pretty good too. Apparently in the early days of the Battalion in Malaya he was with a convoy that was ambushed and seizing a weapon from a wounded squaddie he joined in the defence with gusto - and allegedly helped to save the day. As the Pathan is a warrior tribe on the North West Frontier of India he probably enjoyed the scrap! This gentleman followed us through many camps I seem to recall. Not however into the jungle areas!

Another (very brave man) arrived generally once per week from the A.K.C (Army Kinema Corporation) to give us a film show. These gentlemen, generally Chinese, drove little Ford 10cwt vans equipped with everything required, including generators and portable screens! Their vans were emblazoned with A.K.C but we never heard of one being ambushed - strange because they always travelled alone. The old hands said it was because some of our 'red' friends would creep up and also enjoy the show from adjacent cover - which is perfectly pòssible given that most of these shows were out of doors - in the dark of the evenings! The screen area was generally quite large, as often other units - and the planters and their families would join us! The films I think were fairly new - but I cannot remember a particular movie now. I think there were newsreels too - and no doubt we would cheer if there was anything 'on' about the Malayan Campaign. From time to time when on convoy escort duties we might find ourselves at an RAF base. As stated before some of our destinations included overnight stops - and we were always impressed that the RAF had proper cinemas on their bases. Were they called 'Astras'?

Before moving on it should be mentioned that mail from home was still the most morale boosting thing of all. The army postal services were excellent and we even got our mail via air drops when on long patrols. I could not complain about the amount of letters I received. Lorna (my Sheffield girlfriend) wrote fairly often, even though our romance was fast fading. Ethel, my almost mother-in-law wrote often too - as did Aunty Jones, Marjorie, and some of the girls from work. Some came from a pen-pal girl in Australia - whose address I think came from Soldier Magazine. Those who didn't receive much mail gazed with envy at those that did. Letters from families with no 'personal' contents were often passed to those less fortunate to read. Humorous letters were often read out to mates as were some heavily sexy ones - wow! Listen to this chaps! We wrote back often, as, letters home certainly generated mail back to us .

Some families sent local newspapers which were passed around to everyone. On one occasion we actually received a visit from a reporter from home! *The Yorkshire Morning Post* I believe sent this gentleman. He interviewed many of us and I can tell you it is a difficult thing to answer questions on what life was like in the Malayan 'emergency' - particularly when you had heard your mates before you trying to formulate some sort of non-cliched answer. Anyway in due course a parent back home sent out the *Post* containing all our names and some of the interviews. I think we were impressed!

On another occasion we were stationed near a place called Rompin. At the time I was being sent out from home copies of *John Bull* magazine. Coincidentally, they were serialising the then new novel by Neville Shute *A Town Like Alice*. The story concerns a group of English ladies - prisoners of the Japs during WW2 - who were forced to march from one place to another - starved, beaten and fever ridden, they fetched up at point in the story in the Rompin area. According to narrative, they left several graves behind them when they had to move on - near to a signal box at Rompin! As it happens we were in a position to check this out - being quite close to the location. However no trace of any graves was found. In all fairness the story could have been true, as the bodies might have been moved after the war to an official War Graves Cemetery? Still it gave me something to write home about.

Whereas the army is heavily into sport (to continue the morale boosting activities theme) - in the circumstances inter company sport was difficult to arrange. However in one or two camps we were at, there were rough hewn badminton courts, plus similar football and cricket pitches. It was mainly knockabout stuff but it helped to pass any leisure time that might have been available.

At one camp some of us acted as lorry escort for a pig! Well it was 'our' pig wasn't it? Bought by subscription - the idea was for us to fatten it up and consume it for Christmas. I can't recall its fate. It certainly wasn't consumed by us in 'D' Coy at Christmastide - as this story will cover in due course! Certainly it grew handsomely on cookhouse scraps and we would gather round it of an evening and comment on its excellent steady growth. I seem to recall it liked having its back scratched in its pen as it came up to greet you. Generally pets were not encouraged. If you were patrolling for large periods of your service your pets suffered - as you needed someone trustworthy to feed them.

Now in terms of time scale we are about up to March 1950 and little did we know that we were working up to what might be called in 1990's parlance 'the mother of all jungle patrols'. A whole book could have been written about this deep penetration of bandit country by most of our regiment - plus many others.

CHAPTER SEVENTEEN

The aim of 'Operation Jackpot' apparently was to drive all terrorists over a very broad area into a smaller 'killing zone' where they would hopefully be decimated by a force comprising many units - including the Malay Regiment and the then paramilitary Malay Police Force. One feature of this enterprise was to include bombing and strafing runs by the RAF! Therefore can you imagine a scene whereby many of us who had endured the Sheffield blitz of WW2 watched spellbound as heavy bombers of wartime vintage (Lancasters and Halifaxes) dropped bombs (which we could clearly see) on jungle areas? It could well be asked - how could you see all this when you have stressed the impenetrability of massed jungle trees and difficulties in seeing anything over a few yards? Strangely enough by accident or design, we were on top of a large 'Bukit' - or small mountain - which had knackered us completely in the upward climb, but which afforded us a grandstand seat for the show! After the bombing we descended to take up ambush positions should the terrorists flee in our direction. They clearly didn't - but we were amazed that a nearby broad swift flowing river ran black for quite a long period afterwards!

Anyway I am getting ahead of myself, We had no idea when setting out that we would be in the jungle for 28 consecutive days. It was said at the time that it was a command record - but whether this was true I know not. I assume we had some sort of briefing, but of this I can only recall that we realised we were in for a dangerous, physically strenuous and nerve racking time - all of which came only too true! For a start we were loaded like pack mules and then some. We must have been extremely fit (thanks no doubt in part to the hated PTI's at Strensall) and of course we possessed the elasticity of youth! I seem to recall we went 'in' before first light not far from a Kampong or small village. Every dog for miles seemed to try and break the barking record which awoke the inhabitants - who in turn banged gongs thinking no doubt they were being attacked by terrorists. So much for secrecy we thought.

We nearly had our first casualty the first day when wading chest high across a fast flowing river. There were just two ways of crossing rivers in operational areas. You either waded or swam across or even more hair-raisingly you found a fallen tree that formed a natural bridge and crossed on that. We had toggle ropes to join together to form a sort of chain but for some reason I don't recall we ever used them. Amongst our number was a Corporal Bousefield. An early subscriber to the 'pumping iron' - or body building brigade, he would carry all the extra items that inevitably needed to go when all packs were full. Thus we were wading this strong running river when he slipped and disappeared beneath the flow. The weight of his pack held him down - and he would have been a goner had he been 'tail end charlie'. Fortunately he wasn't and the man behind dragged him spluttering to the surface. We were glad he was OK, for as corporals go - he was a popular chap!

It would have been interesting to have kept a daily diary of this mammoth excursion into nature's primeval lair, alas I have never been a diarist and can only rely on memory of this particular time. We soon got into the usual routine of marching resting and marching again. Brew-ups were manna from heaven and the midday halt was sheer bliss. Soon however it was 'packs on - you're on next' - to quote the unpopular phrase of one of our leadership! We mercifully on most evenings stopped early enough to build our shelters and cook a meal. Joe Slater and I became adept at jungle stew making. This concoction comprised mashed potato powder (a forerunner to Smash) a tin of bully beef, tinned veg. say, peas and carrots, all mashed up in an army biscuit tin and brought to a hot edible stage by heating over a tommy-cooker! Follow this by tinned cake - or tinned fruit with evaporated milk - and you had a meal for the Gods! All this of course carried in our packs - maximum capacity about four days supply. We had become used to the taste of evaporated milk (a prized delicacy at home) - out here were no prime dairy herds - so in the services your only choice was evaporated, or as it was sometimes known 'pouring cream'!

The whole operation of basha building and cooking could take no more than 40-50 minutes on a good day. It needed to be so - for the light went very quickly in these latitudes. One of our re supply airdrops included some fresh vegetables for a change. The potatoes were deemed rotten by the powers that be and dumped. Joe and I went through them surreptitiously, and found some edible ones we made into chips. Much to the envy of our mates!

Frequently your clever catering plans might be thwarted by having to join a recce party when arriving at a night stop location. Joe and I seemed fated with this undesirable (but necessary) chore. Probably two sections would set off to probe the local area, one to get water if we were not adjacent to a stream and one to ensure we were not positioned inadvertently near any of our guerilla friends! This latter fact being emphasised when on one such recce, we were about to cross a stream -

when we spotted a small encampment on the other side. We charged across a la John Wayne to find (fortunately) an empty nest. Had it been occupied we would have been in big trouble obviously! We returned to our camp in some modest triumph and led a stronger force back to examine the site more closely. Newspapers showed residency had been fairly recent and some documents were collected for further examination. We then destroyed the small camp. A diary might have revealed how we coped with that nights cooking and shelter - as it must have been almost - if not dark by the time we returned.

Convenient though it might have been to camp by a stream it did have its disadvantages. Like the time when our (and other,) shelters were flooded during the night after a torrential downpour. We finished up sleeping across our rifles - supported by two large square army biscuit tins. (We must have just had an air drop.) These re-supply drops were a feature of long range patrols and I cannot recall a scheduled drop that did not arrive pretty much on time! The pilots and despatchers were superb and the Douglas Dakota aircraft were ideal for the job!

Every four days or so your drop took place. The pilots would have a rough idea of your last reported position and you would aid and abet this by hacking out a clearing slightly away from the camp. At the appointed hour you would hear the engines approaching and your signaller would try and contact the aircraft on a special frequency. When the Dakota was fairly close, smoke grenades were flung into the clearing which sometimes also had the fluorescent recognition panels displayed to confirm identification,

Several passes might be necessary to complete the drop depending on the numbers being catered for. Down would come the 'chutes with large padded loads beneath. They hit the ground with a fair old crump and you had to watch closely sometimes to avoid being well and truly 'clobbered'. Food, dry clothing, medical supplies and most importantly, mail - came to us this way. The whole thing was over quite quickly except for recovering the various loads (which might have drifted in the breeze outside the D.Z (or dropping zone) the odd load would end up wrapped around the top of a tall tree. This is where your sure footed Dyak (or Iban) came into his own! The supplies had to be sorted and distributed - so a re-supply drop ate up a good part of the day. Did we care? Not likely! Comfortably ensconced on soft nylon parachutes we would smoke our fags and read our mail - utterly content with the world at that point in time. On my last patrol many months later I acquired a parachute and brought it back to base (probably illegally) - but generally they were destroyed by burning or burying at that time. I brought mine home in my kitbag - stuffed down at the bottom. It was rapidly turned into 'feminine unmentionables' by the famous Ethel - who was delighted to see it - bearing in mind austerity Britain at that time! And so, loaded to the gills once more we would set off again on the next phase of the operation.

I have not spoken much about jungle wild life except insects for the simple reason there wasn't much to see. The only creature I actually saw was a very dead armadillo type creature which was being rapidly consumed by ants! However we certainly knew large creatures were around! On this particular patrol we followed a herd of elephant up another steep muddy jungle hill. We could hear their trumpeting from a distance and they had carved a stairway for us up this steep slope - and littered it with their cannon ball sized droppings! Another time on a particular track we came across a pronounced, pungent cat odour - that could have only come from a very large feline - either leopard or tiger! Monkeys certainly we would catch a glimpse of as they swung about the treetops. Their calls were certainly the incidental music to our incursion of their territory. When I watch a wildlife T/V programme today the screeching and calling takes me back in a flash!

I have mentioned snakes already I think - and spoke of an incident to come? Well this is it. Under Sgt. Grimmer we were detached from the main body and sent on some mission or other several days march away. Our trusty sergeant was an unmistakeable figure with his jungle hat slightly Robin Hood style. His personal weapon was a long Lee-Enfield rifle - circa WW1 and WW2! Normally this rifle, when still in service, had been converted to a grenade throwing instrument. However with the discharge-cup temporarily removed - it reverted to being a normal - if elongated rifle, deadly accurate. So there we were then, marching along quite a well defined, good jungle track, when the point man (which we took it in turns to be) signalled a problem. This turned out to be an extremely large cobra (and I do mean extremely large.) Coiled around a tree branch it was, about head height across the track - with it's hood up, daring us to try and get past! Not likely matey! Our leader puts up his trusty .303 and blasts it right between the eyes. It fell dead - still writhing as we nervously went past it as fast as possible! We needed no encouragement to step on it - should its mate appear, bent on vengeance!

I mentioned T/V wildlife programmes a moment ago and the memories they evoke at home. Just recently we were watching a programme about the French Foreign Legion. In a particular episode we saw a mock casualty being evacuated from the jungle on an improvised stretcher. This again took me back in a flash to this very patrol for - when we rejoined the major part of our unit after our detachment - we arrived back to find the body of a comrade cocooned in parachute silk. It appears that two recce patrols set out on the same track with a time interval between them. The idea being that a group of our enemy might hide whilst one patrol went past - but bump into the next group as they hastened away in the opposite direction - less alert. Sadly the only 'bump' that occurred was between the two groups, who unfortunately caught each other up - and despite the new recognition patches - found themselves in a fire fight against each other! Sadly this ended in tragedy. I don't think the manoeuvre was tried again.

It was decided that our comrade should be carried out - to receive a proper burial, with full military honours. Sgt. Major Walton and a small team of the strongest men were charged with this task. It took them three days to get out by the shortest route, where motor transport awaited them. The Sergeant-Major concerned was not one of our favourite characters - but for this operation he was I believe quite rightly decorated and we saw him in another light. We could just about envisage the physical struggle and effort involved in ensuring that our comrade was laid to rest with the proper and due ceremonial.

Our expedition continued and we penetrated ever deeper into the dense forest. Eleven platoon then had its small hour of glory thus. We found an abandoned terrorist camp - which was in a decayed state. Rooting about for documents - or anything of interest, young Cutler (who hailed from Driffield) - found a skeleton! At first this didn't create enormous excitement - it was assumed a bandit had succumbed from disease or wounds and been left behind. However when this was reported back to H/Q in a radio signal we soon realised we were in the news. It was felt we may have stumbled upon the body of a Brigadier Erskine - who had been of recent times in command of our regiments sector, and who sadly had been lost in a storm over the jungle, when on an aerial recce in an Auster aircraft. We were ordered to carry the skull and bring it back with us at the end of the patrol for identification purposes, which we did. It appears that forensic tests showed it to be an Asian skull and not that of the missing Brigadier - who I do not believe was ever found despite extensive searches - even before we had arrived in Malaya.

I mentioned young Cutler - who was a popular lad amongst us with a well developed sense of humour whatever the conditions. He developed a huge carbuncle under an eye when we were on our detachment. Putting theory to the test we placed several leeches on this thing - and lo and behold they sucked all the pus and poison clear away!

Leeches were a fact of life out there. They did not worry us too much - except that they seemed to be able to wander at will about our bodies - without our knowing until we took off our gear. Then we would find a corpulent thing or things, full of our blood - clinging painlessly to portions of our anatomy! What we asked ourselves would happen if one got down the tube of our willies? We didn't dwell on that one too much.

Onward we went, day after day - supply drop after supply drop and we began to reap the harvest. I was covered in Tinea, the tropical skin complaint and a number of leg ulcers, which was mild compared to some of the others. My mate Joe was suffering from a sort of 'trench foot' and limped badly. Our medic 'Skid' Skinner did his best for us - and skilfully patched most of us up to the end of the show. We covered a fair distance on 'Operation Jackpot'. Nearly every sort of terrain was covered from the thickest jungle to dense areas of lallang - a razor edged grass as tall if not taller than a man! Occasionally we hit open country - what a sight, but before long we would be back in the tall trees. Once in an area of open space we all dived for cover when we heard the 'ratatat' of an automatic weapon. The joke was on us as we soon realised it was nothing more than a woodpecker doing his stuff against a tree! Later we found another abandoned enemy camp where we were set upon by a cloud of angry hornets - who put us to flight in very short order.

The days and weeks passed without our coming across an enemy formation. We were told afterwards that we had fulfilled our mission by driving cohorts of terrorists into other less bothersome areas. I think other units did have some success but not us! Eventually we emerged looking I might add not unlike Napoleon's men in the retreat from Moscow - albeit wetter and warmer. We were all examined medically and some despatched promptly to military hospitals - including my mate Joe - whose feet had been oozing blood on the march out. He was in dock for 6 weeks! So ended this operation. We were pleased to have been involved in one way because it showed we could handle the terrain - and look after ourselves in the worst of conditions - even if we weren't regulars! We all knew there was more of the same to come - but for the time being we could rest and relax for a short while.

CHAPTER EIGHTEEN

No longer 'rookies' after the big show we returned to Pertang and luxuriated in the fleshpots of camp life! We now felt like hardened jungle veterans - proud of our sores, and confident of our abilities.

We had somehow survived all that the jungle had seen fit to throw at us - but we were not anxious to enter its portals again for a while at any rate! The inevitable post mortems after 'Operation Jackpot' showed it to have been considered successful by the powers that be - with something like fifty terrorists killed or wounded over a very broad front. We had taken our own casualties of course and there had been many accidents throughout the battalion causing death and serious injury. No doubt there was a similar story throughout all the participating regiments and police units.

After the operation we took to the roads again in our Dodge 15 hundred weight vehicles - looking for trouble. We found it all right by colliding with a bus on one occasion. It was just a glancing blow but it sent us spinning off the road. Fortunately, none of us were hurt - just shaken up a little bit. Our main damage was to the (very substantial) bumper bar which was quietly put right at a local garage thus avoiding reams of paperwork. The bus incidently just kept on going presumably uninjured and not anxious to discuss the matter with security forces, or fill in his own paperwork!

Meanwhile we continued our frequent stop and search operations with more buses stopped and more Asian housewives 'patted down' as discreetly as possible for hidden weapons or ammunition. Sometimes we would board trains and carry out routine identity checks and cursory luggage searches. It went like this. You would approach your passenger and ask for his/her identity card. Then you would say "apa nama" and check the name was the same as on the card, and the photograph bore a resemblance! ' After checking the train or most of it, usually with the train still under way - then we would alight and carry on our patrol. I was never present when this sort of check ever caught anyone out. Nevertheless it obviously kept our terrorist friends guessing and frustrated their leadership from travelling around on public transport which I'm sure they did from time to time. Constant checking was surely a worthwhile idea - as most of the communist leadership were well known by name and description to the security forces - and wanted pictures were circulated all over the place - just like the wild west!

From time to time leading communist figures would be captured or killed and much publicity would be given to these successes. Where possible, deceased enemy were carried out of the jungle for identification purposes. Too far 'in' and it had to be a photo - or a fingerprint!

Another aspect of our activity allied to stop and search was a 'surround and screen' routine. This entailed the encirclement before dawn of a kongsi (village) or kampong to prevent anyone leaving before an I.D check. This trawl might catch possible suspects who had ventured in at dusk for a night with a wife or girlfriend - or leaving with a bag of supplies or money for the guys in the hills. Frequently on this type of operation the whole village would be screened and an informer might be inside an armoured car - invisible from the outside - but able to indicate those who should be detained for questioning as they were paraded past him. Once I was concealed only a few feet away from a pig being slaughtered before dawn. The noises emanating from this procedure almost turned me towards vegetarianism!

After a few weeks the terrorist gangs filtered back into their old locations and the usual murder and mayhem began again. For our part the regiment suffered from a series of road ambushes whereby we lost a number of men to the grim reaper. Some were personally known to us having trained with us and come out east on the boat with us.

Ambushing a road convoy was a fairly simple procedure for a determined enemy. A heavy log across a road was all that was needed to cause a vehicle to slow or stop - and then you just poured fire upon it from prepared positions. Other vehicles would be hit too as they tried to extricate themselves from the situation - by gunmen positioned further back along the road. Sometimes it was a huge land mine that caused the damage. These were exploded by remote control and detonated by scores of torch batteries linked together. Another Sheffield mate, 'Ginger' Pugh, was shot up badly as he drove the Major's jeep - at the head of a routine convoy about this time. He was rushed to hospital and survived, then sent home to Blighty - where we were to meet up with him again, surprisingly, after National Service - in reserve training. Talk about the Army getting its pound of flesh!

I was pleased when Joe Slater my jungle bashing mate returned to the fold after his spell in the British Military Hospital at Kinrara and elsewhere: The latter was up in the Cameron Highlands - the cool mountain country where sahibs and memsahibs of prewar days played after gathering for their annual leaves and social activities. They may well have been still doing so at this time too! However Joe was despatched on convalescent leave fairly promptly to the so called 'millionaires playground' - island of Penang - before another patrol came up. I applied for leave too so I could join him in the fleshpots - but I had to soldier on for a few weeks before permission came through. Needless to say his stories about the fabulous nurses he had been treated by at Kinrara Hospital were highly stimulating to say the least! Not so stimulating were his stories about the badly wounded people up there. We all understood about some of the blokes who were trying to engineer longer stays in their hospital beds - by one method or another, to put off the evil day when they had to return to yet more jungle bashing. After returning from his leave in Penang Joe had a great deal to tell us about the delights and feminine charms of the place. To say that we hung on his every word would be an understatement! So much so that most of us couldn't wait to get there! When we did - 'twas every bit as good as he said!

I think the first patrol that the returned, refurbished Joe was on, was the one where we were awakened suddenly in the night by an artillery battery firing over our heads at a target in our vicinity - which we were certainly unaware of! Be sure that we each hugged the ground like it was a beautiful woman! The thoughts that a stray missile might come our way were uppermost in our minds! Like so many other things in this campaign - we never heard the why or wherefores regarding this firing but presumed 'they' knew we were there! Our nightly radio 'sitrep' (situation report) we always assumed - indicated our position. This we felt would be outlined on the chinagraph covering of some enormous operational map - back at a high level H.Q!

Some of the girls I used to work alongside 1945/54

4A Platoon. Basic Training. Strensall Camp 1949 (Sgt. Reeves)
Picture by R.D. & E. Richards, Strensall and York.

i

On board 'Orbita'. Smithy, Frank Salf, Buffalo Lingard and self.

Major Gillies and his famous hole.

The Malayan 'Musketeers'
Joe Slater, 'Jigger' Johnson
and Leslie.

Bren pit and observation point,
permanently manned, due to our being
overlooked from a hill covered by rubber.
(See page 122)

Relaxing in Singapore
Messrs. Kemp, Bell &
Varity.
(See page 133)

1st Bn. THE GREEN HOWARDS.

CHRISTMAS 1950

The Commanding officer and officers wish you all a very Happy Christmas

MENU.

Roast ~~TURKEY~~ ~~Goose~~ Stuffing

Roast Pork & Apple Sauce

Yorkshire Pudding

Roast & Mashed Potatoes

Brussel Sprouts

Green Peas.

Christmas Pudding & Rum Sauce.

Fruit & Nuts.

Beer · Lemonade · Cigarettes.

MALAYA 1950

Christmas Menu 1950 - signed by various officers inc. C.O.

11 Platoon Green Howards, Bentong, Malaya 1950.

Did I ever look like this?
Bentong 1950.

Done up like a dog's dinner.

Self in jungle gear.

Tarzan at Port Dixon. R&R camp.

Camp Life. Cooks preparing 'tiffin' - note 'compo' tins.

Camp Life. Open air ablutions!

Green Howards Scout-car. Note twin Brownings.

The Rivers ran deep around Yong Peng! Try crossing this with a 'toggle rope'.

The Water Truck of ill repute.

Scenes from camp life. Bringing up the rations.

W.O. Holloway in Company Office and long shot of Officers' Mess and Company Stores. Believed South Johol Rubber Estate.

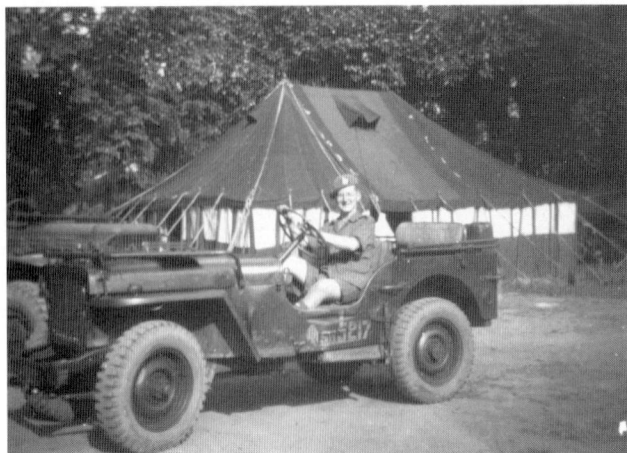

Ginger Pugh and Jeep - in which he nearly 'bought it'.

Ganza our Dyak or Iban tracker - with Cass and Cutler.

A rough hewn Badminton court.

*Left: Officers' Mess
Selerang Barracks.
Below: Officers' Mess
Yong Peng*

A 'Welcome to 'D' Company' sign.

*'Mon Repos'
Home to a section of 'squaddies'.*

Left of picture -'D' Coy. Jeep - that the author had some illicit driving lessons on - before the 'instructor' was shot in an ambush!
Right of picture - 15cwt Dodge weapons carrier - which we used to patrol the roads. These pre-dated the Somali 'technicals' by about 40 years!

Tyre change on a
battalion scout car -
standard 3 ton
Dodge truck
illustrated - right.

Leslie's friend Marjorie (right) at Blackpool early 1950's

Carved shield with Green Howards
Badge & Battle Honours

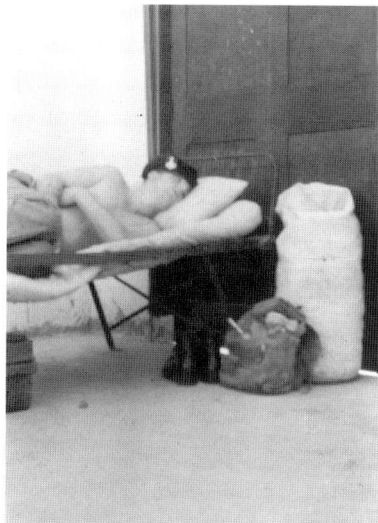
Unknown 'snorer' Selerang Barracks.

Part of Trooping the Colour Parade - Singapore 1951

Capt. Barlow M.C.

A squad on Selerang's intimidating square!

Slow boat from Malaya

'Devonshire'
1951

Old schoolmate, Denis Bullivant Green Howards / Hallamshires.

'A' Company Hallamshire Battalion York & Lancs. Early fifties.

Armistice Day Parade Sheffield 1952

Photo 'Sheffield Telegraph & Star

NORTHALLERTON'S MR. 'JACK' JONES

Ex-Green Howard's death at 73

A man whose life interest was in soldiering and the training of Army Cadets, Mr. John George ("Jack") Jones, Vicars Croft, Northallerton, died in hospital at Northallerton on Monday after a long illness. He was aged 73.

An ex-Green Howard himself he was honoured some years ago when he received from a fellow Green Howard, Sir William Worsley, the Lord Lieutenant of the Riding, a certificate of good service for 32 years with the North Riding Army Cadets.

Later when he finally left the Cadets at the age of 70, he received a long service certificate from Group Captain G. Shaw, having completed no less than 38 years' service as instructor with the Northallerton unit.

Though he was born at Guisborough Mr. Jones spent most of his life in Northallerton where he enlisted in 1915, and served in France with the 4th Yorkshire Regiment, later to become the Green Howards. He was taken prisoner during the latter stages of the 1914-18 war and was one of the last to be repatriated.

On repatriation he was not long out of uniform, for in 1921 he voluntarily took up cadet work. Too old for active service in the 1939-45 war he joined the Civil Defence Corps (then A.R.P.) and remained with it as storeman-driver at Northallerton until his retirement.

He leaves a widow and three married daughters.

The funeral service took place at All Saints Parish Church, Northallerton on Thursday, conducted by the Vicar, the Rev. John Castledine.

The History of a remarkable ex-Green Howard. Mr Jones was the father of Nora, one of our then new neighbours at Tavistock in 1975.

From Durham and Stockton Times.

Leslie and the 'Famous Ethel'.

Lorna - Leslie's girl friend during National Service

The shoe polish counter lassie - when first I met her!

Soon after 'demob' - Leslie with bike.

The English 'Private's' Woman. On 'The Cobb' Lyme Regis 1996

About 1982 - documentary film producer -with award certificates.

CHAPTER NINETEEN

As the year 1950 rolled on - three major events were to take place that affected (A) the whole world, (B) Malaya, and (C) we National Servicemen.

The world event was the outbreak of the Korean War - which soon involved troops from the United Nations - including Britain and later the Commonwealth. We expected to be sent to Korea pretty smartish - as we were a trained infantry formation, ideally placed to get there quickly and perhaps be an asset to Allied Forces. However we were kept where we were and subsequent reading up of the then situation reveals that the seriousness of the Malayan situation was beginning to dawn on the government at home - so there we stayed!

The second of the major happenings which affected Malaya and the emergency there, was the hatching and implementation of 'The Briggs Plan'. This had a tremendous effect on the situation - and sowed the seeds of eventual victory. More of this later.

The third happening that affected we N/S men was the imposition of an extra six months service - and as the late great comedian Tommy Cooper would have said "just like that!" I think we also learned of a three and a half year reserve period in the TA to follow - due to the world situation, although this didn't concern us too much at the time. The extra six months service announcement might have been slightly tempered by news of a pay rise but not much - as many of us had seen the advance notification of what boat we could be travelling home on at the end of our Malayan service - still some months away. As they say in Yorkshire - we were not best pleased with this news and the thought of a further six months jungle bashing - not our favourite occupation.

When the original time for us to return home came up - some of us did indeed get home, but still with the six extra months to do in the U.K. Amongst those that did return on the due date was my 'oppo' - Joe Slater. Birth dates decided it - believe it or not. Up to a certain date you went home - after that you stayed! Joe had been born two weeks before me so he was one of the lucky ones. However I am moving ahead in my story - which was pretty much the mixture as before - but naturally influenced as the months passed by the events mentioned at the beginning of the chapter. One rather startling event was a sudden snap kit check of all our possessions. Rumour had it that many of us had small reserves of ammunition stashed away - and perhaps the odd grenade or two - against the evil day when we might accidentally lose some, and then be in trouble for being deficient! Penalties were high for the loss of just one round (28 days in the cooler) and as for a grenade - they probably threw away the key! So, all kit and kit boxes were searched under the eagle eye of our Sgt. Major Holloway - who I somehow felt wasn't relishing the job. All sorts of anomalies were discovered - and indeed some 'buckshee' rounds were found - but no grenades. Some small punishments were handed down for these - but nothing serious.

However one of our number had lately been employed in the company stores. He had (naturally) come into the possession of many items of extra equipment - including several pairs of the newly issued pyjamas! (We had each been given two pairs of these, which we were quite astonished to receive - and wondered just what was happening to this 'mans army' - but we wore 'em just the same!) The book was well and truly thrown at our friend - who lingered long in the cooler! Being somewhat unimpressed after this treatment - he formed a romantic attachment to a mature but very pretty Chinese lady hairdresser. At a later stage he eloped with her for an idyllic life in the tropics with an adoring lady. Unfortunately he had some years of his service still to do and the M.P's descended and spoilt all this by carrying him off for some more unromantic time in the glasshouse! I personally never saw him again - but we were not unsympathetic of our comrade's predicament - neither did we expect anything else other than that he would have made the most out of his time in the stores. There was this lovely story around at the time that another storeman had made a fortune flogging bush hats in Egypt that were surplus to regimental use. Apparently they were highly prized amongst the fellaheen. (Egyptian workers.)

It should be mentioned at this time that tete-a-tetes with the opposite sex out there were confined mainly to the commercial variety. Opportunities for romance with what might be called 'nice' young ladies of Chinese, Malay or Indian stock were very rare indeed. Chances for fraternisation were themselves extremely few - and the girl's parents would have taken a very dim view of liaisons with service personnel! It may have happened to some individuals stationed in the big towns - but even then most unlikely. As for us out on detachment on a rubber estate - not a cat in hell's chance!

Certainly there would have been more than a few white unattached young women doing various useful jobs for the Raj in Malaya. We certainly never came into contact with them. Possibly officers attending various functions in the larger towns might do - but certainly not us.

Anyway what would a nice well educated young English girl with prospects see in one of Mr. Kipling's licentious and impecunious soldiery? Incidently this isn't meant to be a lecture in class structure - that's how it was then! Things have changed greatly now and I know at least two Brits who have married Malay girls whilst working there. I only encountered three or four English ladies in my time there. They ran the Sandycroft Leave Centre in Penang and were kind, gracious, cool and attractive - available they were not! They were the sort of English ladies - who together with their menfolk went forth and colonised half the world.

Anyway to return briefly to the snap check of our kit boxes - I heard along the grapevine that because of the general tidiness of my kit box and the cleanliness of the stuff within it I was being considered for promotion to the dizzy heights of lance-corporal! This all being subject to other considerations of course - so I was being watched. Needless to say the other considerations must have fallen by the wayside as the great day never dawned, and I remained a private for the whole of my service! To the best of my knowledge the only one of our draft promoted was a chap who was found to have aerial 'photo interpreting skills'. He became a sergeant overnight and disappeared to some far off H.Q. It is not surprising that promotions were thin on the ground at that time for us newcomers. The regiment was stuffed full of experienced people who had seen much action in WW2. Believe it or not there was even a man with us who had been with the original Chindits in Burma - and he was only a corporal! Had I ever made the grade as an NCO I would have needed one hell of a lot of training to have been capable of navigating and leading a section of men around the Malayan jungle.

Soon we were to move to a new encampment near the town of Rompin (as mentioned previously regarding the signal box graves story!) The area was within the state of Negri Sembilan but I can remember very little about the move or much else about this place. More often than not we would just be relieving members of another regiment - who themselves would be going on to relieve someone else! On very few occasions did we occupy a virgin site - where we had to construct a camp from scratch. I well remember the one where we rolled out a parade ground one Sunday - after borrowing a heavy roller from the plantation manager!

The event that sealed the fate of a communist takeover in Malaya was launched in the middle of 1950. 'The Briggs Plan', touched on earlier - was a major contributor to the eventual defeat of the insurgents. The plan was named after its instigator, General Briggs - and tackled head on the problem of support for the terrorists via illicit food, money, and medical supplies, without which they could not function effectively. This supply organisation called the 'Min Yuen' - was their equivalent of our Royal Army Service Corps. At the time much of the foodstuffs, money and other supplies were collected from a network of small farmers, smallholders and squatters. These latter farmed small parcels of virgin land and their activities had been tolerated by the authorities until the Briggs Plan.

Because of their scattered nature - these small enterprises were easy prey to the guerrilla's - who descended on them at night, threatening their families with unspeakable horrors unless they delivered the required food, money or medical supplies. We sympathised with these unfortunate people - and wondered what we would do if confronted by these armed and desperate men. Give them what they wanted was our considered opinion! Something drastic needed to be done to shut down the major supply routes to the insurgents - and Briggs did just that. Basically the plan was simple - but fraught with potential hazard and political dynamite. Deny access to all the potential victims by moving them in large numbers - goods, chattels, livestock - the whole blooming lot, to special areas where they would be protected by troops, police and an armed, specially raised, home guard. Their homes to be rebuilt in new villages - surrounded by barbed wire and watchtowers! These areas would have (and did) schools, stores, medical centres and even tea houses - the works!

And work it all did eventually. It was a colossal gamble but it paid off. Obviously it wasn't put in place overnight as the protected sites had to be built and there were many teething troubles. However the people thus uprooted found their lives were much improved overall - neither were they threatened any more - by having to hand over a considerable portion of their crops and income. The government provided land, seeds and implements as an encouragement and I believe a trickle of converts then became a flood!

Needless to say our 'Red' friends did all they could to frustrate the plan by raids where they saw weaknesses. Watchmen were killed and had their arms stolen, plus other atrocities designed to intimidate. However the plan began to pay dividends - eventually forcing the guerillas into cultivating their own foodstuffs deep in the jungle and adjacent open areas. From the air these crops could be easily spotted - bringing air strikes and other deep wrath upon them. This all meant that the security forces were able to concentrate their efforts on the towns and larger villages - where transport was needed to move illicit goods around - and where apprehension was so much easier.

We listened once to a live hook-up on Radio Malaya to an ambush position just off a main road somewhere - where a car carrying contraband was expected - plus a team of carriers was presumed to be waiting on the jungle fringes. In the end I think the carriers escaped but the car, contents and driver were caught thus breaking another vital supply line. Our part in all this (the Briggs Plan) was to find isolated squatter areas and persuade them to move to the new locations. Sometimes this necessitated the burning down of huts and sheds as a final inducement to the naturally reclusive peasants involved. Many of the hutments were beautifully made from local materials and it was a great shame to burn them down. Most of the constructions were of bamboo - even down to the furniture. However all this was sanctioned by the local Sultans who each governed a state - plus other civic powers, who saw quite clearly the need for positive action in the face of a determined foe.

Success in Malaya would have opened the door to a huge swathe of communist states dominating the far east - not a pleasant prospect for the British and other governments with territories in the area. The authorities must have breathed a huge sigh of relief when the gigantic project was seen to be working.

For a short period during this period we found ourselves patrolling in mostly open country. Quite a novel experience and one which certainly had us 'swivel necked' as we progressed around the countryside and paddy fields, feeling extremely naked without our normal jungle cover.

CHAPTER TWENTY

Whatever the outside world was doing - our lives continued the same familiar daily pattern. As previously mentioned we had done our bit to help in the transformation of the countryside by the 'Briggs Plan' - which took up a lot of army time - but eventually involved the resettlement of something like half a million people - quite an operation by any standards!

An opportunity now came up for me to escape all this for a while and enjoy a few high jinks in the millionaire's playground of Penang! Being unable to join my mate Joe on his convalescent leave, my application had finally ground through the mills and I was the proud possessor of a 14 day leave pass and a railway warrant for Penang. My finances must have been in reasonable order as well, as the army were well aware it was likely to be an expensive experience - which indeed it was. There were several of us fortunate ones who boarded the train fully armed, and watching the stations pass as we sped to the (hopefully) sun kissed shores of this blissful island of dreams! One station made us sit up and be a little more alert. This was Kajang - home to the notorious 'Kajang gang' - who were a byword for cruelty and murder and whose exploits we were constantly reading and hearing about.

Apart from this I cannot remember much about the journey - the train eventually depositing us by a broad stretch of water. A long road bridge now spans this waterway - but in those days a ferryboat took us across. Once over - we relinquished our weapons at a military police depot and thus assumed we were on relatively safe ground! Two weeks of sun, sand and palm trees beckoned as we made our way to the Sandycroft Leave Centre which I recall being some six or seven miles out from the island's main town of Georgetown. Of Sandycroft I can recall nothing at all. Did we have separate rooms - or sleep in small dormitories? Were meals served in the centre - or did we eat out? (Probably there was a Naafi style catering service I would imagine.) I have no memories at all of the basic amenities that the centre provided. It was well run, I'm certain of that.

All I can recall clearly is that when signing in, the signature and home address of a guest - just above my own, was of a young RAF man who lived just a few doors away from me in Walkley Street Sheffield. I did not even catch a glimpse of him once during my stay there! Gorgeous, palm fringed sandy beaches were adjacent - that's for sure - and needless to say that's where we spent the majority of our days - basking - swimming and relaxing, recharging our batteries! Evenings were mostly spent at the renowned City Lights Ballroom in Georgetown. This was undoubtedly the place to be of an evening without any doubt. It housed a gorgeous array of young pretty females known as 'taxi dancers' - for the simple reason that you paid to dance with them! The number of tickets you bought equalled the number of dances you were entitled to from these exotic young things.

Many of these girls pursued other nocturnal activities of an intimate nature - and many assignations were made on the dance floor. Over your leave period dancing with these ladies could prove to be an expensive business - and a strategy was called for to avoid blowing all your funds too quickly. This entailed being as nice as possible to your favourite - buying her cooling drinks and plying her with cigarettes helped you claim a few free dances when she wasn't booked by anyone else. Being a reasonable dancer helped too as they were always getting their feet trodden on by over enthusiastic learners! Come the last waltz with your favourite in your arms - you hugged her as tightly as possible, and hoped for a few kisses when the lights dimmed or went out as they usually did for a few moments. For you were starved of pretty female company, lonely, and a long way from home. When the lights did go up the scene resembled a scene from *la Dolce Vita* as couples disentangled themselves from some very tight embraces. Hardly a couple would be dancing in the strictest sense!

My favourite lassie was called Shirley I think. She was a good dancer, attractive and a giggler. My fellow leave mates dared me to take her out in the conventional sense. I was surprised when she accepted - so were they! As I recall we had a drink and a meal - and then went to the Cathay cinema to see a film. I think even then the cinemas were air conditioned - and certainly the very latest Hollywood productions were on offer. The films would have normal English sound tracks - but subtitles in Cantonese would be flashed on a small screen underneath the main one. During the film no doubt I got amorous (as in an English back-row cinema situation) which she no doubt tolerated in a patient sort of way. She was probably surprised that I did not seek her professional favours overnight - but I resisted the temptations - much to the amazement of my mates who had hatched this little plot to presumably relieve me of my virginity no doubt. However in my minds eye still lurked the images from the V.D film we had seen en-route to the east and so I resisted the temptation. Probably I was the only squaddie ever to come home thus, in the history of the Malayan campaign!

Temptations were enormous for all - needless to say. Penang swarmed with delightful young ladies - who made their living at that time by being intimately nice to servicemen (and the local population generally I suspect.) After the City Lights turned out there would be a another large contingent of lovelies waiting in trishaws for the disgorgement of further randy soldiery who had not made arrangements inside. Aside from this it was interesting though to be in the company of a local and not pay the full tourist whack for things like taxi's and trishaws. She would say, "pay him this - or that" - usually about half the normal tourist rates. Trishaws I should add were bicycle powered rickshaws piloted by lean and tanned men generally wearing black with the typical conical straw hat of a Chinese working man. They were pretty hot stuff in cycling terms - and many would have done well if they could have got to the Tour de France had it been operating in those far off days!

The final story about the City Lights dance hall concerns my missing the last bus - or 'passion wagon' - back to Sandycroft, towards the end of my stay. I must have gone there on my own otherwise a group of us would have no doubt hired a taxi and shared the fare. As it was, probably I was getting short of funds and couldn't contemplate paying for a taxi. I set out to walk back. No problem walking back these few miles for a jungle bashing Green Howard I said to the M.P's - who stopped to check my bone fides. "That's all we do - march, march, march - jungle jungle, jungle." They gave me a lift back the last few miles to Sandycroft - and dropped me off pretty smartish before I started on the war stories no doubt. Actually I had been very pleased to see them as every hamlet or village I walked through seemed to have a ferocious pack of hounds who would follow me through the place barking like the devil and staying just out of boot range. I was fearing for my safety when the redcaps hove into view!

On reflection it had seemed surprising that an area of service recreation would need a contingent of redcaps to police it but fairly recently I read Pte. Scurr's book on his time in Malaya. (Later than mine.) In it he mentions that his battalion H.Q was in Penang - but most operations being carried out over on the mainland. Therefore many other troops may have been stationed there, necessitating a police presence!

All too soon my leave time was up, and broke but happy I and my leave mates said farewell to this lovely part of the world where we had spent two weeks of tropical bliss. We had worn nothing but our bathing trunks by day and the obligatory tropical uniform by night - this consisting of white shirts and generally grey coloured slacks. We had spent most of our savings of course - but certainly didn't begrudge a penny of it. I daresay much of our spending was on food. We were still eternally hungry. Much to the surprise of many a waiter we would eat a substantial meal - and then ask for the same again! In those days I found it hard to put so much as a pound on. Drawing our weapons once again from the island's arms store we prepared to make our way back to the battalion and our day to day existence - far from the delights of the tropical jewel that is Penang. All too soon then - back to 'D' Company it was - to regale our friends and comrades with greatly embroidered tales of our doings. Now people were hanging on to our words! Was it worth it - it sure was. May I go again some day - soon.

CHAPTER TWENTY ONE

I had written home during my leave to say how nice it was to be luxuriating in our tropical surroundings - gazing at distant jungle clad hills and not having to sweatily climb up them, loaded like a pack mule! Now it was back to the grind once again. The next really notable event for us was the arrival of our new company commander after a series of temporary ones. He was a Major LLB (Bertie) Beuttler. He had been a Colonel during WW2, and like many officers wishing to carry on their careers in peacetime - he had dropped to the war substantive rank of Major. He was a different sort of guy to all we had known before, and we were about to witness a lesson in leadership enacted before our very eyes!

Within a few weeks we found we had a pretty good bloke at the helm - and one who knew what he was about. After only a very short while as our leader - we would have followed him literally anywhere! Forgive the old cliche - but we would! The difference between leaders is an indefinable 'something' - some have it, some don't. Our Major certainly had it in abundance. He was a tall spare, slightly aristocratic looking man frequently given to showering with us in the 'other ranks' ablutions block! This was something we had never experienced before - and I think he was saying something to us along the lines of "look - I'm built no differently to you chaps - we're all in this together, so lets get to it eh!" He was no soft touch mind you. Get on the wrong side of him or do something stupid - and you got a bawling out of ferocious proportions. Most of us I think would have preferred a collision with the enemy!

After duty, he and some of the other officers would wander round the camp dressed in sarongs and playing imaginary test cricket. Bats, balls and wickets being purely imaginary you understand. "Round the twist" - we would say, shaking our heads sadly, but we were secretly amused - as well as getting the subtle message that the officers of this company were a pretty united bunch and were quite prepared for a spot of corporate lunacy! Nowadays this sort of think is probably advocated by your management training guru's! Anyway it certainly worked on us - we liked and respected our new Major. Whatever 'gongs' he got in the war - he was to add the award of the MBE to his string - undoubtedly for his leadership in the Malayan campaign! I very much hope he finished his career as a General - probably not as he was far too unconventional.

One of the major's first positive actions was to spot that our .303 ammunition was wartime vintage - marked something like 1944/5 and well passed its sell by date. Obviously it couldn't be dumped so the order was to use it up as soon as possible. This was achieved by opening up on any likely ambush points as we sped along the roads - 'brassing-up' tank men call it. Mobile wild pig shoots were organised by the headlights of our 'technicals' and I recall one night a large family of wild pigs slowly moving quite nonchalantly away from a hail of lead from our various weapons - pointed lethally in their direction. Not a one did we get. We had a Chinese liaison officer with us at this time, who set out the next night to show us how it should be done. He returned with a wild pig he had bagged around his neck - probably from the same herd! Still I think we all got a slice. So, most of our old 'ammo' got used up - the ceramic insulating pots on telephone posts copped it a bit too as we sped past. Not us gov! Terrorist action obviously!

One other tale if I may about our 'mad' major which illustrates possibly our affection for him. He carried most times a genuine gangster type Colt .45 automatic that he had acquired during WW2. "Goes like a train" he would say. One day - whilst cleaning this thing he accidentally fired off a shot through the thin wooden wall of his company office. The slug came through the wall - narrowly missing the head of one of our number who was perusing company orders on the notice board beneath. With anyone else there would have been dark mutterings - and someone would have blabbed to 'head office' - not a word was ever heard, and the potential victim thought it quite hilarious and enjoyed a few free pints as he retold the story over and over again. If the top brass ever heard of the incident (which I doubt) nothing was ever done about it.

On the subject of senior ranks, rumours began to percolate about the visitation to be expected of a very senior being from our pantheon of military gods! This visitation required that a smart guard of honour be produced at fairly short notice, that would not only look good - but know their drill, despite spending much of their time immersed in primaeval forest. As I recall we were not informed as to who the great man was to be until close on the time - but in the meantime the squad needed to be chosen and put through their paces. I'm glad I was picked as the visitor turned out to be one of the legendary heroes of WW2! So our 'best' boots were recovered from long stored kitbags, and once again we sat spit and polishing like the training days of yore. We found that we had qualified for the General Service Medal and this meant that we had to wear the ribbon - mounted on a little brooch affair - on this special parade. Needless to say our national servicemen's chests swelled with pride - that is until we saw what ribbons some of our regular colleagues were sporting.

Here's a humorous vignette. Regimental Sergeant Major to guard of honour party - after extensive rifle drill. "Stand-easy," followed by - "adjust your medal ribbons" - "not you, you 'orrible little men, I'm talking about real soldiers, with real medals!" The ceremonial party as you might imagine was under the eagle eye of the battalion RSM - who was putting us through the requisite paces, indicative of the quality of our expected visitor. Whether we went to battalion H/Q for rehearsals - or whether he came to us I cannot recall, but I'm pretty certain most of the guard - if not all were from 'D' company. He was a distinguished looking geezer the RSM, tall and well built and a very large clutch of decorations nestled on his chest! As we neared the great day, on one rehearsal I must have been about an inch out of line after a drill movement, and with one huge hand he lifted me up by the belt and dropped me gently down in the correct position.

I have mentioned previously that a key element in our morale during camp life was the services of the 'char-wallah'- well another gentleman from India came into his own prior to the visitation from on high, and this gentleman was of course the 'dhobi-wallah' or laundryman. By some quirk of memory I can remember his name even after all this time - Bannerjee! He did all our laundry, following us from camp to camp - as did the char-wallah. Like most Indians of that time he spoke excellent English - but addressed you with that fluid side to side head movement that is so characteristic. Anyway he came into his own before the big parade and produced garments so heavily starched that they would have stood up on their own! We had learned that the visitor was to be no less than the CIGS (Chief of the Imperial General Staff) himself - just about the highest rank you could achieve in the army of that time. His name was as famous to us as Caesar's was to his legionnaires - Field Marshal Sir William Slim, hero of Burma - and leader of the 14th. Army. This one time private soldier had hauled himself up by the bootstraps through the ranks to become Field Marshal and turned defeat into victory over the Japanese in WW2. Now he was our 'governor' and in charge of the Malayan emergency. Even the hard bitten old hands were impressed!

Dress of the day for the visit were our olive green bush shirts and shorts, worn with whitened belts and gaiters with hose tops and the green regimental tags atop. Boots as already described were 'highly bulled' and our blue parade berets topped off the ensemble. Each of our back pockets contained five .303 rounds (in case of trouble) - but there was enough security around that day to put off any would be assassins. Anyway, came the great day and we were lorried to a nearby airstrip at Bahau lined up, inspected yet again and stood awaiting the great man. As I recall we weren't kept too long before an Auster aircraft made an appearance, circled then landed and taxied towards us - at the same time sprinkling us with dust as the pilot swung round ready for take off again. Helicopters were few and far between in those days so personal transport for the top echelons were Auster single-engined high-wing monoplanes that were maids of all work and planes that required very little in the way of take off and landing room. Anyway the great man alighted with a couple of ADC's in tow and we did our guard of honour stuff - after which we were inspected by 'his nibs' who spoke to one or two of the guard as he progressed. After the inspection our leaders were congratulated on our turnout (despite our fine coating of dust) and we were called around him for an impromptu speech. I think he stood up in a jeep to deliver this - but he reminded us that he too had stood in guards of honour on many occasions - and had marched for many miles, dusty and thirsty - as he made his way up through the ranks. It was probably the same speech he gave to every such inspection - but it was sincere there was no doubt about that! On the current Malayan campaign - he used some ripe barrack room language to describe our opponents and the communist regime in general and admitted it was going to be a tough assignment to beat them, but beat them we must, the government and the nation were behind us in our efforts he acknowledged.

A further 'present arms' and he was up and away - once again showering us with a fine coating of dust as the aircraft lifted off. There is a sequel to the great man's visit. A dinner in his honour was arranged at a Brigade H/Q a few days later and one of our number who was originally in the Field Marshal's parent regiment (The West Yorks I believe) was invited to represent our battalion's other ranks. Our friend, who was another Smith I think, had the soldierly good looks of a recruiting poster, and despite being seated well below the salt, had a very nice evening of wining and dining with what might be termed 'senior management' - sadly to be back on compo rations very shortly afterwards! I seem to recall him having to be issued with a white, formal, evening 'mess' type of uniform - not a rig that most of us were very familiar with!

Back went our shiny boots into kitboxes once more - not to be seen again for quite some time - and then in circumstances we would not have believed had someone made a forecast. Meanwhile it was back to reality and the jungle trails with our new Major. Patrols 'under new management' were little different to what we had known before - the terrain and climate saw to that. As previously mentioned, unless something specific or interesting happened operations tended to blur together in a haze of sheer physical effort. Some patrols lasted for weeks others just a few days, but the former were more the norm. One of the shortest was a 'panic' show - initiated by a civilian team of forestry inspectors, who reported hearing what sounded to them like a serious battle taking place at a particular map reference. As it happened some of our guys were in this particular area and so we were rushed in with a team of medics - with ambulances standing by at the nearest possible road rendezvous. For some atmospheric reason this particular patrol couldn't be reached by radio so the worst was feared! However when we eventually met up with our blokes they were extremely surprised to see us. No, they had not been in a battle, neither had they seen hide or hair of our elusive enemy! As for the forest surveyors - they were probably advised to take more water with their 'stingahs' or 'chotah pegs' of an evening. On another jungle bashing expedition my mate Joe, now back to normal duties - found a fine species of large aggressive scorpion in our basha one evening. So he took it on in mortal combat and emerged the victor. However bits of said hairy beastie tended to have flown around the area somewhat, including the tasty stew I was at that moment bringing to the boil! Needless to say - being hungry we didn't think twice about scoffing it - after all it was well cooked.

On another occasion we were in ambush positions and just before the pale of dawn we observed some lights moving to our front and so we prepared to open up with everything we had. Whether we would have hit anything with the intervening screen of trees I don't know, but action was aborted when it was realized that we were near to the fringes of a rubber estate and the lights just might have been an early morning shift of rubber tappers en route to work! At daybreak we worked our way down to where the lights had been seen, but no clear picture emerged as to who our visitors might have been. Certainly this event would have been reported 'in' later, and had our friends not been workers then at least intelligence would have been aware that some 'hostiles' had been seen in the area. Had they come down the track where we were positioned then there would have been no hesitating in terms of firing upon them. Needless to say we were not aware of the other track which was several hundred yards away.

After Joe Slater had returned home to the UK (of which more later) I shared a basha on some patrols with one 'Jigger' Johnson, a large amiable character who was the platoon signaller. He needed to be large - as the radio set he carried weighed a ton. Joe, Jigger and I had been a bit of a threesome in the limited social life available to us - so I knew him well. We weren't always together on patrols as skilled signallers were at a premium on operations, frequently having to stand in for others who might be sick - or be required on special 'do's' where more than one sparks might be needed. A great mate to have around was Jigger. On patrols he would frequently carry your Bren for you when you were knackered - as well as the awesome weight of the wireless set on his back! This was comradeship of a very high order!

Anyway, on the first patrol as his 'mate' I was deeply asleep one dark night when I awoke thinking I was dead and had gone to heaven. Only those who remember the war years and just after, will recall the late, great, Tommy Handley - and his hit radio show, ITMA. (It's That Man Again!) How was it I asked myself could I clearly hear - albeit faintly, an episode of this much loved show deep in Malayan jungle? As I awakened fully it became clear that Jigger was having a clandestine listen in to a recording of this hit show on Radio Malaya, and what was coming across to me was 'fallout' from his earphones! Battery life being what it was this was somewhat on the illegal side but had I been ignorant enough to mention this, no doubt the answer would have been "just testing old boy, just testing."

Anyone reading this narrative might wonder if the author and his platoon ever met up with our elusive enemy? Only once in my time did we do just that! The result was somewhat inconclusive as the following account will show. We were some distance from another platoon - but relatively aware of their approximate position. We had stopped for a midday rest and meal break in an unusual location comprising a small clearing surrounded by thick jungle. As it happens I was posted on guard with the Bren pointing down the track the way we would be proceeding. Suddenly, about 30 yards away and hidden by the jungle came a tremendous commotion and a babble of voices which were pretty obviously Chinese. The terrorist group (which is certainly what they were) then took off at a rate of knots back whence they came without showing themselves at all. They probably smelt our tobacco smoke or our brewing-up! Had they come just a few yards further then there would have been some action and they would have been vulnerable to the Bren. Should one have sprayed the trees in the hope hitting one of them? Possibly, but it was all over in a flash. A quick chase was out of the question as we might have bumped the other platoon which is exactly what our Communist friends did. There was a brief but intense fire fight which we heard very clearly even though it was a little distance away by then. There were it seems, no casualties on either side, although young Plows (he of the PIAT fame) distinguished himself by a close encounter with a terrorist - giving him a full magazine of Sten gun rounds. No body was ever recovered, but the guerillas had a basic training instinct to get away - however badly wounded, to build up a legend of invulnerability amongst their supporters! We set up hasty ambush positions lest the birds come back our way - but needless to say they made their escape by another track. So, once again 11 platoon drew a blank - but we continued our patrol with a heightened sense of awareness.

In another slightly macabre incident we slept the night in a Sakai Cemetery - the Sakai being a native jungle people who I may have mentioned before. Albeit accidentally - our overnight stay in such an unusual location was due to our days march ending later than usual - giving us no time for the niceties of basha building etc. Here we pitched our makeshift camp - and only next day did we find where we had spent the night! In our small clearing there were a number of low wooden structures rather like bed headboards planted around. I think it was our tracker who identified what they were. We hoped the spirits of the place would not be too offended - but being jungle nomads they probably understood our needs well enough.

To almost complete this litany of 'unusual' patrols, the one which will stay in my mind forever is when 11 platoon marched for some hours along a track - so clearly defined that cyclists could have used it - to where a small Malay kampong lay. We sort of force marched our way along this track which was mainly (and surprisingly) on the level - and to the extent that one or two of our less fit were in the early stages of exhaustion by the time we got there. We were never told the reason for our stay at this kampong - but we suspected that intelligence had picked up that it was going to be raided, for some reason, probably for the watchman's shotgun. Our destination was a typical Malay village where the houses were built on stilts surrounding a small padang (or village green.) The Muslim villagers were a friendly lot and allowed us to camp below their houses which offered good shelter from the almost inevitable nightly rain. No doubt some of their livestock were pushed out in the process!

The village was celebrating a male birth and a feast was being prepared - to which we were cordially invited. Never have I (before or since) tasted so beautiful a curry as we were served that day. It was absolutely delicious - and being served up on a large banana leaf, with fingers acting as cutlery - only added to our enjoyment. A cabaret was provided by a village goat who got his head stuck in a large army biscuit tin (they had a round access hole at the top.) He then galloped around the padang colliding with trees and other immovable objects to the delight of the visitors and villagers alike - who all fell about at the sight of it. Sadly very few patrols were as pleasant as this one was. Obviously the all clear came after a few days, and we speed marched back whence we had come.

Shortly after this we were on an excursion which almost gave us heart attacks all round. A section of us under a corporal had to shelter for the night in an old, tumbledown squatters hut. We had again been caught by the swift onset of nightfall. Where we were going - or what our mission was I know not - but one of our number had a nightmare, and shouted "stand-to, stand-to, attack - attack," during the night. You could say this created something of a panic amongst us as we tried to organise all round defence in the pitch darkness and unfamiliar surroundings. Sighs of relief all round and deep embarrassment by the culprit when it was realized it had been a false alarm. We probably wakened him - as we began to crash around, trying find our weapons and probably screaming things like "where's the bloody Bren gun!". Don't think a lot was said about this one when we finally returned to base at the end of the mission - whatever it was.

Camp life could have its dramatic moments too - what little time we spent in them! The small impromptu canteens mentioned before, were organised for us generally by the quartermasters staff - and helped take the edge off the boredom generated on isolated rubber estates. One particular night we were sitting around smoking and drinking our ration of Tiger beer, some were playing cards but mostly we were just sitting around talking, little groups of mates together. Well into the evening one of the two armed prowler guards came into the tent - for what reason I know not - probably for cigarettes. However the man in question was the guy who claimed to have been a member of the wartime SAS. This fact was disputed by some of the old sweats and in just a few minutes the old argument flared up again.

Drama struck when mad with rage, our friend brought up his Sten gun and pointed it at his tormentors. We froze. This is it we thought and made ready to dive for cover! Sitting just below the angry man with the gun however was a young soldier from our draft - noted for happy go lucky ways. He calmly reached up and took the magazine out of the weapon before anyone realized he was doing it! It was magnificent, and completely defused the situation. We suddenly found it necessary to involve ourselves in deep animated conversation as the culprit was quietly led away. I do not know what the outcome was but the incident was never mentioned again. We suspected there would have been some very frank talking into several ears and maybe the odd transfer took place - more I cannot recall. One thing is for sure I doubt if anyone ever took the mickey again!

Continuing the subject of camp life - we shared a camp with a Gurkha contingent for a brief period. This came about as we were at that time part of a Gurkha Div. (17th I think.) Where this camp was I cannot recall but it was one of theirs. We were invited to a film evening they were having in a very large tent. The smoke from a hundred cheroots was a bit overpowering and the film being Indian and dubbed in Gurkali somewhat incomprehensible. However there was no denying the welcome from these generally small mountain men. They had been in the emergency since it first commenced - and their track record was unsurpassed for bravery in the strange conflict we were involved in. No-one insulted a Gurkha unless he were mad. I think they had a custom of not sheathing their kukri until blood had touched what they considered its sacred blade!

Only one memory remains with me from that brief liaison. It seems that when a Gurkha was up before his superiors on a charge - one of the worst things that can befall him is to be denied guard duty! To be denied the honour of guarding your comrades seemed a strange sentence to us (we may have even welcomed it) But to a Gurkha it was considered a complete disgrace. From time to time our paths crossed with these fierce hillmen from Nepal. We were glad they were on our side!

CHAPTER TWENTY TWO

There were some lighter moments to our camp life however. I think it was when we were in the Tampin area of Negri-Sembilan State we had access on very occasional weekends to a living page from a travel agents brochure. This was a place called Port Dickson on the Malacca Straits. Here were golden beaches, sparkling blue seas - fringed with palm and a million miles from sweaty swamp and jungle. (Pretty much like Penang I guess!) A large villa had been placed at the disposal of army personnel - reputedly donated by a wealthy Chinese businessman and once in a rare while, 11 Platoon frolicked there! We lazed in the sun, swam and read and generally relaxed. Food was courtesy of our own cooks I'm pretty certain - and the only thing we were missing was female company. I think we glimpsed the occasional Chinese family enjoying the beach but alas no shapely maidens in skimpy costumes came our way. What we would have made of topless bathing in those days I cannot think; died of apoplexy I imagine. All too soon - like my leave, these brief treasured moments were over and back on our trucks we went - to what might be termed reality.

A brief footnote to this particular item is that years and years later I was reading an account of the life style of the wealthy sahibs and memsahibs of the prewar Raj, (before the Japanese invasion) and it seems that Port Dickson was a favourite spot for high class social gatherings - beach parties and the general fun and frolicking of the great and good! At one of these beach parties it seems a beautiful young socialite was enjoying an energetic swim some distance from the others. She was attacked and badly mauled by a predatory shark - and so badly injured that she died. I cannot remember ever hearing a warning given to us about possible shark attacks! Certainly one of our number was always on guard during our stays - but then we were still in bandit country! Our splashing about in the water and youthful *joi-de-vivre* might well have invited our triangular finned friends to lunch - us! Nowadays it would cost an arm and a leg to pay a visit to this lovely spot? I would love to see this area again sometime - but my memories will always remain tied to that particular time when we were young, full of zest and banter, and surrounded by good mates and comradeship.

Back to reality - our new CO had made an appearance. Not that we saw much of him you understand! One CO was pretty much the same as another we had reasoned. Modern COs (according to T/V dramas) are pleasant folk - happy to involve themselves in the daily activities of their merry men. (See the ITV current production of 'Soldier - Soldier.) Not back in the fifties they weren't! They were autocratic beings - probably even towards their own officers I suspect, but no doubt expected to be so as that was the form then. However our new commander was a Lt. Col. D'Arcy Mander DSO. There was a 'bags of jankers' look about him - the old sweats said, and we assumed they were pretty psychic about these things. As it happens 'things' remained pretty much the same - although one of the aforesaid old sweats had an early close encounter with his nibs. The camp had been spruced up for the CO's first visit and the guard was ready to be turned out for a ceremonial present arms and inspection. As the entourage neared the camp entrance they observed a private emerging from a side turning carrying a large bundle of clean laundry from the dhobi-wallah's hut. Our colleagues arm hit the salute at the same time as the clean dhobi hit the deck, earning him a withering look from our new be-medalled leader. It is recorded that our new CO was considered a first rate commander by those in higher authority. As we were frequently placed under the control of other commanders during large scale operations - watching over 'our' best interests - plus other political niceties, required considerable diplomatic skills which we of course knew nothing about. For his services he received a 'Mentioned in Despatches' citation - not often the prerogative of Lt. Colonels I understand. He had a big thing about hats did our new C.O. Sometimes on the move in our 15cwt. 'technicals' or on convoy escort duty - it was very hard to keep your hat on, be it beret or bush hat. So, to avoid losing it overboard a blind eye was often cast when it was tucked away till journeys end. However heaven help you if you should run into 'the boss' minus hat!

CHAPTER TWENTY THREE

Much lower down the social scale and a sad time for me was the departure of my mate Joe Slater, for home - as per the original schedule. Six extra months service had been grafted on to our time due to a dodgy world situation (as I may have mentioned earlier.) Joe, and the others who qualified still had their extra time to do, but served it at home in the U.K. Birthdays decided who stayed and who went. Joe's birthdate was 2 weeks earlier than mine - thus was the dividing point.

Joe had a really delightful Mum who was naturally overjoyed to see him home again in one piece. However she was considerably unimpressed that his mate had to soldier on out in the 'badlands' and actually lobbied her M.P to try and get me home as well! I thought this was a pretty nice thing to do - even though there wasn't much of a chance of it happening as obviously a good many more were in the same boat. We all wished our mates well - glad they were homeward bound - but naturally very envious, and hoping for a swift passage of time so that we could follow in their footsteps. However quite a few adventures were to befall us before we too headed for home.

One of these was to affect me personally and took place soon after Joe had gone home. It might not have occurred had he been there to watch my back - so to speak, which is what we always tried to do. What happened (a small affair in reality - but frightening for me) could be called character building I suppose - but I realized as it was going on that the army was no place for the faint hearted. To tell the story I must first preface it by setting the scene. This is on a normal morning first parade you understand, undistinguished from any other except for a somewhat unusual happening. It was customary to have weapon inspection on this parade which was also attended by those who had done guard duty the night before. After the order 'for inspection - port arms' the drill movement was a bit sloppy, so the 'ease springs' command was given - meaning that bolts were closed again - and the trigger pulled before the movement was repeated. There was a tremendous bang as a rifle from one of the night guards went off, the bullet narrowly missing the man next in line. The firer was inside the guard tent faster than his feet touched the ground - as the saying goes, and in due course he saw the inside of the regimental clink!

The net result of this unfortunate event was that guard commanders were ordered to be personally responsible for the unloading of weapons of the night guard standing down, which meant a close inspection of rifles and ammunition, obviously. My fright began shortly after this as I was notified of a guard duty soon after. Part of the procedure was to routinely draw and sign for, fifty rounds of ammunition in a canvas bandolier from the arms kote (or store.) This I did late afternoon and as usual stuck the bandolier under my mattress before heading for the shower. When I got back - shock - horror no fifty rounds to be found - they had disappeared completely! Everyone in the tent denied all knowledge of seeing them and I came to fear the worst as there were Chinese contractors working in and around the camp. It seemed likely that my bullets were already on the way to Chairman Mau's lads - and I saw ahead of me a lifetime behind bars! The loss of one round constituted 28 days in the cooler - so I supposed after losing fifty they probably would throw away the key. It became pretty clear to me very soon that I was in one hell of a predicament! In a short while I would parade for guard duty - be rigorously inspected by a guard commander minus a very important item of essential kit - namely fifty rounds of .303 ammunition! My very first thought was to go to the Sergeant-major and report my loss - but I chickened out of this one and wondered if I could somehow bluff my way through.

Well, I wound up on parade with the rest of the guard expecting the worst. Luck was on my side as the guard commander, being completely unimpressed with someones general turnout proceeded to harangue the culprit as is the way of NCOs - completely overlooking the fact that one of his guards was deficient in an important respect i.e no bullets! As we patrolled in pairs and my 'oppo' knew my problem (I could use some of his if a problem arose.) Mercifully it didn't - but come the morning the worst ordeal was to come, due of course to the new rules about the unloading of guards weapons! When the dread moment came I just couldn't believe my luck. Concealed somewhat in the rear rank I rattled my rifle bolt with the rest of the guard and again the guy didn't spot my nakedness in the bullets department. Boy! It was a hairy few minutes - and I just couldn't believe it when we were dismissed without my being spotted. However - just one minor problem presented itself. Having signed for fifty rounds, then fifty rounds had to be handed back! Panic again and a hectic further search of the tent and the general area without success. I say minor problem, but of course it was major obstacle. The chips were well and truly down and I was in despair until the thought came to me that I should break into the arms store somehow and pinch another bandolier - and then hand this in within the time limit allowed. Now arms stores - even in tents, are not exactly walk in and help yourself shops for obvious reasons. A swift recce revealed that there was a way into the back of the tent which involved a degree of energetic wriggling but calling for concealment and fieldcraft of the highest order.

Observing the storeman going for his tiffin and making fast his domain - all my training was put into practice and squirming my way in from the rear (being extremely thin helped a lot) enabled me to help myself to a full bandolier. Repeating the procedure got me safely out, and bold as brass it was then possible to return the ammunition booked out against my signature, phew! The whole thing would have remained on my conscience for years as you did not need to have too vivid an imagination to realize what fifty rounds of ammo could do in the wrong hands. However, soon another dilemma confronted me, a platoon member from the same tent, returned from two weeks leave. Drawing his kit box from the stores and opening it up revealed - guess what? Yes, tucked away in its recesses was of course my original fifty rounds of ammunition. How did that get there he said with some choice military language. The other guys who knew about my little problem chorused - "must be thine old lad!" Here was very serious dilemma number two. It was one thing to do what I had done to save my neck - but now I was stuck with fifty very illegal rounds, which in the light of a possible snap kit check say - would have again put me in the cooler for a large period of time! Again I was in deep despair. Various possibilities crossed my mind, burying the bloody things, taking them on patrol and 'losing' them or, contriving to throw them into a deep fast flowing river. All ran the risk of being observed of course - so in the end I repeated my previous strategy, and heart beating loud enough to be heard all over the camp, once again wriggled and eased my way back into the arms tent and replaced those accursed bullets. Mercifully I got away with it and breathed a very large sigh of relief - whilst also thanking heaven for my deliverance!

The whole thing was brought into sharper focus for me when shortly after, one of our number accidentally let off a round after climbing off a truck in Kuala Lumpur - after an escort duty ride. Sure enough he got 28 days field punishment for this which we were all sorry to hear about - as it really was so easy. You were indeed a very tense individual exposed on the back of an uncovered lorry. Needless to say you had a round 'up the spout' from the moment the wheels turned - and the safety catch was most definitely off. Great relief when you get to the other end without incident, you jump down and could completely forget about your cocked weapon! Sure enough you might well badly injure a mate - so we all knew the score on this one and hoped it wouldn't happen to us. But 28 days in the cooler is a long long time!

No doubt it was pretty much the same on the other side! They of course did not have a constant stream of replacement ammunition as we - plus the fact that a round, discharged in error might well be heard and bring down a pack of security forces around your neck. We never heard of other sources of supply for the terrorists than what had been stockpiled during the war against Japan.

CHAPTER TWENTY FOUR

It might well be asked how the emergency was going at this time from the British point of view. As ordinary squaddies, if asked we might have said 'with difficulty mate'. At times we wondered who was chasing who! We read the newsheets avidly and listened to the radio bulletins whenever possible - and in those days of 1950 we were just about containing the situation I would say. The news was rarely good at that time for murder and assassination plus the general cruelty involving ordinary people (who you would have thought that the communists would have wanted to win over) seemed to be the order of the day

Certainly at this time mechanisms were being put into place that would eventually lead to victory, and free Malaya from the threat of a Communist take over. However when it was as late as 1968 before the last 'hard core' terrorists came down from the hills to surrender - you have some idea of the calibre of our opponents. The Green Howards scoreboard of terrorists eliminated was gradually rising to equal that of other regiments, as training and experience began to pay off. Our own guys suffered too. Not just in battle or ambushes but in the day to day activities of troops in a hostile environment. Drivers were particularly vulnerable. Not just through terrorist action, but a moments lack of concentration could see you plunge over a jungle clad gully - perhaps 200 or so feet down! Your hat might fly off - an instinctive look back to where it went could see you floating off a hairpin bend, down, down, down - without the benefit of parachute. Accidents too with firearms were sadly not uncommon. Climb to the top of a jungle clad mini-mountain and say "hells teeth, that was some climb," perhaps emphasising the point by banging your Sten gun down. This could easily blow your brains out as the working parts respond to the pressure exerted upon them. Like all young men with guns we 'played' cowboys sometimes - quick on the trigger etc. etc. This too had its repercussions as perhaps sometimes the safety catch might just be off. Easy to forget you have a loaded weapon in your hands! Easy too the accidental 'bumping' of two patrols - not necessarily from the same outfit. A brief firefight in the gloom and sadly you have casualties. Passwords were the order of the day needless to say - but not always heard or understood!

So it wasn't just the man with the funny hat with the red star on it that could see you off chums, although needless to say they tried hard enough. Just one little lapse of concentration could put you in hospital, or even worse. But overall there was a gradual, imperceptible change for the better - brought about without any doubt by that very elusive hearts and minds process. The average British squaddie was pretty good on the P.R, front even though the word probably hadn't been invented then! The older guys amongst us - many who had children of their own, cared a great deal about kids and made a big fuss about any we came across in our daily lives. There was a sweets and chocolate component with each compo ration pack. These were regularly saved up and thrown out to the kids as we passed through the villages and kampongs. One question we never did find an answer for was, often, when driving slowly through a village, kampkong or small town the kids would appear like magic - lining the route as it were - and saluting. It certainly wasn't the sweets because we didn't always have them. Word was that had they not done this during the Jap occupation, there might well have been a spray of bullets to demand some respect. How true this was we never knew, but turn out and salute they did.

Up to 1950 the general population might have been standing back a little and watching developments. On the one hand the Japs were now gone and the British were back - but the Communists were Asians after all weren't they? Might they not be the prequel to self rule? Perhaps they might well have argued lets see what develops, and no one could blame them for initially thinking this way. However, ignoring the hearts and minds theme themselves the terrorists waged a savage war - not just on security force personnel but on every class of the general population, so that eventually the penny dropped that the red star brigade were not necessarily good for the nation's health - or that of the ordinary individual! Indeed far from it. The news said it all. Trains were regularly blown up. Buses ambushed and set on fire - bombs thrown into shops and crowded dance halls and many many other atrocities. Pure terrorism in fact - hundreds of innocent people murdered to try and influence the others.

Despite all this mayhem an interesting fact began to emerge that Malaya was beginning to prosper again with its massive tin and rubber production. Also, Singapore was assuming her former place as a world trade centre (no sign of austerity there) so all in all things were perhaps looking up, and this too was a nail in the communists eventual coffin. As mentioned before, your average British tommy played a considerable part in the overall P.R game - together with the renowned fairness of British administrators, plus the growing success of the Briggs Plan. These and many other factors began to slowly tip the balance against the Red menace. I have subsequently read that terrorist 'successes' or 'incidents' peaked in 1952 - and from then on the initiative passed to the security forces and despite setbacks was never lost again. More and more terrorists after this time began to give themselves up. A trickle became a flood as the likelihood of victory for their cause diminished as each month went by. Most of us who plied the jungle trails had a respect for our opponents and their forest skills. Their bravery was not in question either, but their methods and murderous activities particularly against innocent civilians got our backs up - for those were days when terrorism was not a household word as it is today.

Quite obviously back in the early days of the campaign large quantities of money and supplies were getting through to the enemy enabling them to operate closer to towns and centres of population - where their supporters lived. However as time went by and the supply and money runs were gradually closed down the terrorists went deeper and deeper into the forests - thus extending their supply routes further and further.

Talking of money - and the money 'couriers' of our enemy, it was the old sweats dream to catch up with such a person and relieve him of his wealth. This to be shared amongst the rest of the patrol of course! Needless to say it never happened, (to us at any rate.) The other wistful dream was to run across and capture a contingent of pretty female terrorists - preferably a long way from base - so that the journey back might include some passionate interludes - (some hopes!) Real life revealed that the female of the species was as fanatical if not more so than some of the men. The most ambitious fantasy of all of course was to find the two elements together - a money courier and a troupe of females in tow. All this is forgetting of course the strict rules about captured 'assets' - very little chance of getting away with either sort of loot unfortunately!

CHAPTER TWENTY FIVE

The next camp move that I can recall was to the South Johol Rubber Estate - near to the town of Tampin. This followed the ambushing of the estate manager who was seriously injured. I can recall little of this place other than it seemed more 'open' than many other rubber plantations - maybe because it was so vast. On our many vehicular travels to and from the place we saw a weird sight. This was an enormous area of dead rubber trees, standing like ghostly sentinels - row on row, completely devoid of foliage. At night their stark whiteness reflected back from the headlight beams like gravestones, giving off an extremely eerie feeling! It was said that they had been poisoned en-masse, preparatory to new trees being planted? Seemed unlikely to us but that was the story. If my memory is correct our camp was based at the foot of a large rubber encrusted hill - seemingly giving good observation and ambush potential to our foes. A permanently manned light machine gun post was positioned to counter any threat from this direction.

One particular night to remember was when we were enjoying an A.K.C film show (as usual in the open air) - when we were alerted by the assistant manager's wife to the fact that he was long overdue from a remote corner of the estate. The film was abandoned and we set off at high speed expecting to find a bullet riddled car and occupant on one of the estate's lonely roads. What we found however was the gentleman in question trudging along the roadside - the victim only of a broken down vehicle. To say he was pleased to see us would be something of an understatement. No more eerie or dangerous place could be found in those days after dark, than a vast area of rubber plantation with nature's own suspicious sounds and every shadow quite menacing. Bearing in mind the earlier incident on the estate, we imagined our friend would be in need of a pretty stiff drink when he was reunited with his family.

Needless to say jungle (or ulu) bashing continued as normal from the South Johol Estate. In we went at frequent intervals but we in 11 platoon were still not successful in engaging any enemy. However we were assured that our very presence was a strong deterrent to our red friends - keeping them away from the precious rubber - and also more importantly keeping them on the move! We continued to be astounded at the success of the 'air drop' supply system, and grew adept at making a clearing in the forest enabling the circling Dakotas's to see us. We had watched and marvelled at how our Dyak or Iban trackers went about the job with their small but razor sharp Parang knives. Some smaller trees would be chopped half through, so that when larger ones were felled, they brought down the smaller ones already part cut. Seemingly in very little time a sizeable clearing could be created. The patrolling mixture was pretty much the same wherever you went - the ulu (as the Malayans called the jungle) was a test of endurance for friend or foe alike.

Occasionally something interesting would happen that helped you recall a particular patrol - as opposed to many others where you could think of little else but fatigue and a remoteness from any sort of civilisation. One of our number slipped from the moving line to answer a call of nature on one of our excursions and as he squatted, he saw to his amazement a Malay gentleman, complete with traditional velvety black hat regarding him before he melted away like a ghost into the surrounding jungle. Stunned our friend grabbed for his rifle which he had laid down, but was too late to get a shot off at this apparition. Needless to say he was questioned very thoroughly about what he had seen after an abortive search in the vicinity revealed no trace. What we did not know at the time and what I subsequently read about, was a famous Malay man, who was a highly successful money courier for the terrorists. This in itself was unusual as most Malays were certainly not in the Communist camp at all. However for whatever reason, this particular gentleman was a highly successful courier, and it could well be we almost had him within our grasp? The old sweats might have got their hands on some red money after all. Sadly not even a reward was available to service personnel if large quantities of money or weapons were ever found. It is also very unlikely that the platoon commander - be he sergeant or officer - would have gone along with a bit of grand larceny in the field'

Talking of officers, platoon commanders mainly, I have not mentioned many names in this narrative as they seemed to come and go fairly frequently. More often than not it seemed that our very experienced sergeant was in charge of us when on jungle excursions. This is what memory serves up but in real life it might have been that there were far more officers than I can recall - although it's pretty certain they were somewhat stretched. I know we had two second lieutenants fairly quickly at one stage, one of them being only recently out of Sandhurst. He distinguished himself very quickly by putting people on charges whilst on patrol and in jungle situations for pretty trivial reasons. These charges were quashed rather swiftly on our return to base and words were said in certain ears leading to a more liberal approach. Needless to say the jungle is a great leveller. Co-existence was the name of the game - mutual respect was necessary at all times because we all depended on each other - not dissimilar in a way to aircrew or tank crew, albeit with a larger number of people. We certainly knew who our leaders were, and in the main they were worthy of our trust. Some throughout the regiment personally disposed of terrorists, and many were decorated, as were a number of NCOs. The jungle itself tended to be even handed to those who dared enter its portals, both leader and lead. Snakes, leeches, falling trees and swift flowing rivers were impartial as to their victims as were the enemy of course. He, naturally would prefer to knock off patrol leaders - particularly officers - so we all wore the same gear, most carried the jungle carbine (at that stage) and were pretty indistinguishable one from another. We changed 'point' man every day for he was the likeliest bloke to cop it should there be a bump or an ambush situation. No one queried that the officer or sergeant in charge should be back somewhat from the sharp end for obvious reasons, although they were very soon up front if a query arose - or their presence needed.

So our daily lives progressed throughout 1950, day in - day out. Jungle, convoy escort work, guard, rest - screening operations and beating up the roads in our fifteen hundredweight Dodges. Unknown to us fate was taking a hand in our next quite unexpected move! This came completely out of the blue as far as we were concerned as, with little or no warning, we found ourselves heading hot foot for Singapore (a fair distance away.) So urgent was the call it meant some of us being pulled straight from the jungle - and still in patrol garb, lorried down country at great speed. Some went by train but 11 platoon went by truck I'm certain of that as I have a distinct memory of our lorry being directed to our destination which turned out to be Selerang Barracks, our home for some time to come.

CHAPTER TWENTY SIX

We were unsure at first what all the fuss was about - there was talk of serious rioting, but until we reached Singapore we were completely in the dark about the causes and who was involved. It was hard not to think that there was a Communist inspired rising afoot - but we couldn't have been more wrong, as the troubles were the fault (if that is the right word) of a judicial ruling in the High Court.

The story ran thus. During the war, and at the time of the Japanese invasion - a Dutch family became separated from their young daughter in the chaos of the times. Eventually they assumed she must be dead - and she apparently thought the same about her parents. They were taken into internment and she was adopted and taken in by a kindly Malay family who brought her up as one of their own. At the age of twelve she was married to a Malay boy (as was then the custom) and some time after the end of hostilities word reached the authorities of this event and an investigation took place - identifying this young lady as the long missing, presumed dead, Maria Hertzog. She was then reunited with her parents who took the case to court to try and get the marriage annulled, which they succeeded in doing. When the judgment was announced the Muslim population demonstrated their disapproval outside the court, becoming more and more incensed because they felt their faith had been impugned. The demonstrations turned into some very serious rioting in which we heard many atrocities were committed.

Fearing that the matter was getting out of hand and beyond the local authority powers to contain, all available troops were rushed down to Singapore to help quell the uprising. Anyway there we suddenly were. Rather as if a body of men from the Outer Hebrides had been called suddenly down to London. We were completely astonished by the sheer magnitude and size of the place. We heard all sorts of stories about the scale of the rioting - the looting and the bloodletting and also that at one stage the Gurkhas had gone in with the bayonet to safeguard life and limb! Without doubt any Europeans caught up in the maelstrom were in for serious manhandling (if not worse) and centres were set up for beleaguered ex-pats to congregate at for their personal safety. It later emerged that our CO's driver (who had recently taken delivery of a then brand new Standard Vanguard motor car,) was also caught up at an early stage and the car was very badly damaged. It came down the line that the driver had only just escaped serious injury or death by the skin of his teeth and was not desperately impressed by his nib's concern for the car. As this was naturally phrased in soldier speak, laced with many four letter words - we found it amusing and not an unexpected reaction given the times.

We were initially based at Selerang Barracks - not realising that this was to be our home for the next few weeks. The original deployment here was because of the proximity of the notorious Changi jail. It was feared that maybe the rioters would attempt to spring some of the violent prisoners incarcerated there. The barracks itself was also expected to be attacked if the insurgents got that far - obviously to try and hi-jack the arms store! The Changi prison building was a stark edifice and could have been nothing else but a prison and a place of execution. Of recent times it had been the home of many British P.O.W.'s and really should have had a sign up reading, 'abandon hope all ye who enter here' so grim looking was it. Of more recent times Changi has been in the news regarding the harsh punishments meted out to drug smugglers. T/V footage showed that since our day cosmetic attempts have been made to 'soften' its outlines by building modern looking administrative buildings at the front - but nothing could ever hide the desperate gravity of the original building. It took me back nearly fifty years in a flash!

Anyway the situation began to ease a little and when it was perceived that there was no threat to prison or barracks we were withdrawn and based near the centre of Singapore. Here some roads had been closed off and we had to direct traffic and pedestrians along other routes. By night we guarded the famous Raffles Hotel - our base being the nearby Union Jack Club (for servicemen) - where we slept on tables when not on duty. So it was that 11 platoon (of dubious social skills and graces it must be said) guarded arguably the world's most prestigious hotel at that time, from a mob who would have liked nothing more than to have torn it down! The hotel needless to say was home from home to your Royals, your Hemingway's and the international glitterati of the times. The smart set played and danced - the music and clinking of glasses could be plainly heard as we marched up and down outside its illustrious portals. To be fair many of the people enjoying themselves inside were planters and their wives probably escaping from months of virtual imprisonment on their fortress rubber estates up country! Being, as I have said before some of Kipling's 'licentious soldiery' we did not set foot inside the hotel.

One day I would like to go back, and with the memsahib on my arm - wander in and perhaps take a Singapore Sling at the bar whatever they are, and maybe stay a night or two! I might ask someone to show us around - and then become a boring old fart (to anyone I can grab hold of) - and tell them how it was fifty years ago when the fate of The Raffles Hotel rested with No.11 platoon of the famous Green Howards Regt. Perhaps a slight exaggeration this - but then, who can deny it, for I and we were there!

Strangely enough I have met many ex-servicemen in my time who served in Singapore and Malaya - none of whom had had an involvement in this fracas - or who had even heard of it! All except one that is. He being a distinguished ex-RN type currently a retired harbour-master in Plymouth. A chance pub conversation led to talk of the far-east and the various people who had served there - and it emerged that he too had been involved in the Maria Hertzog riots with all available Navy hands! As for Maria Hertzog herself I have never heard or read another word about her! Hopefully she found happiness and fulfilment in whatever she did. But I wonder if she ever realised the trouble she caused at the time, and that the immediate future of one of the world's great seaports hung in the balance for a few days in 1950 on account of her doings!

Although we had not heard the rumours prior to our dash for Singapore, it seems that the Regiment had been earmarked for R&R (rest and retraining) for some time. Thus we were somewhat ahead of schedule and were eventually caught up by the rest of the battalion who came down at a more leisurely pace. After the excitement of the riots all units were posted back to normal duties and we began to take stock of our new surroundings at Selerang. The barracks here were I suppose quite modern as they go. The accommodation blocks surrounding a large intimidating 'square' were light and airy and pretty much as described by the elegant major - who sold us the original idea of volunteering for some 'real soldiering'. He was wrong in one respect however in that we did not sally forth from here to duff-up terrorists! My memory tells me that the barracks were three storied affairs, and colour washed in a sort of creamy colour. Each block had a balcony and those nearest to it had the benefit of cooling breezes to augment the large bladed propeller fans which hung from the ceilings.

During the war at some stage Selerang had been a P.O.W camp and centre, and photos could be purchased-taken back in those days, showing the whole square packed with transport of all shapes and sizes together with what appeared to be thousands of men beginning their captivity. A footnote to this story is that, after a prolonged heavy downpour, beneath the colour wash on some buildings - Japanese 'characters' indicating the nature of the building could be clearly seen. The only other evidence of the war we came across was a wrecked Jap armoured car - up to its armpits in sand near to one of the beaches, where it was standing its last watch I guess. When the whole regiment was in situ - we commenced what can only be described as 'peacetime' garrison duty in a tropical location which to the uninitiated meant drill and bull and spit and polish to equal anything we had had in basic training. Regimental pride was the name of the game, and company commanders were anxious to see their men in the forefront of the competitive system in operation. One of the manifestations of this was the regimental quarter guard and its ceremonial mounting.

This was the 'day' guard, with ceremonial to equal the Buckingham Palace mounting! Each company supplied a suitable member and he was turned out as if for a recruiting poster and then some. Only the best physical specimens were generally chosen - which fortunately left pretty average little old me out of the frame. Your man's uniform (still olive green) was starched to such an extent that it would have stood up on its own! Badges brasswork and webbing were works of art - and the mirror shiny boots even had the undersides bulled, the studs were polished like chrome also. The brasses, belts and other items may well have been borrowed from willing mates who possessed finer specimens than the guard himself. It was not unknown for a man to be carried to his parade position by comrades to avoid desecrating the soles of his boots! Needless to say all this was done in the name of brownie points and being flavour of the month with the sarn't major and senior NCOs - particularly if you were to be chosen from the rest to be CO's 'stick-man'.

A great honour this and in effect meaning you were the CO's orderly for the day, doing no guard, but running any errands as required by the great man and following him around with an ornate message pouch and ceremonial swagger stick - hence the title 'stick-man'.

Even normal 'night guard' meant a great deal of bull and ceremonial. You were inspected rigorously by the officer i/c and woe betide you if you didn't come up to scratch - names were taken and punishment inevitably followed. I only did a night guard once and it stays in my memory because my 'oppo' and I were patrolling in the vicinity of the officers mess in the middle of the night. By chance we saw the orderly officer emerge, obviously about to check up on the guard's wakefulness - and if he felt a bit mean, turning out the guard for inspection! We crept up on him and with a rattle of rifle bolts proceeded to ask the 'who goes there' question. We hoped this might alarm him just a little - sadly it didn't but we felt he was a bit impressed! He walked a way with us chatting normally until with a gleam in his eye he set of for the guard room no doubt to try his luck down there. Did we earn a brownie point or two for the company? We hoped so!

Meanwhile a rumour circulating for some time turned out to be completely true. To celebrate The Green Howards premier battle honour, The Alma - earned during the Crimean War, we were to 'troop the colour' which is an ancient ceremonial now seen by many people on television - celebrating The Queen's official birthday. The battle of the Alma saw the Regiment, then the 19th of foot, distinguish itself against superior odds in the Crimea in 1854, forcing a huge Russian attack to flee in disorder and helping to win the campaign. Our Colonel obviously saw our splendid barracks as a suitable backdrop for such a ceremony.

So, we became intimately acquainted with the Selerang barrack square and rehearsals would begin at about 5 a.m! In view of the 90 degree heat at mid morning it was a sensible hour to start, but it meant being up and around at 4.0 am, bright eyed and bushy tailed (and pretty smart at that.) The colour trooping ceremony was choreographed hundreds of years ago when it was necessary for men to be able to recognise their 'regimental colour' - it being a rallying point in battle and also a challenge to opposing forces - and a great disgrace if it were captured. Being escort to the colour in those days could be both an honour and a death sentence! The whole set piece lasts about an hour or so apart from the preliminaries and is very challenging in the stamina department!

As on television, the piece de resistance is the march through the ranks of the colour and escort - with a drill movement widening the ranks to accommodate this. Apart from that, most of the ceremonial consists of drill movements we had all done many time before - but the precision was awesome. To illustrate this on one rehearsal my bayonet came off during a 'slope arms' before a march off and by some miracle this was not seen by the RSM. No doubt he would have commented on my parentage had he noticed, as I was in the front rank! I cannot recall what bit we were doing but we returned to precisely the spot we had moved from - so that when stood easy I was able to recover my pig sticker and slip it on before being spotted. The participation of many officers in this parade and the amount of shouting involved saw (for us) the amusing sight of those perhaps less vocally blessed, having for want of a better word, shouting lessons under the RSM (Raynor.)

So, we rehearsed and rehearsed and rehearsed, until we were every bit as good as guardsmen. For the big event we were issued with a new type of puttee to replace the old gaiter which normally topped off our boots. These looked very smart but the securing ribbon was a pain to fasten correctly till you had mastered it.

For whatever reason the band of The 1st. Cameronians were also resident at Selerang - and as they were constantly playing our regimental march we assumed they would be supplying the music for the big event (our own band being in the U.K.) Whether you were regimental or not - there is nothing quite like the feeling of swaggering around the barrack square to your own regimental march! However, regimental pride being what it was in the end the corps of drums, bugles and fifes did the honours on the day. Pretty good they were too - but sadly not quite the power and glory of a big military band.

Although our kit was being bulled up because of our sojourn in tropical barracks we certainly had to go the extra mile for this big effort. Come the day we gleamed and our starched olive greens were examples of the dhobi-wallah's art! And so the great day arrived and in beautiful weather conditions the parade took place. Taking the salute was no less a person than the new C. in C. - General Sir John Harding. All went decidedly well and we performed before a celebrity audience of senior officers and even had radio coverage on Malayan state radio! Apparently the march in review order (not easy) was considered to be as good as anyone had ever seen so all were very impressed. Various official celebrations also took place in officers and sergeant's messes with many distinguished guests.

I cannot remember what was laid on for us but there must have been something official. Certainly there was an inter-company athletics match the next day where most of us were spectators. Most of us were glad it was all over - but pleased we had been involved I guess - even perhaps a sneaky bit of regimental pride creeping in! Not bad we all thought for a bunch of jungle bunnies, all this ceremonial stuff eh! But not being particularly anxious to re-acquaint ourselves with the green stuff just yet please sir.

CHAPTER TWENTY SEVEN

Meanwhile we began to appreciate the benefits of being based in Singapore. It was a island city/state flowing with the proverbial milk and honey - and it was as if the war had never happened - not like back home in austerity bound Britain. Seemingly it was not targeted by terrorists, although no doubt many of their supplies were obtained in Singaporean shops and filtered up country. Robinsons famous department store was an eye opener for us and was the Harrod's of the far-east. We supposed you could get anything there.

Motor showrooms had brand new cars available. New models coming in from the U.K. (and I suppose elsewhere) were pretty amazing to us. Cars like the Standard Vanguard (as mentioned earlier) and the equally new Triumph range, including the Renown and Razor-edge, as they were known were on display. At home it would have been the mid-fifties before you could have strolled into a showroom and bought yourself a brand spanking new car. Everything was for export in those days! .

An amusing story came down the line from one of the batmen concerning an officer who was appointed escort to the CO's wife. The riots being over it was deemed safe to visit shops again with due vigilance. Visiting the Robinson's store our first lady reputedly was intrigued by some falsies and said something along the lines of good heavens - look at these they've even got nipples on them!" The officer escort was allegedly quite embarrassed by this informality, as generally men were not thick on the ground in lingerie departments in those days. The story had us agog. Naively we asked what were falsies? How were they worn and why etc etc? Don't they show up when worn - how can you tell? As the wags said it would be fun to find out! How innocent many of us were then.

So we became accustomed to our new life in these tropical barracks. Although starting our day pretty early because of the afternoon heat - after tiffin the day generally was free for sport or a trip into the many delights of Singapore. Army food at this stage wasn't bad as our cooks were part of the regiment - and were I suppose under gentle pressure to produce reasonable fare. I personally was still not attracted to oriental food and rarely touched it at all, Similarly with alcohol. By now I could drink a pint or two of Tiger beer and enjoy it but was equally happy with Frazer & Neave's soft drinks which were the best of the bunch out there.

However Singapore had many restaurants and cafes serving European cuisine. Here many of us spent our money and often again would amaze waiters by polishing off a large plateful, and then asking for the same again! We all continued to be staggered at the sheer size and scale of Singapore. Even in those days it was a clean and tidy place. The buildings were on a human scale then - not as today I understand, with a skyline like a mini New York. I'm told that many of the old 'traditional' buildings have been demolished to make way for more modern high-rise architecture, and many landmarks of our time have long since disappeared. Sad in many ways, but progress is progress as the man said. However, I understand that a halt had to be called into this great demolition drive while any parts of the old Singapore remained standing. Concrete looks pretty much the same the world over - and once destroyed the atmosphere and charm of old buildings can never be recreated.

This all being in the future of course. In terms of getting about, Singaporeans enjoyed a first class public transport system at that time comprised mainly of fast buses. Fares were cheap and on any bus you would find a cross section of the population - ranging from Chinese, Malays, and in a slight minority Indians - who seemed mainly to be Sikhs at that time. Just the very odd European might be encountered on a bus.

All would be smartly turned out, with many ladies in their native finery. Chinese girls in general had not yet, all adopted western styles. Most housewives therefore wore a black two piece pyjama type outfit but young girls wore chongsam dresses with a revealing split skirt. These were figure hugging garments that really kept you looking in their direction. The menfolk though seemed to favour the white shirt and grey or light coloured trousers, pretty much the same as we when off duty. Again with the traditional row of pens in the top pocket. The number indicating the status of the individual we supposed. In our case, although shorts were worn off duty sometimes, in the main trousers seemed to be the favourite for the man about town whatever the time of day. Jackets were rarely seen or needed.

One feature of bus travel was the number of ticket inspectors who climbed on the bus between Selerang and the city centre on any day. We assumed they were seeking fare dodgers or checking on staff honesty - but you might have four or five during the journey. Trying to be seen as polite gents, we would offer up our seats if the bus became crowded - preferably to young ladies who we would have liked to have impressed.

Some hopes. They would accept our seats, smile and giggle but as for a conversation or contact, not a chance!

We roamed all over the place in our off-duty hours. Good beaches abounded if you wished to laze in the sun or swim in tropic seas. Open air swimming pools were available too. One I think was at a servicemen's club - of which there was a choice as I recall There really was much to see. Botanic gardens and well kept parks were there to be enjoyed, plus of course the famous Tiger Balm Gardens - presented to the island by the multi-millionaire owner of Tiger Balm, which was an ointment famed for its healing powers over a multitude of skin and other problems.

Down by the harbour and dockland, huge warehouses (called 'godowns') testified to the area's trading status and growing prosperity. Many fine Colonial buildings graced the edge of the waterfront area and gave a sense of power and prosperity to the already impressive overall scenario. Midst all this the lush green of the island's major padang (or green open space) stood awaiting cricket, hockey or other sporting events, possibly polo? But not I think just at that time. There was however a distinct air of the Raj about it and you half expected to see soldiers in red coats drilling under mounted officers.

For film buffs like myself (but most of us were in those days) - Singapore was a Mecca. Numerous large, cool (air conditioned?) cinemas offered the very latest in screen entertainment. For two or three hours you were transported away from drill, bull and army life in general to the fantasy land peopled by the great film stars of the era.

Those amongst us who found feminine charms irresistible and paramount were also spoilt for choice. There was the notorious Boogie Street, amongst others, crammed with ladies of the night and their establishments. For those whose desires lay elsewhere there was a particular area known colloquially as 'gobblers green' - where the gay fraternity met. 'Gay' in those days of course had a different meaning to today! Both areas were raided from time to time by the M.P's - but were operating again by the next day. The sex 'industry' as it was in those days was a pretty flourishing affair, but seemed to carry little stigma. Les girls were everywhere and for many of them - long before the growth of Singapore's industrial might - perhaps one of the few well paid jobs available if you were uneducated? I'm reliably informed that Boogie Street has long ceased to exist together with many others, torn down in the quest for progress.

Quite a few interesting things happened during our stay. On one occasion we were invited to a quiz show being broadcast on Radio Malaya. One of our number, young Sheldrick from Hull, was chosen to participate. He was doing really well till the six million dollar question which was to complete the following famous phrase from Hamlet. "Alas, poor Yorick...." We were willing him on as most of us knew the answer, but sadly the gong went and he lost out on a big money prize. (Big for those days anyway.)

An opportunity arose for some of us to fly on RAF missions, bombing and strafing deep jungle targets upcountry, where terrorist camps had been pinpointed. Can't quite remember how we were picked for this - but those who went came back considerably impressed. Neither can I remember what type of planes they flew in. Obviously some sort of fighter-bomber of that era - not exactly flush with passenger room we gathered. What the success rate of these attacks were we never knew but the sheer noise factor from the rockets and bombs must have been pretty nerve racking if you were underneath and anywhere near it at all.

Out on the ranges we got our eyes in again re-qualifying on rifle, Bren, and a new replacement for the time expired Sten gun. This was the Owen gun from Australia. I can't remember much about it except it was safer and had similar principles to the Sten but was better engineered and the magazine springs didn't weaken as did the Sten's (which could let you down when you least wanted them to!) Another little plaything we tried out, was of all things a fearsome flame thrower! This we did not fancy. A large circular pack/tank fitted on your back - and the nozzle emitted streams of a liquid toffee like substance which was projected and ignited in long streams of flame as the trigger was depressed. Very few jungle situations could have called for such a deployment, apart from burning down abandoned enemy camps, but usually a box of matches could take care of that aspect. We were glad not to see this particular weapon again! The usual wags did remark on its brew-up and cooking capabilities!

Officers were issued with a new piece of gear too - in the shape of an American infantry carbine. This was very light and seemingly insubstantial compared with our own rugged .303's. I cannot remember the calibre of the American weapon - but the bullets* (or shells) as our Yank cousins have it were pretty small by comparison. However apparently it was very accurate and its major feature was an automatic facility which in our slam-bang type of warfare was a useful attribute.

*since identified as .300

Firearms experts all - we laughed at the apparent fragility of the piece - a point brought home to me when cleaning one of these American things. It had a small spring concealed in its innards - which had a desperate tendency to fly off into the undergrowth in a speedy arc as you despairingly tried to refit it - leaving you grovelling on your knees trying desperately to find it - knowing there were few if any replacements available! However I have no doubt that the carbine was a pretty viable gun - as most G.I's carried them throughout WW2. New anti ambush techniques were being 'worked up' as I may have mentioned earlier - including a smoke emitting device, which was fitted to a demonstration vehicle. It blanketed the ambush scene totally - hindering friend as well as foe unfortunately!

CHAPTER TWENTY EIGHT

Whilst we were at Selerang amidst all the bull and the retraining - Christmas suddenly came upon us. This was my second one overseas and I suppose these days there might be a modest mutiny if you missed two Christmases at home! At the time we didn't think too much about it. Were then now - no doubt we would be on to our mums via our mobile 'phones, complaining like mad! I cannot remember too much about Christmas 1950 except that the cooks excelled themselves with a magnificent spread. All ex-servicemen will know that humble other ranks are waited upon by officers and senior NCOs on Christmas day. This ceremonial starts with early morning dixies of tea laced with rum, delivered to your block and then bedside mug by no less than the Sgt. Major himself. This tea is traditionally known as 'gunfire' and pretty lethal it can be too!

Needless to say, there is much mickey taking and ribaldry throughout this day, but I don't recall it ever going over the top. Jokes, tipsy speeches and much bonhomie were the order of the day. Still being a little chary about alcohol since my jungle rum experience I went a little easy on the 'sauce' but non the less enjoyed the comradeship of the day! After the feast, those who wished to (and were able to,) journeyed into town for further revels. I recall Sgt. Major Holloway giving us all a lecture on the lines of "if you must have a bloody jump - for Pete's sake pay a decent price for it, that way you might avoid the clap!" Did I go into town? Can't remember - but if I did, it would have been to see yet another film. Hard to believe anyone would do this on Christmas Day - but then we were all positively nutty about films in those days, and just couldn't get enough of them. Major film 'stars' enjoyed a popularity hard to understand these days. Our much anticipated Christmas mail had been augmented of course by cards and small gifts. I say small because weight restrictions and long delays in parcel post (which came by sea mail) not to mention the quite significant cost involved - favoured very small packages. On my 19th birthday for instance, a cake had arrived from home - which must have cost a fortune to send - and then was sadly inedible due to the length of time in transit. As I might have said before, normal letters by air mail were pretty swift taking approximately a week to reach us. Obviously there were moist eyes from some of the guys whose wives and young families were at home in England - but overall morale was very high on receipt of an extra large issue of mail and good wishes from home.

I seem to recall one letter telling me (somewhat ironically) about an International Peace Conference being held about that time, in Sheffield's magnificent City Hall - still scarred from the heavy Blitz of scant years before! Anyway this large gathering included such eminent world figures as Picasso, and the superb bass baritone, Paul Robeson. Naive as most of were about art - I don't think many of us were in the Picasso camp for even then we were aware of his strange reproductions of the human face and figure! In the main our art world experience had been gleaned, from the Sunday 'promenading' through the Graves Art Gallery and Museum in Weston Park in Sheffield where we would hope to meet similarly inclined young females, also on the look out for new friendships. Paul Robeson was a different kettle of fish. I would have walked a very, very, long way to have heard him sing - which indeed he apparently did at this august gathering

It is a sad reflection that whatever genuine aims this congress might have had in relation to world peace - unfortunately there wasn't too much of it about just then. The Korean War was raging in the far, far east, Indo-China, Aden and Suez were soon to come - not forgetting Kenya and the Mau-Mau plus Cyprus and The Belgium Congo! .

Should anyone ask, I could not tell how the Island of Singapore celebrated its Christmas. Certainly the Chinese and Muslim calendars do not recognize the Christmas feast but as the colony had been British in operation for a very long number of years it's pretty certain that some of our colonial celebrations and festivals must have rubbed off. Certainly bars, restaurants, cinemas and servicemen's clubs did a roaring trade - as did the ladies of the night! Hard to recall just how long our Christmas leave was at that time. Probably just a day or so. I have a dim recollection of being given a lift back to camp by an ex-pat Briton from the Civil Service sometime around the Christmas /New Year period. Our conversation was very desultory as we had so little in common - but at least he did stop and pick me up. (Obviously the 'missed last bus syndrome' again) - just where had I been? I certainly envied his posh car but I doubt he would have wished to change places with me!

However, one last word about Christmas - whatever distractions there might have been in spending the festivities in a lush tropical setting, it was no substitute for the festivities at home, whether freezing or no! The ones with wives and young families felt it most of course. However great the comradeship of best mates - there was really only one place to be.

Once the festivities were over of course it was back to normal with a vengeance. We renewed acquaintance with our huge barrack square again - and continued our weapon training. Rumours began to percolate about our next operational area 'up-country', but when and just where remained a secret almost to the end. In the meantime it had begun to dawn on some of us that we were only two or three months away from stepping on to the big boat home. We kept our excitement close to our chests - just in case the powers that be added further time to our overseas service. The war in Korea had widened to include the Chinese regular army and we felt that anything could happen. Most of us squeezed the last drop of our army 'credits' (savings deducted from pay) and began shopping around for presents to take home. Singapore even then was a shopping mecca so there was no problem in locating suitable gifts, paying for them was more the problem.

However bargaining was a new skill we had learned and this method certainly helped your dollar go further. We all pretty much bought the same type of large suitcase. They were made of a sort of leatherette-cum-compressed cardboard - but looked pretty luxurious and imposing. Mine is still in our loft at home - quietly decomposing. I keep it there for sentiment I suppose but it has always been too large for holiday purposes over here. Some chaps kitted themselves out with a suit, as these could be made up quickly and efficiently - nor did they cost an arm and a leg. I was tempted - but the material seemed a little too lightweight for home climes - particularly the fair county of Yorkshire!.

The explosion of superb quality cameras from Japan had not yet happened - otherwise I might well have bankrupted myself to get one. I did however buy a very second-hand one from young Hardy. This was even then a vintage piece, being an early '30's 616 Kodak. Where it had been picked up I don't know, but it was in lovely condition and in your 'genuine' leather case - no plastic stuff in those days! The print size was quite large (getting on for postcard size) however the shutter speed and stop openings needed to be guessed or calculated from the booklet that came with it. No built in light meters around just then. However I found it took reasonably sharp pictures and used it for quite a long time when I got home. 'Twas swapped later for an old typewriter which of course I regret now. Some of the illustrations in this book were taken by this old Kodak.

One new camera I did buy as a novelty/gift was a small miniature thing - which actually took quite good photographs from a miniroll of film, for which there seemed a quite a plentiful supply. I cannot remember who it was gifted to at home - but I see they fetch good prices these days. I did treat myself to one small luxury item which was a Breitling wrist watch - which was also a 'stop' watch. It was very reasonably priced at the time and came from a jewellers called, A. L Abdeen & Sons. (Where are they now?) Somewhere I have a receipt for it - and much to my surprise Breitling watches are highly prized and older ones have a rarity value - although mine is currently in need of some expert attention.

So our time in this oriental island city was gradually running out. I suppose we were somewhat softened by our tropic surroundings (apart from prickly heat, tinea etc.) I don't recall there was a mosquito problem in Singapore although I suspect we were still taking our Paludrin. Did we still use our mosquito nets? Can't quite remember. I have subsequently heard that Mosquitoes do not operate much higher than first floor level - so, perhaps, being on a second floor we were not on the receiving end.

Needless to say we were not anxious to re-acquaint ourselves with damp foetid jungle again, and the harsh conditions of patrolling - but that of course was what was in store for us. Just prior to our departure for more rigorous adventures I had seen the M.O. (Medical officer) about the need perhaps for an eye test - as I found small print difficult to read. An appointment was made and on the day of the test I reported (as you did) to the medical centre and found myself with other squaddies with a variety of problems, on board an army ambulance speeding into Singapore! The appointment was in a civilian establishment which was modern and efficient. The following week the same procedure - this time to pick up the specs. These were 'fitted' for me by a really lovely Chinese lady technician, whose close proximity gave me thoughts other than those of the optical variety. No doubt about it I could have come out of there with plain glass lenses so smitten was I! The glasses proved very effective and I could now read for long periods in comfort. Sadly in one respect they led to the slippery slope of eventually having to wear them all the time.

CHAPTER TWENTY NINE

I dare say a good many books have been written about Singapore and these brief descriptions of mine have hardly scratched the surface - or done the place justice! Suffice to say we were sorry to leave it behind, and once again head up-country to resume our normal lives in far less salubrious surroundings. At least we couldn't take 'the elegant Major' to the Trade Descriptions Court, (even if there had been one in those days) - as indeed, we had stayed in excellent tropical barracks just as he'd said, even if only for a few weeks. Exactly how long after the New Year celebrations it was before we departed for the 'badlands' up-country is not recalled at all. Certainly we enjoyed letting in 1951 - but what I did, again is beyond my memory. What I do remember is being wished the seasons greetings by 'our' Major as both he, and we, were returning to barracks in the small hours. (He in a taxi - we on foot at that point.) He also said something along the lines of "hope you had a good night lads - did you behave yourselves?" The grin on his face indicated that he hoped we hadn't particularly - said it all really. As far as we were concerned he was still an 'ace' bloke, to quote the vernacular!

So, the day of departure neared and we were locked into an orgy of packing. When a regiment moves - so does an awful lot of gear and baggage! Our new location had been announced - it was to be a place called Yong Peng in the State of Johore - not as far up-country as we had been before. At the time we did not know anything about the place but, we soon found out that was known as a hot-bed of terrorist activity with quite a bit of local support. Charming we all thought! Having mentioned our major in the last paragraph, by coincidence, another guy and myself found ourselves in charge of his, and some other officers' personal baggage. We waited patiently at the designated pick up point for a baggage truck to arrive - but come it did not. After some while it was established that we had been left behind, and no way could we catch them all up. This meant travelling up by rail the next day - and having the unexpected bonus of another night in the metropolis!

Come the morn, the truck arrived, eventually depositing us with baggage at Singapore railway station. The mountain of gear we had with us nearly caused a diplomatic incident. You cannot take this on the train soldier gentleman sahib they said. (Or words to that effect.) "Oh! Yes we can, we said!" This stalemate continued until we convinced various levels of officialdom that we would probably get shot at dawn if we did not arrive with our very high ranking officers baggage on time (this time.) We might also have mentioned the Sultan of Johore, for we had heard that some of our guys were to spend a very happy period guarding his palace. Whatever we said it did the trick and we were assisted to get the gear aboard. Where we detrained for Yong Peng I cannot recall but a look at the map would suggest Kluang - from which Yong Peng is slightly to the north. The journey was uneventful and eventually we arrived at our new unpretentious home - yet again on a large rubber estate. A few desultory cheers greeted our arrival - but all were busily engaged in making camp and getting organised in new surroundings. Accommodation was again in tents - the officers not a great deal better - their abode being in a large hut formerly a storeroom - and thatched for effect with the ubiquitous 'attap'.

It may well have been at this camp that we hacked out a rough Badminton court within the camp precincts. One of my few sporting endeavours out there was to take up the game - which is I think still the Malaysian national game? I was doing quite well really till I met up with a Chinese Liaison Officer who beat the pants off me. Talking of sport in the services in Malaya - all varieties were played, subject to prevailing conditions. If you were good there were occasional opportunities to represent the company - or battalion, giving the individual a break from the normal grind. The company second in command (or 2 i/c) was a star rugby player. This officer - Capt. Barlow played for the army team and flew about all over the place to take part in matches. Once I was detailed to heat a tank of hot water for the captain as he was coming in still filthy, from a big game somewhere or other. I think we were then virtually straight off out into the jungle. Scrounging some petrol from the cooks I eventually got a good blaze going - under the tank after being chased back by a stream of fire by over enthusiastically dousing the logs from the jerrican! I certainly beat, or equalled the world sprinting backwards record. A lesson well and truly learned.

Fairly recently I read an account of a retreat in the Western Desert in WW2. It seems a wealthy Egyptian, on hearing that the hated Brits were in full retreat, hastened to a vantage point to watch this debacle. What he witnessed was an orderly withdrawal - with convoys properly spaced and the Eighth Army boys brewing up at each halt. Almost immediately after, impromptu games of football would begin - stopping only when the order to embus was given. Our friend returned home convinced that the Brits were there to stay - as indeed they were. So it was with our guys - whenever an opportunity occurred a football would appear as if by magic, and a kickabout or five-a-side, four-a-side, or whatever would commence. Not in the jungle of course - but just about everywhere else!

Three things we soon found out about our new home. The rivers ran swift and deep around Yong Peng and there was a great multitude of them! There was also a great deal of swamp in the vicinity - but I cannot recall 11 platoon being involved heavily in swampy conditions. The third thing was that Yong Peng had been the site of a huge battle during the British retreat down Malaya in WW2. Despite several patrols throughout the area no trace of this fighting was ever visible - even though it was only a few years before. One assumes there must have been a huge military cemetery nearby somewhere - but we never came across it.

Somewhat ring rusty after our dalliance with the fleshpots of Singapore - we approached the jungle and our foes with a degree of apprehension. Nothing much had changed. The same foetid odours assailed our nostrils and the same debilitating clammy heat exhausted us after long days of marching. The jungle looked the same even though the map may have changed! The familiar hugely buttressed trees soared heavenwards, dressed overall with their rigging of creeper and lianas, thick enough for a sailor of Nelson's time to scramble up for a view of the enemy. Exposed roots and ground creepers everywhere on the narrow tracks to plunge the unwary to the ground with a crash, as every metal bit you carried resounded through the forest undergrowth. The rain poured into our crude basha's once again till we got the hang of building them properly once more, and the seventy or so pounds upon our backs reminded us we were not quite the athletes we thought we were!

The bloodsucking leeches and mosquitoes welcomed us back too the leeches in particular, worming their way into our boots, clothing and just about everywhere else. No wonder we all smoked - it was the only way to get their teeth out of your body. Pull them off and the heads remained clamped to your flesh to go nicely septic! We had lost too, the 'habit' of the deadly debilitating night guards, which were our lot most nights. The heavy hand would shake you from the deepest slumber and you struggled to keep awake during your spell of guard - or 'stag' - terrified sometimes still by the noises of the night. Come dawn the 'stand-to' ceremony still held sway and 'chatty' and scratching we would take up our positions of all-round defence. The sketchiest of breakfasts and a mug of 'char' saw us on our way again to meet up with heaven knows what or whom! My Tinea returned after a few weeks plus a nice set of leg ulcers.

We had however one new luxury innovation with us this time around. One per section I think it was, so you got at least one night's dry warm accommodation in it per patrol. This was, would you believe - a waterproof hammock! It came complete with mosquito proofed sides which you zipped up to keep the world at bay and a strong monsoon proof roof, heavy duty base fabric and guy ropes to secure you to two trees. The designated user to be, carried it during the day - handing on to the next lucky recipient before marching onward again. The only pitfall attached to this innovation was to choose the two trees supporting it with care. Too slender your 'bearers' and you could find yourself on the deck - one end of you or the other as heavy rain could easily erode the roots of your supports. Frequently you awoke doubled up in a 'u' shape as your smaller trees had succumbed to your unaccustomed weight - larger ones generally were too far apart! In terms of an emergency getting out quick could pose a bit of a problem I guess - although you slept with your 'blunderbuss' by your side.

Having mentioned the swift flowing rivers around Yong Peng it is natural that we needed to get across some of them on our designated routes. No bridges in the jungle or even rope bridges - a la Tarzan, however precarious! A particular crossing gave us all food for thought as we stood on one bankside - gazing across a raging brown torrent to the other. Marching along the bank we eventually encountered a huge tree that had fallen across the river - producing a pretty fine bridge - if you didn't mind your bridge covered in slippery moss, fungus and lichens. The torrent raged some forty feet across and twenty feet below, from bank to bank, but our Dyak tracker Ganza was over like a monkey. Getting the rest of us over was not quite so easy as we were loaded as usual like pack mules. Our rubber soled jungle boots were excellent for pounding the forest trails - being almost knee high, they supported the ankle and calves. What they were not good at was gripping slippery surfaces - which there were in abundance on top of this tree trunk - massive though it was.

Eventually all were over safely but needed the helping hand of Ganza (who barefoot met us half way across) to guide us foot by terrifying foot over the chasm. Don't look down was the operative word! Anyone falling in would have stood little chance of survival. Those with a touch of vertigo or of a nervous disposition - had their equipment taken across separately and then like tight rope walkers, were virtually willed across by those who had gone before. "Cripes! We surely said as we gasped at a timely fag - never again!" Alas! there were still a few times more of this hairy character building activity game to come! Crossing a less raging torrent sometimes in the oppressive heat was a blessing and wonderfully cooling despite how it looked to those at home who saw us performing on the newsreels.

Thus did the remainder of my time pass with the army in Malaya. It would be a fitting climax to write perhaps of being part of a successful ambush team - or returning victorious from a firefight with the enemy. None of these things happened - and so my rifle never spoke in anger as Hawkeye, last of the Mohicans might have said! However, the regiment was becoming very successful in adding to its scoreboard of terrorists disposed of - throughout its widely separated companies. It was just after I left that 11 platoon had its moments of glory - Capt. Barlow winning an MC in one of the dramatic actions. I served out my time in the usual routines we had so become accustomed to. I cannot remember much about the final patrol. I think it might have been the one where, after an airdrop or two - we were requested to bring back as many used 'chutes as possible. No doubt they were not cheap - and re-use was a distinct possibility we supposed. Help in carrying these ungainly bundles came from a man from a Malay Kampong we passed through on the way back to the road. He carried most of them in a huge bundle on his head for quite some way. As a reward we gave him one - which pleased him mightily and salaaming effusively he set off back to his Kampong in high spirits - to be welcomed no doubt by his womenfolk who would turn the silk or nylon into feminine garments. He probably found a good use himself for the shrouds - which were immensely strong.

I do recall to some extent my last convoy escort duty. Where we went, and for what purpose I know not. I distinctly remember thinking 'twould be just my luck to get shot at on my last trip, but it was quite uneventful - except for the huge green monstrosity of an insect that alighted on my chest after passing under some low tree branches. The stuff of nightmares it was - all tendrils and other ghastly bits. Somehow it was dislodged (difficult when you're clinging to a Bren at speed) and I saw it no more! Very likely it was quite harmless! Phew!

As this is a 'warts an' all story', back at base a small incident had occurred, and as these things do sometimes - it probably influenced my future life. When most of us look back and consider why we did this or that, we find do we not, some small happening completely changes our lives? In this example, we blokes due to go home had been asked (naturally) to consider signing on for a regular engagement - minimum three years. It was a sensible suggestion from the command point of view, as we were well trained and experienced in most aspects of jungle warfare and had proved we could stand the heat in the kitchen so to speak! So I suppose the loss of a bunch of guys like us was considerable from a replacement point of view. Hence asking us to stay on. In my case, many things about the army appealed to me. I liked the ceremonial, the traditions, comradeship and the sense of purpose out there, and admired the current leadership. I can't say I enjoyed the jungle - none but a masochist would - but much else of army life had a certain appeal. So I was mulling it over - and considering for instance the large increase in pay for a start! I might well have taken the plunge until just before decision time I and others were detailed for a fatigue party - unloading stores from trucks and carrying them into the Q/M's store.

Carrying a large box which made me unsighted I put my foot down a post hole and did a really good 'base over apex' manoeuvre resulting in a badly gashed hand. Better get it dressed my mates said - so I went off to the medical tent sharpish - this was manned as always by a Cpl. Skinner - (cheerful sod) who cleaned up the gash, dressed it and swathed the hand in an impressive bandage! Strangely enough a piece of glass from this wound stayed in there for thirty years - before working its way to the surface. (Our company nurse took it out for me!) When I returned to the working party the Q/M (quartermaster) had taken exception to my absence. Despite an obvious problem with my hand I got a good bawling out for slipping away without permission, although at the time he wasn't there to ask. As a punishment I had to clean four or five rifles used by an officers hunting party - which proved a bit difficult with a painful hand. In the army there is no appeal - you obey the last order - but I certainly cussed and swore at the unfairness of it all. This incident made up my mind for me and I determined to become a civvy again! Had I stayed on I would not have had the civilian career I subsequently enjoyed - as the all important timings would have never again come about. Most of our last days at the Yong Peng camp are lost to memory now. We had said our last goodbyes and were paraded before the Major who gave us a humorous farewell speech, complimenting us on our service to the regiment and wishing us well in civilian life. We gazed for the last time on comrades going about their business - some preparing for yet another assault on 'the green stuff' - as we ourselves had gazed at similar parties heading homeward before, envying their good fortune.

CHAPTER THIRTY

The familiar Dodge trucks revved up and we were off - back to 'Blighty' - England, home and beauty (as they say!) The journey to Singapore was uneventful enough. We found ourselves once again at Selerang Barracks - and joined all our old mates who we had not seen for months and prepared ourselves for the 'slow boat from China'. It was great to join up again with Smithy 'Buffalo' and Frank Salf - all of whom had many tales to tell of hairy jungle moments. We were all pretty much unscathed although many took a long long time to get over their experiences. Even when safely home a few people found they had mental problems that lasted for years. I had nightmares for quite a while. Always the same - I would be alone, under a tree guarding something or other - and aware of a large force of enemy encircling and closing in on me. At the penultimate moment I would awake sweating like a man in a sauna!

Still with all that behind us, we spent a last couple of nights 'on the town' - not that we had much cash left to spend - and early one morning we boarded the troopship *Devonshire* for the long journey home! We stood on the deck to take a last look as we eased away from the dockside and stayed there until we were well out into 'the roads' with Singapore and Malaya slowly disappearing into the haze.

The voyage home on the *Devonshire* was as near as one could get to a luxury cruise on a 'Trooper'. Discipline was very relaxed and all on board were pretty cheerful, for, were we not all homeward bound? We soon accustomed ourselves to shipboard life again, the seas were calm and the hot sun beamed down upon us as we lazed on the decks doing as little as possible. No seasickness to grasp our vitals as on the outward leg of our journey! We were once again escorted from time to time by Dolphins and flying fish and as before tropical sunsets at sea were marvellous to behold.

When first en-route out to the East on the old *Orbita* - I mentioned being 'pressed' into the ships carrying party ferrying goods about the ship. I cannot recall being involved on the way home in anything special - perhaps just the odd fatigue party - in the kitchens possibly? Certainly nothing strenuous as the earlier carrying party certainly was. Some of our bigger lads were detailed to become temporary 'ships regimental police'. This entailed once again segregating the lower decks from the upper - wherein lay any female passengers - officers and warrant officers and possibly civilian male personnel. They also had duties in the ships 'brig' - or lockup. We were fascinated to hear from them about an officer prisoner, en route home for court martial - or to begin sentence. He was a Captain I think in The Pay Corps and had been 'done' for allegedly drawing pay for Gurkhas away on leave - or had invented some to draw their pay - I forget which, (possibly both.) Seemingly, when a Gurkha went on leave - he might well be away for several months. In those days with very few passable roads in Nepal your soldier would need to walk most of the way home on first arriving in the country - hence the length of leave given! Needless to say we were absolutely dumfounded that an 'officer and gentleman' - the type we had been trained to admire and look up to - would forfeit his officer status for a few hundred pounds. We really were 'gobsmacked'. Even more amazed to hear many others in our friends' pay office were allegedly 'at it'.

All in all our mates reckoned he was quite a decent bloke really - for an officer. They saw quite a bit of him as they had to supervise his exercise - as well as guard him. Mind you I don't know where he could have escaped to - surrounded by millions of miles of ocean. I forget who else was in the cooler alongside his nibs - but I think there were one or two more. Events like this helped us to spice up our letters home. Naturally we had all written home before embarkation to advise of our approximate arrival. Nothing more than a guestimate could be given in those days - no time table as you would confidently expect these days! Just somewhere around about a months steaming - give or take a day or two!

We all hoped for a faster crossing than our voyage outward. Those in the know on the old *Orbita* reckoned that a 'side-boom' we had carried, jutting out amidships, was a signal meaning 'ship proceeding under impaired engines'. How true this was I've no idea - but *Devonshire* seemed to take just about the same length of time between ports of call as did *Orbita*. These worked out roughly a week between calls. One week approximately to Colombo - another seven days to Aden and about the same to Port Said. The last and most important leg as far as we were concerned, the U.K run - also lasted about seven days.

Thanks to the Forces Post Office - mail could be posted on board for onward despatch at points of call. Similarly mail reached us regularly as before, again at points of call and was as welcome as ever. World news, dominated at that time by the Korean War - came to us over the ships Tannoy system and the odd newspaper came out from home amongst squaddies mail. (Plus the occasional one picked up I suppose at ports of call.) Could be there was a ships newsletter too but I'm not sure.

Those running the ships entertainment programme tried very hard to break up the monotony of sea travel for us. As before, boxing tournaments, talent contests, Bingo sessions and film shows were laid on. There may well have been the odd dance 'upstairs' too - and as mentioned before - the only time we were allowed up aloft - apart from the odd sing song around the piano if it was windy on the decks. Card schools flourished. (I still couldn't 'go misere' in whatever the mysterious card game described earlier was) - despite all my efforts! By this time we could all play brag and strictly amateur poker (very, very low staked poker indeed.)

We obviously reminisced a lot, for indeed we had all had some pretty hair raising experiences one way or another. Some of the guys had seen action - having taken part in various operations where they had been under fire or indeed had taken out terrorists. My own 'under fire' experience had taken place in a less grim scenario which included all of us in 11 platoon. Can't quite remember when it was, but there had been a significantly large air drop. So as to deny any possible booty to the terrorists everything that couldn't be carried was burnt. Parachutes, the webbing around the containers, discarded 'olive greens' - worn jungle boots - an amazing amount of unwanted stuff really.

The blaze was just starting to go well when, suddenly, the bonfire started shooting at us! The first bang was assumed to be a tin of something exploding. Several more sharp cracks and a few pings (as in western movies) convinced us all that there was live ammunition within the blaze. At least fifty rounds! Hastily taking cover till the fusillade stopped we then destroyed everything useful to an enemy completely. Before moving off we had a rigorous inspection by our platoon officer to check that each man's bandolier of fifty rounds was 'present and correct'. Had anyone's been missing there would have been a spell behind bars for the culprit. Where the cartridges had come from we never found out - but they hadn't come down with the 'chutes that's for sure!

We all had our souvenirs too. I had (and still have) a Malay Kris - a traditional dagger in a wooden sheath and a Gurkha Kukri - the fearsome chopping knife carried by all Gurkha warriors. This one had a curious history. When many of us were due to go home originally, (before our extra six months service) - one of our number bought a specially produced Kukri - highly polished and made to hang on the wall at home. Quite expensive they were too. Absolutely the real thing but spivved up a bit by a sort of silver plating. For whatever reason, our friend took it out on a patrol or two - where it soon lost its presentation lustre. It also lost the two little knives that accompany the big one in little sheaths attached. Short of a couple of dollars for beers - or whatever, our friend sold it to me, and I too took it on the odd patrol. It remains now pretty much as it was, with the case or sheath wrapped in parachute shrouding (or cord) - to keep it together. The blade is somewhat blunted and indented by some real life hacking and slashing, augmented by some wood chopping etc. at home.

As the ports of call came up en route to dear old Blighty - I and many others decided to stay on board and declined the 'run ashore'. This was mainly due to being hard up - as we had probably lost our local overseas allowance on leaving the country, which had certainly boosted up our pay when we first arrived in Malaya. It may be that we didn't receive our full pay whilst on board either - but I cannot really recall. As mentioned before, most of us had almost bankrupted ourselves to get suitable presents for the folks back home. So, as well as being broke - at the back of our minds there may have been the fear of being left behind when the boat sailed - a horrible scenario. So I personally carried on trying to read my way through the ship's library - with the aid of my new army issue reading glasses of course!

We all gave a great deal of thought to our future once home and demobbed. Many planned to return to their old jobs and marry their long time girlfriends. At that point I was undecided. It was unlikely that my romance with the fair Lorna would lead anywhere. It is fairly easy to pick up 'vibes' and affectionate thoughts by letter, and as mentioned previously, it was fairly obvious from her correspondence that the relationship wasn't going anywhere. I had been away too long I feared. Marjorie, my little 'cigarette girl' whom I liked very much, had married - so my future on the romantic front looked a bit of a washout!

In terms of work I really wasn't sure what to do. I had had a secure job but it was certainly not well paid. Listening at various times to conversations on pay and conditions viz-a-viz various jobs - I had realised how low down the ladder I had been. For instance, Joe my best mate had worked on the railways as a trainee fireman (the guy that stoked the boiler on steam trains.) With various bonuses for mileage covered plus salary he was earning four times my own wage. I knew my old job paid the full adult wage only when the employee had reached 21 - but even then my salary would still have been nothing like his! So there was much to think about!

It is interesting to consider too that we were to arrive home after spending many months in a multi-cultural society whereas in Britain at that time it was exceeding rare to see a coloured face at all. I remember a joke being played at school whereby a report circulated that redskins had been seen in a shop just along from the school premises. Virtually the whole school decamped to see these wondrous persons - only to find of course that the 'redskins' were in fact tomatoes in a large fruiterers! No doubt the shopkeeper was somewhat confused by half of St. Mary's School peering in through his shop windows!

The multi-cultural population in Malaya (which we had observed at fairly close quarters) had it seemed worked very well. We had not seen any apparent friction amongst the nationalities involved - despite hearing occasionally that Chinese and Malays didn't get on. I think the truth of the matter was they all needed each other and the Chinese and Indian populations with their trading traditions brought prosperity and colour to the community.

In the fight against terrorism all of the nations represented did their bit. The Malay Regiment was beginning to establish its traditions and perform better and better against the enemy. Chinese liaison officers and members of the police force were also in the forefront of the conflict and suffered very heavily during the period before security forces emerged most definitely on top. The same honours went to the Chinese 'home guards' - who helped defend the Briggs Plan settlements. Indian members of the community were also involved, mainly through the Sikhs - who have of course a strong military tradition. It could be also argued that the Gurkha's strongly represented India in this conflict - and if so - what a representation!

So, the *Devonshire* ploughed her stately way through the tropic seas and not a lot happened of an exciting nature - except for the piano of course. Called on deck parade one morning The Green Howards contingent was accused of vandalism, namely that a piano which soldier passengers had access to - had been badly damaged. If the culprit did not own up pronto then the whole returning draft would have to pay for the damage and also be banned from that particular recreation area! Typical military thinking we thought - punish all for one person's misdemeanour. However to our complete astonishment - one of our number who was a pillar of rectitude, stepped forth in answer to the charge and was carted off to be interrogated forthwith. We were then dismissed to wonder what would happen to our comrade. As it happens he was back with us shortly after and explained that he had had any charges against him dropped. It seems he was really quite a good pianist and while playing the instrument the previous evening - suddenly - without warning, virtually the whole keyboard had collapsed about him.

No doubt he had to prove his piano playing 'bone fides' - but once proven it was the end of the matter for him. In reality it seems that years of energetic service had just about knackered the thing and on the fateful night his tickling of the ivories was just about the last straw! So, neither he nor we heard any more about it.

So, the ports of call came and went and the *Devonshire* sailed smoothly on in the direction of home. Like I said, those wishing to stretch their legs ashore did so - also those desirous of exotic female company on a short term basis. Eventually we made our final port of call at Port Said - after negotiating the Suez Canal for the second time. This superb tribute to man's everlasting ingenuity, cuts like a knife through featureless desert and so peaceful was it that anyone forecasting the eruption of the Anglo-French invasion of just a few years later would probably been sat on! The approach to Suez and Port Said were coloured for us by a huge sandstorm in the distance, which looked tremendously dramatic - as indeed it would have been for anyone caught up in it. It had cleared by the time we reached Port Said where as ever the bum-boatmen did very well from those wishing to top up their present list for those at home. Many servicemen will remember the skill required by these blokes who somehow got the goods to the recipient and the cash in return - from decks some 40-50 feet higher than their flimsy craft!

The temperature was noticeably cooler hereabouts and we were detailed to change from our lightweight 'olive greens' to U.K battledress - which we had not worn for something like eighteen months. We proudly sewed on to our upper sleeves our 'Divisional Sign'- which incorporated crossed Kukri's, and also above this a Malaya flash. Finally the medal ribbon (bloody well earned was the general opinion) was put up in the appropriate place. Ah! Vanity, vanity! This'll knock them dead at home we thought as our chests swelled. After all we'd been there, seen it - and got the scars to prove it!

The dreaded Bay of Biscay was relatively kind to us when we reached it. I don't recall being sick myself - nor was anyone around me. A far cry from the outward journey when we were all, to a man, violently ill as I recall. Anyway the great day came when we sailed up to what were I suppose the white cliffs of Anglesey, and many of us gathered on deck to take in the vista of our approaching homeland. To my amazement, standing next to me in the uniform of the RAF Regiment was one Walter Spitzer - a former colleague from work. To say we were amazed would be putting it mildly! Of all the boats in all the world, etc etc! We had a quick chin-wag before going down for breakfast - but were not to meet

151

up again until a few weeks had passed - when we rejoined our former firm. Walter back to the gents tailoring department and I to footwear. He and I must have been called up just about the same time. Later he was to leave the firm for another job before I did.

I never saw Walter again after that (on the vessel) until civvy street. However as for not meeting up with him on board ship is I suppose indicative of the size of those old troopships. I think Walter had got on at Port Said - but I hadn't seen hide nor hair of him till we both stood at the rail contemplating the U.K. .

We anchored outside of Liverpool for an hour or two before proceeding to our berth, and we were all struck by the brownness of the water surrounding us - assuming that we were 'parked' where the River Mersey discharges itself into the sea. It was a bright cold day - but boy, were we a happy bunch of squaddies! We couldn't wait to get off that boat, believe me!

CHAPTER THIRTY ONE

Disembarking was swifter than we would have imagined and hinged on access to the holds where our 'not wanted on voyage' gear was stowed. This - in most cases - involved our normal service kit-bag and a large suitcase. Eventually we found ourselves filing down the gangway to good old terra firma, British terra firma - to parade by the ships side for roll call and brief inspection. (No one would have missed this roll call!) The first hurdle for many of us as we made our way towards customs was that our kit-bags and cases were seized by large burly gentleman porters who brushed aside our protests that we were perfectly capable of carrying them ourselves. As we proceeded in most minds I suspect was the same dilemma - with what were we going to pay these guys? For reasons that became pretty clear soon after, we had not received the pay due to us before disembarking and all I had were a few coppers. Obviously we would not be able to tip our burly friends as we might have wished to! I personally had to dig around to find twenty (or was it fifty) precious fags to placate my porter. Having dispensed with this hurdle, the next was to negotiate the customs and excise boys. These 'gentlemen' treated us as if each of us was an international smuggler of Carlos the Jackal fame. What contraband they thought we might be bringing into the country on a private's pay beggared description! They poked and probed into our gear and had us peruse a notice board indicating the dire penalties for smuggling various illicit items - having fixed us with the steely eyed gaze of a High Court Judge - (of the infamous Judge Jefferies variety!) All these customs men we decided had been recruited from ex-Military Police Sarn't Majors of debatable temperament. I have subsequently read that all incoming servicemen from time immemorial were subjected to this treatment, which we definitely thought over the top!

Having survived this bruising encounter to our egos and with a last look at the vessel which had brought us home safely, some 8,000 - miles, we boarded transport to Liverpool Station. (I assume this would have been Lime Street?) Who, and how many NCOs were in charge of us I cannot recall - but I'm pretty certain there were no officers. At this point, were we arriving home today - we would have been on our mobile 'phones to Mum announcing our arrival in the U.K. But as it was in those times, very few families had the luxury of a home 'phone. One of our number who did - and managed to get to a 'phone box had the slight consolation of being able to wave to his folks as the train whizzed through his home station without stopping - which makes me wonder today if ours was a special troop train - not unknown even in the fifties. There were R.T.Os (Rail Transport Officers) on most main line stations for many years, even after that. On a more social note, as the train pulled out of the station and picked up speed we noticed that almost all household chimney stacks were festooned with curious ironmongery in the shape of a letter 'H'. Word got around that these were the aerials for the new-fangled television sets we might dimly have heard of in newspaper reports. To our complete amazement nearly every house seemed to be sporting one! As a matter of interest - when we all finally got home to Sheffield there was nothing like as many aerials to be seen there at all. (It was probably 1952 before I actually saw a T/V set working. This was in the house of a friend of a friend!)

Meanwhile, as our destination was The Green Howards Regimental Depot at Richmond in North Yorkshire - I suspect we first had to detrain at a major railhead - such as Leeds, to catch a connection to Richmond. If we had anything to eat or drink en-route then I cannot recall it. Most of us had little or no money to buy anything with anyway. Should you ask how many of us Green Howards were there on this homeward bound draft probably about forty to fifty would be my guess.

Eventually, somewhere around 9.0 p.m - and in the dark, we arrived at Richmond. Shouldering our kitbags and cursing our heavy suitcases we made our way to the barracks. Richmond is a hilly place, but does memory deceive when I recall us going down from the station? In our dreams we imagined ourselves as sun-bronzed heroes arriving - and led by a resplendent band marching in triumph (past swooning maidens) in bright sunlight through the town to our famous barracks! Reality was a little different - when we finally arrived at Regimental H/Q - weary and decidedly peckish, to our considerable surprise we were not expected! Not for at least two more days apparently. So perhaps our journey on the *Devonshire* had been slightly quicker? As no preparations were on hand for our arrival we slept in a freezing barrack room, on bare metal springing, covered in our greatcoats - and slept the sleep of the weary and exhausted.

In all honesty I cannot recall whether the cookhouse could open up for us at that hour or not - probably not. Whether we were advanced any pay to visit the NAAFI I cannot recall either but again probably not. Next morning we woke to the familiar sound of the 6 a.m bugle and a new existence at Regimental H/Q began. An analogy of our new life at that point could be described as distant members of a large family arriving out of the blue (so to speak) - and expecting to be greeted and treated as closer members might expect. Most of the inhabitants of Regimental H/Q at that time were permanent staff, plus the regimental band, who were gearing up to go to the battalion in Malaya from whence we had just come. However the new day saw us kitted out with all essentials and an emergency issue of pay. We became officially 'on the strength' and so could be fed and watered in the dining hall. We were strongly reminded that we were still very much soldiers and would be treated as such until the day of our discharge. What day of the week it was when we arrived is beyond recall - probably a Wednesday - but one fact soon percolated down to us and that was there would be no leave for us that weekend! Nowadays this might spark off a minor mutiny - or scores of angry Mums arriving with writs of Habeas Corpus to get us out - but in those days that's how it was. Orders were orders!

It emerged that the Depot was soon to be inspected by The G.O.C (general officer commanding) - with a view to its usage by a much larger formation. Therefore it had to be made spick and span, both inside and out. Quite a task given the scale of the place, which was huge - having barrack rooms on two or probably three floors, with several blocks. The whole place strongly resembling (in more ways than one) a medieval fortress! Many of its barrack rooms had been unoccupied for a long time and a great deal of effort was to be needed in bringing them up to scratch. So we laboured throughout the whole place, painting, scrubbing - even gardening as there were some large plots in and around the barracks. My first chore was to clean all the windows in the medical centre. These were many and multi-paned. Diffidently I enquired about some warm water and a chamois leather. Where do you think you are sonny - have you never heard of cold water and newspaper? Lucky to find a bucket I suppose. Anyway I guess I made a reasonable job of this - not being harassed or desperately short of time.

So, with our suntanned Malayan hero status somewhat undermined by these lowly fatigue duties - we were more and more anxious to get home before our deep tans wore off. As previously stated there was no home leave for us that first weekend. We were allowed into Richmond however, where we strutted about showing off our fancy shoulder flashes and single medal ribbon - hoping to impress any spare young ladies about - also some fairly new National Servicemen who were around the town too - possibly from Catterick Camp. We felt sure they would gaze in awe at our splendid insignia and deep tans, redolent of far campaigns. If they did then they were unaware that we were hard up, fed up, and wanted desperately to be allowed home to be reunited with our loved ones!

Leave was finally allowed on our second weekend in the U.K. after another week of hard graft in the 'elements of refurbishing' programme. (To mention the now famous quote from an American Ambassador - taking up residence in the U.S London Embassy!) I think we might have had a 48 hour pass on this first home leave, and our feet had wings as we flew to the station, desperately keen to get home at the earliest opportunity. Our 'wings' were slowed somewhat by the large suitcase most of us were encumbered with - containing amongst other things the gifts we had hauled some 8,000 miles across the world. Most of the things that I had brought back were intact except for a saucer from an ornate tea service - and most embarrassing for a rough, tough squaddy (?) - a bottle of perfume had broken. Whenever the case was opened it gave off the aroma of the boudoir, not the barrack room! So it was that those, Sheffield bound, drew into the Midland station early on Saturday afternoon. We stood on the platform making our farewells to mates, sniffing as we did the old familiar acrid smell of our steel producing city. Yes! We were certainly home.

It was a moment to savour, the next (happy) dilemma was where to go first - girlfriend - home to Aunty in Duncombe Street, or what? Roughly guessing that early evening might be a better time to arrive I decided to visit my old place of work which was just a short tramride away - and still on the route home. Thought I'd show off my tan to some of the scrumptious young women I'd worked with - before it faded away, (again vanity, vanity) and have a look at the old place which I hadn't seen for about two years. Entering the store by a side door I asked a very pretty young Miss if I could park my suitcase behind her shoe polish counter. She agreed smilingly and metaphorically speaking it has remained there for the past 47 years! (But that's another story.)

All the lovelies were still there and more. These were the girls who taught me to dance in the stockroom, helped me polish up my social skills and sympathised with my tales of juvenile woe about lost loves etc. Most of these kindly lasses were older than I, and by the time I returned had themselves become engaged or indeed married. They said nice things about my tan and new maturity and hoped I might be coming back to work there - which boosted the old ego more than somewhat of course. However it was very noticeable that there were many more sweet young things around - which had a bearing on my comments to the assistant manager, Harry Tillman. He came over when he saw me, and asked if I would be returning to work there when my service time was up. Well, I thought I can give it a month or two - and move on if I don't like it! (I stayed for another four years!) I met up too with my male colleagues as well - who also asked if I were coming back.

After this pleasant interlude it was time to turn homewards and within twenty or so minutes, I was reunited with the first of my loved ones and it was every bit as joyful as I had anticipated. My gifts were well received and the famous Ethel regarded my ex-airdrop parachute with delight. Apparently it was transformed very quickly into 'ladies unmentionables' still in very short supply normally - despite the war being over for some six years. Amongst many other things Ethel was a whizz with a sewing machine! In my training days she had saved me from an unpleasant interview with higher authority - as I had badly scorched the cuff of my best battledress blouse. Back at Strensall they tended to jump on you from a great height if you defaced The King's uniform - whether by accident or no! Whatever she did to it 'twas as good as new. Britain still had an austerity programme in force, with many things still under ration - or in very short supply - including sweets and chocolate would you believe.

On the romantic front, Lorna and I got on very well together still and went out together for a few months after demob - but it was obviously, sadly, a doomed romance and we drifted apart. I remained friends with the family for some time though and visited them often. However, how nice it was to be home again and enjoy Aunty's cooking once more, and appreciate her continued kindness towards me. On this my first leave and for a while subsequently, most of my civilian mates were doing their own National Service - so I didn't see too much of them - but sufficient old chums were around to make my eventual homecoming far from lonely.

The first weekend's leave was over in a flash and we were all back again, soldiering on at the Richmond Depot. The cleaning up programme continued apace plus other fatigues and we were reunited (if that's the right word) with our old R.S.M from Malayan days. He had returned home before us as his overseas service time was up at that point. RSM Peacock, it must be said was greatly respected by most of us for his general fairness, commanding figure and unusually for an R.S.M - a well developed sense of humour. He had a chestfull of medals including the D.C.M and M.M - so you knew he had seen it all! As may have been said before, he was not averse to borrowing a comic or magazine from under a squaddies pillow - where they normally resided. If seen doing this he would say gruffly "it's for the kids" - we knew differently, and thought no worse of him for it!

As well as a touch of guard duty, he obviously thought a bit of drill would be good for us, so we strode around the square at Richmond barracks - sometimes to the tunes of the regimental band - practising for their journey to Malaya - sometimes not. We thought it a touch humorous that we should be drilling like this again, with our demob just around the corner so to speak but we guessed the army was going to have its pound of flesh from us, whatever! The square held no terrors for us. Had we not been guard of honour to a Field Marshal - and done a Trooping the Colour to boot? No sweat!

Once we got to know the permanent depot staff, then things became much easier. We found there were many characters amongst them and generally they were much older than we - most having been in, or through WW2. Wherever we were in the depot, the strains of the band could be heard. They were good, and since that time I love to hear the sound of a good military band. The regimental slow march 'Maria Theresa' was being practised a lot and when I hear it now on televised military occasions, it takes me back in a flash to those far off days.

Work continued on the refurbishment of the depot and jobs were switched around to avoid boredom. My time came around for the gardening 'chore' - which was much disliked as, I suppose it involved a fair amount of physical effort. As I recall there was a goodly amount of ground attached to the barracks, some of which was cultivated for vegetables. Who normally attended to this we never found out - but dig it we had to. The R.S.M used to pop up frequently on the gardening detail, and on more than one occasion I or we, would be about to salute him - till we realised in time who it was. R.S.M's as I may have said before were the highest ranking NCOs in the army. Their uniforms were of officer cut and quality, plus they wore 'Sam Browne' belts with cross shoulder strap and the sabre-tache of commissioned ranks. They also wore officers S.D hats which really fooled you from a distance! It was definitely not done to salute the R.S.M. Although I think ours might have earned one.

To return to the gardening chore - digging was definitely not one of my strong points - being a stranger to spade, fork and hoe. I tended to go at it like a berserk Morris Dancer probably digging around in a circle and knackering myself in the process. I will be eternally grateful to Frank Salf of the musketeers. He, being more experienced at this lark, showed me how to dig in a straight line and how to pace the digging process. Two or three gardens of my own later have benefited from this early 'masterclass'. So, slowly our few remaining weeks slipped by with pay parade our most exciting moment. This was conducted by a most punctilious officer who demanded the most meticulous military approach to his table with a crashing halt and salute worthy of a guardsman! Failure to comply meant doing it over and over till 'his nibs' was satisfied. No doubt these days pay goes straight into the squaddies account - but I speak of a time when the words 'current account' would have people thinking about their electricity bills!

Weekend leave was not guaranteed because of the work in hand and we were very pleased when our disembarkation leave finally came through. This was the traditional two weeks following overseas service and I think our efforts in sprucing up the barracks had to be finished before we could go. Hard to remember what one did on this leave period, but we had a lot of living to catch up on! I do remember coming home by 'dawn's early light' on more than one occasion! We returned to Richmond after this Nirvana, even more eager for our demob, and actually finishing our two years service on June 3rd 1951. By this time we had become fully aware that three and a half years service in the TA (Territorial Army) lay ahead for most of us - due to an unstable world situation. (Those not near enough to a TA depot were put on special reserve - were fully equipped, uniform and kit wise, and had an emergency military base to report to - if the balloon went up.) We did not give this reserve training too much thought at the time as apparently we would be free until late 1951.

However we did have to report, all of us, direct from Richmond barracks to our Territorial H/Q in Sheffield. Rail warrants were provided and transport awaited us at the Midland Station in Sheffield.

Our departure from the Regiment was purely routine! No farewell speeches as I recall. (Not that we minded.) Various documents had to be signed and sealed and it was a lot of puffing billies, who rushed up the hill to the station to find that the train was actually on the platform. Hurried goodbyes to mates from further afield who we would never see again and then off to be civilians once again. A couple of vignettes of this occasion remain with me. Thinking the train would leave without us, most of us put a spurt on - which had us knackered before we hit the platform. One of our real Geordie hardcases, whom I never had any rapport with, seized my heavy suitcase and carried it the remaining distance to the train - much to my astonishment. (Our Geordie's seemed to be either tough or mild, and we had a fair sprinkling of both!) The other is of seeing the handle come completely away from another lad's 'composite' suitcase as he hurtled for the train, and chucking it over his shoulder, (the handle) - he somehow managed to scoop case, kitbag and all up, then, almost bent double he finally made the train.

In 1997 a famous T/V programme hit the screens - entitled 'They Think It's All Over! - or something similar. Perhaps we thought this too about our military life. We soon found out differently though when we duly reported to the Hallamshire's H/Q at Endcliffe Hall, Sheffield. The Hallamshires were a famous T/A Battalion of the York and Lancaster Regiment. They earned undying fame in WW1 - on the Somme when bravely charging forward they were mown down by machine gun fire during those terrible first days of July - many were lost! Their worst losses however came before the River Selle in 1918 when two thirds of their number were killed or wounded.

Here we learned of the three and a half years we must serve with them, which entailed three full weekend 'camps' and a two weeks annual training period - where we could be engaged anywhere in the country. "Just in case you think you can't be bothered" said the informant in charge of our induction. "You'll get sent straight back to the regular army for all of the time you've missed, plus a bit extra!" This concentrated our minds just a little bit, but after a quick tour of the place we were civilians once again until our first weekend camp in late 1951. At least we had almost a half year off before we donned uniform again! This reserve period was all part of the National Service Act - and employers had to go along with it. Not very popular I guess - as they had to give you your paid holidays as well!

So, on June 3rd 1951 I became 'Mr.' Ives instead of private or 'ere you', Ives! My completely undistinguished military career was over. However, as (surprisingly enough) - the period with The Hallamshires had a bearing on my subsequent civilian career - I will stay with this narrative a little longer. So it was then, like many other demobbed squaddies - I returned to my former job. This was as a salesman in the footwear department of a department store near the centre of Sheffield. My romance with the fair Lorna was obviously coming to an end so I played the field a little and went out with a number of young charmers - several from my place of work. I resumed my ballroom dancing again, mainly tea dances - held usually on the half-day closing of our store, which happened to be on a Thursday.

Many if not most of my dancing partners were still there on Thursdays, and it was great to be back again and enjoy their dancing and company. At one time - not so long ago, it was estimated that something like two out of three marriages were initiated on the dance floor in the 50's and 60's! My long time pal Brian Stevens - met his wife to be on the dance floor at the 'City' - which was what our City Hall ballroom was nicknamed. My own better half did not come via this statistic. I had already met her, but knew not then what the future held in store at that time.

I also picked up many threads of my former life. Snooker and billiards at the Walkley Reform Club. The odd pint with mates who were not doing their National Service. Contact was made with Joe Slater my fine chum of Malayan days. He had returned to work at British Rail and we got together from time to time whenever possible. Unfortunately he lived at Normanton near Leeds which was a fair distance away in the days before everyone had cars. Still the brief times we were together were very pleasant. Later on I was to be best man at his wedding and we have been in touch ever since! Sadly his lovely Mum died just recently. She it was you may recall - who wrote to her M.P to try and get me back home sooner than was possible. In her book, if her son was coming home so should his mate - as we had both gone in together!

I also took up cycling again. Had a much better and newer bike than I'd ever had before - when I did some quite long distances on an old wreck - but somehow after a trial run to Bridlington (about 75 miles away) - I realized my heart wasn't in it any more, so this lovely machine was just used for commuting and modest runs around Sheffield and Derbyshire.

CHAPTER THIRTY TWO

Anyway I digress as they say. This narrative being about my military service - I was still (theoretically speaking) carrying The King's Musket - and wearing his uniform, albeit as part of a reserve formation. Talking about clothing - I could really have done with a demob suit but National Servicemen weren't eligible alas! Obviously becoming a salesman in a department store required a certain standard of dress. Suits cost dosh - and I didn't have a lot. However I had to bite the bullet and dig into my meagre Post Office Savings and kit myself out with a blue double breasted suit - of a style now coming back in again!

It came to pass eventually that word was received to attend an inaugural TA weekend later in 1951 - and included in the document were a list of weekend 'camps' we could choose to attend - plus the date of the two week exercise period we most certainly had to attend. All were of interest to my particular employer at that time as, working in a store, Saturday was our busiest day! Anyway I went to this first weekend 'military seminar' you could almost call it. It was great to see many former army mates there. Very few of us had remained in touch as we had gone back to our old districts, pals and jobs of course. What was obvious was that the minute we were in uniform again - and all together it was as if we'd never been away.

Oaths returned to our lips like before and the same jargon held sway also as before! We crashed about in our ammunition boots as in days of yore - as we exchanged news updates with particular references to current female company.

Much of the programme of that first weekend escapes me. Did we fire rifles again up at Totley Ranges? I think we might, but certainly we spent the weekend under canvas - returning to H/Q on the Sunday for a briefing on the Hallamshire's role in the current scheme of things. It seems we were now part of an armoured division (49th) - and our job was to clear the way forward for tanks when held up by opposition from anti-tank weapons etc, manned by opposing forces. Films were shown depicting this strategy in practice - and we saw for the first time pictures of armoured half-tracked vehicles in which sections of infantry were conveyed as near as possible to enemy positions. After the lectures volunteers were called for to take driving lessons and I was surprised that everyone didn't put his hand up. I certainly did, and unconsciously took the first step to a very rewarding civilian career - the likelihood of which I was most certainly unaware of at the time. My mate Brian Stevens also volunteered for the driving cadre but was well ahead of me in practice as he had had experience of Bren Carriers whilst with the York and Lancaster Regiment in Germany.

Within a week or two the courses started and were held in the evenings - as most 'pupils' held down jobs in the daytime. We were taught on a variety of vehicles from five ton trucks to Land Rovers - which I think were just coming into service then. Certainly there were jeeps too - but of half-tracks there were none. Indeed they did not appear until some months before our last annual exercises. Brian and I went up as often as possible at least twice or three times a week. Obviously you only got 15-20 minutes per session as there would be a truck full of learners awaiting their turn. Sometimes less - sometimes more.

In retrospect how smart it would have been if an instructor had said to me " what rubbish Ives," "what happened to your last instructor?" Then I could have honestly replied - "he got shot Sarn't," - which of course Ginger Pugh did - as I have mentioned earlier. Needless to say I was never asked the question, but doubtless from time to time I was rubbish.

Mind you it was easy for us all to be rubbish on some evenings - the vehicles then mainly had 'crash' gearboxes. This meant dipping your clutch twice, i.e once to get the gearstick into neutral and again to slip it into the appropriate gear. Ah! The sheer bliss of being able to change down with the pleasing 'rev' on the throttle - as you found second or third!

Imagine our complete surprise (going back to Ginger Pugh) of seeing him alive and kicking and still having to do his T/A service! We couldn't believe it. Had he not been badly shot up driving the Major's jeep back in Malaya at the head of a convoy? Was he not carted of to hospital and invalided home to Blighty? Indeed all these things had happened, but he had recovered well at home and finished his two years off in a less stressful role. He even got a wound pension! Those were the days when a pound of flesh was the thing guy's - yours!

Brian and I passed our tests at the same time and so we became members of the fraternity known as M.T or (motor transport.) Although still technically in 'A' company, we were slightly segregated from our mates as on weekend camps, and on the annual training fortnights - we were drivers doing the various jobs that the title entailed. At the time the full licence we got entitled us to just about drive anything on the road. Some of the lads got driving jobs (including heavy goods) on the strength of their new licences! Not many people were privileged to actually be paid to be taught to drive as we were. Still not yet on my full salary at work because I was under 21, meant that there was no way I could have afforded driving lessons on my earnings. No-one of my acquaintance had a car at that time so there was no chance say of learning on a friend or relative's car.

As I may have possibly mentioned before - this driving licence was the first step - unknown to me then - towards an extremely happy and fulfilling career. The timings being as they were, without the licence it wouldn't have worked out the way it eventually did.

Our first annual camp was at Castle Martin in Wales. This was a tank training and firing battleground. Here we learned about our new 'tank protector' role in the great scheme of things. We drew a vehicle each from the issuing centre. Mine was a Morris Commercial of about two tons. It was a fully equipped wireless truck and I had visions of a cushy 2 weeks driving this thing around and laying up for long cosy periods whilst signallers did their stuff within. Wishful thinking I fear as it was soon passed on to the rightful owners. I then received an Austin also of about two tons. All these Austins were quite amazing. Being equipped with very large wheels they could go almost anywhere a tracked vehicle could go - within reason. This without four wheel drive too! We used them in all sorts of terrain to the drop off points - where they joined mock attacks on anti-tank positions. Those in the know may say why not Bren Gun Carriers - which were tracked armoured vehicles? These would have been perfect except they were limited in the men they could carry, and also were being phased out at that time.

In reality of course 'soft skinned' vehicles as these lorries were, would have been useless doing the real thing. They would have been shot to bits before we were anywhere near to the target area. The half-tracks that came later were tailor made, being fully armoured all the way round. Once again I'm getting ahead of myself. Our first lecture on the nature of armoured warfare was delivered at the side of a tank by a Sarn't Major of our 'twinned' armoured outfit. He was burnt black from the sun and appeared to be the very essence of a glamourous tank commander! I was much amazed later to find he was Marjorie's boss (my little cigarette lady,) - from English Steel! He described the essence of the tank business and our part in it very well. However seeing the cramped insides of this steel monster - most of us agreed we would prefer to stay with the infantry. At least said the wags - we can dig a bleeding great hole to hide ourselves in can't we!

So we did our thing charging up and down this training ground, taking advantage of any useful cover to deliver our sections into attack positions. At least the weather was good and being outdoors all the time knackered us completely, so we weren't at all put out by there being nothing much to do in the evenings apart from checking up on our trucks for the next days activities. I cannot say I was the best of drivers in those early days. Despite having the licence I did not get much, if any practice - as I only got a chance to drive on TA weekends and camps. Brian was streets ahead - as he drove a Ford van for his Dad's firm every day. Still somehow we got there right enough but the guys in the back of my Austin had a rough ride occasionally. On the whole they were pretty patient with me.

Come the first weekend, we had a pass and transport into Tenby - which was very nice. We found some amenable girls just about the time to head back for 'the passion wagon' which was a little unfortunate. There may have been a similar vehicle available on some nights to go into the nearest town for R&R but many of us were too knackered to go. Here again letters were important - phones were not then the communications tool they are now. (I think the sweet young thing from the shoe polish counter was writing to me by then.) One night on camp we had an unforgettable film show. The film in question was the original version of the French classic - *Clochemerle*. A well scrubbed version of this was seen on our T.V screens recently, but the original movie is - or was, quite a naughty film. It is mainly about the impact of a new gentleman's 'pissoir' (or urinal) in the sleepy town of Clochemerle. Suffice to say it is riddled with affairs and sexual 'goings on' - and to see it in the company of, and to the ribald comments of - upwards of a couple of hundred squaddies was an unforgettable experience, and made it a night to remember.

When I look back on those days I cannot help but think that the TA units of that time had never had it so good in terms of manpower. Thousands of young men - well trained - and often from active service areas such as Korea, Malaya, Kenya and Aden were seconded to them, bringing them not only up to numerical strength - but also with a wealth of experience of the sharp end. To help ease the situation a large number of experienced NCOs were then seconded to the TA from the regular army. Long service people - probably moving towards the end of their service careers in the main. How do I know this? Well, probably in the second year of territorial service - those of us who knew it well - heard the dulcet tones of our old 'D' Company Sergeant Major from Malayan days, W.O.1 Holloway. He too was one of the seconded ones. He remembered us all right and hadn't forgotten our names. We were on the range at the time and plugging away at a target I heard this familiar voice say "bloody hell Ives, tha's gettin' bloody better" although in reality I was still the same classification. He must have seen a few bulls going down as he approached. What I cannot recall though was his rank. I suspect he had come back as R.S.M!

Not that there was much wrong in reality with our company Sergeant Major - whose name completely escapes me now. He was a manager of a steel complex I believe - and easily identifiable as he had a small 'port wine' stain on a pleasant countenance, a la Michael Gorbachev. He had been through the war and was a kindly man but there is an amusing story attached to my comments. He was taking us for drill during our first camp and to be honest he wasn't the best at giving the executive command at the exact split second required. After we had come to a shambolic 'halt' a plaintive voice from the ranks said "sarn't major, if you could give us the command on the left foot we might all come to bloody stop together - sir!" There was a pause - he laughed - we all laughed, and didn't we come in second in the drill competition, much to his delight!

During our T/A service various 'old faces' turned up as they were demobbed from National Service. One such to appear was Carl Russell - a friend and neighbour from boyhood days. He had been with 'The Duke's' - in Korea - where there was some real soldiering done. He described facing the Chinese regular army in the fearsome winter cold - and conversely the baking heat of summer. Apparently one morning a Chinese tank broke cover and attacked their positions. Although being swiftly put out of action by a P.I.A.T or rocket, everyone was amazed how this thing had appeared opposite them without being heard - tank engines being particularly recognisable. How they found out I know not, but apparently this tank had been pushed into position by a very large force of men!

Another Korean veteran (whose name I cannot recall) entertained us with graphic illustrations of his prowess in the various red light districts of whatever area they were in at the time. Judging by his antics it was obvious that the Korean ladies were keen to show that the *Kama-Sutra* was not necessary confined to Indian couples. He certainly had us in fits - for his descriptions were unbelievably humorous - as were some of the positions undertaken!

Later on, Dennis Bullivant an old schoolmate came back from The Green Howards in Malaya with an update on how the old mob was doing. Seemingly it was doing OK - and 11 platoon had really got themselves onto the scoreboard of bandits disposed of since I had left it! Capt. Barlow had been awarded the MC - and believe it or not, the regiment had its own armoured train! This was to counter a growing increase in attacks on trains and anything appertaining to the railway system which because of the sheer length and breadth of it - made it very vulnerable to attack. I wondered how my old mates Joe Slater and Harry (the) Wragg would have viewed this? No doubt being professional railwaymen they would have liked to have been involved. Incidently Dennis - who gave me the update has been mentioned before in this narrative.

Not much else remains in my memory about our first TA training fortnight. Except of course that it seemed we had never been away from the army. We were all pleased though when it was over - and we could return to our civilian lives and pursue our careers - and as many young ladies as we could. On this subject - the lassie on the shoe polish counter had become a significant item as far as I was concerned. We sort of got together (as you did) on a departmental outing to Blackpool or Morecambe, in the company of various young people who moved about in little parties - determined to have a good time in the short period we would have in the resort. Incidently the shoe polish counter was not where she worked normally. She was an assistant in the children's footwear dept. From time to time all did a stint on this particular counter - fine in summer but loathed in winter - as two doors opened almost directly onto it, both bringing a howling gale in from the streets beyond.

When mulling over the section of this narrative about service in the TA - I had thought our second fortnight's training camp was in Norfolk. Some small research tells me otherwise. It seems we were 'on' Salisbury plain - where countless sqaddies have done their stuff since time immemorial! I can remember just a few happenings from it. The first was that we were performing (at one stage) in a big exercise - seemingly watched by an international brigade of 'top brass' - including it was said The Duke of Edinburgh no less. Supposedly we did well and 'twas said that the observers could not believe 'we' were just reserve formations. Be that as it may - all we did as drivers was get our sections to their mock attack start positions and then zoom back from whence we had come to evade simulated fire upon our vehicles. I assume that the blokes doing the mock attacks were the stars of the show and all the credit went to them, quite rightly.

We did some night driving exercises on this particular 'camp' and here we discovered that staying awake whilst concentrating on the tiny patch of white light - shining down from underneath the truck in front's rear, and only slightly illuminating a small area of white paint on the differential - had a hypnotic effect in the wee small hours. As you can imagine the idea of this was to show not even the smallest light that would make a convoy visible from the air. On our exercise quite a few left the road - which must have been exciting for those on board in the back! Don't think there were any serious injuries though. Heaven knows how I kept awake myself at the wheel - as here is a man who likes his kip! Having said that, when woken to refuel by jerrican (simulating active service) in the middle of the night - I was wide awake in seconds!

Another (I hope) humorous vignette of military life occurred at this camp. I may have said already that we lived under canvas on all these TA exercises and because of this, seemingly, just modest tidiness was all that was required of us - except maybe perhaps before a drill competition. Anyway it was announced that there was to be a commemorative church parade on the mid Sunday of our two weeks. Other units would be there including our tank chums from down the road whom we had been exercising with. Hussars, Dragoons or Armoured Corps? I cannot remember. (Research shows they were from 8th Armoured Brigade anyway!)

Smarten yourselves up a bit was the general cry from our leadership - so we dug out our best battledress, polished our boots and breathed on our brasses - but blancoing was out, due to there being no facilities for such avante-garde activity (we felt.) Also from a drivers point of view - as we were messing about with trucks most of the day - a little grubbiness was par for the course was it not? So there we were, feeling pretty smug about how smart and soldier like we looked despite the adverse conditions - lined up waiting for the armoured mob down the road to arrive. We then were to tuck ourselves in behind them and march to their band as they led us to church. We heard them coming from afar as they were led by their pretty impressive band. As they came over the hill in the morning sunlight they literally gleamed! As they neared we could see why. Each man was 'bulled-up' as if en-route to Buckingham Palace! Knife edged creases, gleaming boots plus brasses of dazzling perfection - and to cap it all medals, I ask you medals! Glinting and clinking in the sun. Feeling distinctly down-market, we tagged along behind this gleaming cavalcade and threw out our chests - basking in the reflected glory. We reasoned that every man amongst 'em had a personal iron with him - plus access to a plug, blanco etc - therefore their accommodation must have been far superior to ours!

Our own personal humorists had it that they all had their own 'bleedin' batman - as well as an iron and a power point! Still that's the cavalry for you. They were no strangers to Brasso that's for sure! We also imagined their superiors saying to them - "now you chaps, lets show these beastly infantry people who are the superior beings around here!" I jest of course but the whole thing was very impressive and showed a high degree of esprit-de-corps particularly as they were a reserve formation, with many ex - N/S men like us! Rather like the guardsmen on the boat en-route to Malaya - not allowed to be seasick like the rest of us. Very little else comes back to me about this particular fortnight's training - except I got home with my right arm in a sling. This was because of a badly gashed hand nearing the end of the two weeks, for I had caught one of the fuel tanks on my truck against a protruding tree stump. Examining this I slipped and fell - catching my hand on the torn metal as I went. Some stitching was required - and so the last day or two was spent in the passenger seat - or helping out in the M.T tent/office. Aunty was quite upset when I came back apparently 'damaged' - however the wound soon healed, although the scar is still with me today!

On the home front another opportunity had occurred which I'm glad I took advantage of, as it was again another of life's small but significant staging posts. These are present in most people's lives - and are often only apparent as you look back over your working life. In this case it was the offer from the firm to take up training for a window dressing position. This offered some pleasing prospects and I was glad to say yes! Having done the course and gained practical experience I found it very enjoyable work and it stimulated an artistic strain that I never knew I had. In many ways window dressing is like painting a portrait. You start with an empty window as your canvas and gradually create and build up a picture. This picture is in the shape of the various products you need to display as artistically as possible. When you put your training into practice - and the shop windows you are working on are on a busy main road and adjacent to well used bus stops - you really feel that the world is looking at you and it is quite challenging! (This small step was a career catalyst for me.)

We were all now of course 'soldiers of The Queen' - due to the passing away of King George the Sixth in 1952. There was general sadness at this event, for, to most of us at that time who had lived through world war two - he had shown the utmost dignity, courage and leadership. This throughout a period which in the early days looked like curtains for our country and commonwealth. Someone on high was on our side - that's certain, for even small boys like me were conscious of our country suffering defeat after defeat - until slowly but surely we began to win a few battles and the tide turned in our favour!

CHAPTER THIRTY THREE

When 1954 dawned many things were changing in my personal life. It was also the final year of TA service for me - and those of us who had been called up at the same time. We all looked forward to our release as the three weekends and a fortnight's compulsory camp were beginning to become irksome and impinged a little on our social lives - even though it was good to see old mates again and hear their news. I think my old mate 'Smithy' was married by this time and already had a young son!

I had also become engaged to the fair young thing on the shoe polish counter and was looking around for better prospects to fund a wedding - hopefully in the next year. By chance I answered an 'ad' in the local paper and found myself accepted for the post of travelling window dresser for a local brewery. I think the official title was display manager - which gave me a bit of a kick as it was the first time I had managed anything! The job - after gaining experience of the type of work involved was an absolute dream - although not without a fair amount of travel and general 'dashing about'. So, with the little Ford 8 van provided I sped around South Yorkshire, some of Lancashire and even a bit of Lincs. In those days most off-licences had shop windows available for product displays and some were in shops owned by the brewery - other 'free' houses allowed competitive breweries space from time to time so we would have our turn with the likes of Mackeson Stout, Guinness and later Watney's who had moved up into Yorkshire from their fiefdom in the London area.

So I would whizz around, van full of crepe paper, dummy bottles and showcards - and make my area beautiful with 'Jubilee Stout' displays - this being the company's major product, and a big seller too! What made the job so interesting was the variety of work involved for, as well as window displays I did displays above the bars in working mens clubs - also stands at exhibitions when they came up. We also did decorated floats for carnival processions and the like. The company was an excellent one to work for - being at that time owned by the Carter family who were very paternalistic and treated the staff very well. As with most breweries there was a generous free issue of beer per week for employees, plus you could buy wines and spirits at discount through the firms Wines & Spirits Department. Prior to working for the brewery I was not much of a drinking man as I have mentioned earlier. However I joined in with the swim and since that time have enjoyed a modest tipple (or two!)

When the brewery threw a party - they really threw one I can tell you. This new life style really opened my eyes as I was not aware of such things as, for instance, working mens clubs and their influence in the brewery world. Many were extremely large and had top class entertainment at weekends. The 'Dial House Club' in Sheffield for instance was enormous - and had a stage about the size of the Sheffield Empire Theatre! Big name entertainers performed here to hundreds of enthusiastic members whose consumption matched their enthusiasm! At this club, by the way, I had to change the display over the stage frontage which as I have said was enormous - balanced on top of the highest steps I had ever seen. Still I had a good head for heights in those days! Often I would be in attendance at the opening or refurbishment of a new pub - armed with a superior camera and flash which gave me my first taste of 'commercial' photography. This experience I was able to put to good advantage over the years!

Drafted over to Manchester one time on my 'circuit' I was taken to 'The Long Bar' of the Gaumont Cinema. Here I was to dress out a large showcase with the brewery products. I was taken there to be introduced by our area manager - who said to the bar chieftain something along the lines of "here's our nice new young display man, keep an eye on him for us won't you - we don't want him corrupted by any of your fast ladies - looking for custom." It appeared that this establishment was a well known picking up-point for ladies of the night (or day for that matter.) I was tickled pink by all this and assumed I had some innocent look about me. I could have told him that anyone who could pass up on the lovely ladies of the far east was unlikely to be tempted to sensual pleasures during business hours. Anyway, even had I been tempted - a busy schedule wouldn't have allowed it! (Nor would my wallet.)

Later that day or week - I was picked up by this same area boss and told to follow him to my next assignment. He had taken delivery recently of a new Ford Consul which could go a bit. He forgot poor old me in an underpowered little van and shot off at the rate of knots. I tried my level best to keep up but soon lost him. Then thinking I saw him ahead having just gone through some lights I hastened after this guy and followed him for many miles through the suburbs of Manchester. He was greatly surprised when I followed him up his driveway because as you will have already guessed - I was following the wrong man! Somehow I was reunited with my senior colleague who had backtracked, looking for me.

Anyone reading this could well by now be saying - what on earth has all this to do with soldiering and TA service? Surprisingly enough it has some relevance which I shall now relate. All this driving practice I was getting helped me to perform behind the wheel a great deal better. There was much night driving and also plenty of travel along the major trunk roads for me - so by the time our final 2 weeks training camp came along I was getting pretty hot stuff at the wheel! My little van had also tuned up reversing skills - for it had only two tiny windows in the back doors - necessitating leaning out with the drivers door held slightly open (with one hand) as you lined up your manoeuvre by squinting down the side of the vehicle. This was pretty helpful experience when backing up a lorry or half track - for again much of the time you could see nothing of your back end at all.

Now I must mention the brewery for which I worked just once more. The advertising office which was my base was in the centre of Sheffield - close to the City Hall and just off Rockingham Street to be precise. I was actually 'in' one day doing some paper work - when the door opened - admitting no less a person than my TA 'A' company commander, Major Hutton. I looked at him and he at me and we both said simultaneously "what are you doing here?" (Should I salute and call him 'Sir' I asked myself?) I jest of course - but it was a strange situation. Seemingly he represented a company which supplied publicity items to breweries like showcards - beer mats, bar towels, ashtrays and that sort of thing. His company was a regular supplier, and he was here to see my boss who was a high powered lady called Miss A.S Hart. Miss Hart was the first woman boss I had worked for and she was a formidable lady with a kind heart concealed 'neath a brusque exterior. Her kindness to me personally was immense - but that's another story. Amongst many attributes she was the only woman at the time in England to hold a speedway promoters licence - and she was also a director of the then flourishing Belle Vue complex in Manchester - some lady! The end of this story comes just a little later as we were being briefed on our next (and for me last) TA Camp

In the meantime the Hallamshires had just taken delivery of their half-track vehicles and we got to know them on one or more weekend schemes. They were magnificent beasts! Weighing about 7.5 tons, they were of U.S manufacture and thus left hand drive. They had a famous name - White's - a company then part of General Motors I think. A five litre engine rested beneath an armoured 'bonnet' and upon revving it up - all you heard was a muted, almost genteel 'swish'. There was nothing muted about the performance. With a section of squaddies in the back

172

- the thing would almost climb up a house side when warmed up! Fully armoured all round and with tiny slits for visibility when all the visors were down they would go anywhere. Two large front wheels guided a tracked rear system - which could be linked to a 'four wheel drive' unit which gave even greater traction when required. A huge winch lay across the front end, perched on the bumper - if so substantial a thing could be called a bumper! This ferocious looking beast had not been seen overmuch on British roads and it was illuminating to see other drivers give way when you were stopped say at a halt sign! The thing had a fifty gallon tank but only did a very modest seven miles to the gallon! I have to say I got on very well with this vehicle and felt very much at home in the driving seat.

Anyway, onward to the briefing session regarding our next camp, which was to be held at a battle training area in Norfolk slightly to the north of Thetford I think. Prior to the briefing we delivered to Endcliffe Hall our kit for the forthcoming camp, and for the first time I was able to drive up in my little brewery van instead of carting it up on the bus. Many and varied were the conveyances doing precisely the same including the knock-out new Humber Snipe 'limo', a 21st present to one of our number from a wealthy haulage contractor Dad! Being one of the lads - he had brought his mates and their gear up too - in a style to which they were completely unaccustomed!

Major Hutton took the briefing and explained that our new CO wished us to march down to the station - led by the recently formed regimental band. He then added a joke for my benefit on the lines of "young Ives will dress a few off-licence windows on our way down! (Nice one.) The march was of some four or five miles - through the town centre eventually and thence to Midland station which lay adjacent. So this we did and had a good audience of Saturday shoppers as we crunched our way through. I think we did it 'proper' with rifles and fixed bayonets - as the regiment had the right to do that in those days.

The last camp for me passed speedily I'm glad to say, but some memories remain. Again we were under canvas but the weather was lovely. We exercised with tanks as before - but this time we could do it as prescribed with the benefit of our half-tracks. These were waiting for us on the camp and 'my' guys in the back expressed their pleasure at my new found driving skills. SMOOTH! They would shout as we pulled away without a single judder! Having experience of being in a tangled heap on the floor - as it was when we hit the bus in Malaya - I could understand their feelings. Sometimes it was quite an adventure - line abreast with some twenty or so half tracks dashing across open country taking every obstacle in your stride! At the end of week one, during one exercise, I heard an ominous clanking sound from the direction of the steering as a tight turn was made.

Declaring me 'U/S' - my blokes were transferred to another vehicle and departed, having promised to call up the R.E.M.E to cart me away. So there I was in the wilderness listening to the Larks singing on high and wondering how long before aid came. It took a long time before help arrived - during which time I had written to my beloved and caught up with my correspondence in general. Eventually in late afternoon help arrived in the shape of a R.E.M.E corporal-fitter who said something along the lines of "it's unusual to have anything go wrong with one of these - they're built like bloody tanks - what have you being a-doing to it!" An appropriate joke as we were playing with tanks at the time. "Will it drive he said?" Yes I said - "so drive it back then said he." We trundled back and I got some queer looks from our friend as the thing behaved perfectly! (Typical garage scenario wasn't it.) "There's a funny noise coming from the steering chums!" Which, when you go to pick it up generally elicits the cheery response - "we can't find anything wrong with it!"

This was the case here, and I was getting hot and still hotter under the collar, expecting a big rocket from both the fitter and my officer. Just as I had given up hope and was turning into the vehicle park, mercifully it did its expensive crunching noise, which had our friend leaping about a bit and deciding a major refit was necessary. As there wasn't a spare bus about, young Pagdin - a fellow driver, found suddenly he had an unexpected co-driver whether he wanted one or nay - so it was on with the show! We did various exercises simulating for instance, brake failure - necessitating driving on gears only. Good one that - try it some time. Other things included emergency recovery, a bit of maintenance and quite a lot of night work. I think we spent all night out on at least one occasion which made you appreciate any bed - even in a tent. For even in summer, a vehicle is a cold bedroom! We had a contingent of motor cycle despatch riders amongst us too - most trained like we were. They zoomed up and down convoys - directed traffic at junctions and generally showed off on their B.S.As. Dangerous caper this one was - and not for me chums! Many of these 'Don R's, as they were called in army parlance were like I had been - not able to afford a vehicle or driving lessons - whereas the TA offered the licence and something to drive too!

Not a great deal of excitement happened during our time in Norfolk. Night time R&R was a 'passion waggon' into Thetford. I went just the once to this pleasant olde-worlde town and can recall little of it. The middle weekend saw us with transport laid on, having almost a full day in Great Yarmouth. All I can remember over the years now is what a lovely day it was and I have no doubt it was a pleasant interlude during a hectic fortnight of training. Our new CO had strong ideas about smartness and we did a fair amount of drill. This time - with no 'sciving' off for drivers either! We also continued range firing of rifles and Brens - for even in the TA you had to keep re-qualifying!

Not much else about this final annual training stays in my memory except that our new platoon commander decided I would be his driver at next years camp. "Oh! No I won't I said - time's up for this warrior." " You'll be signing on again won't you Ives - think of the extra cash etc." Anyway promising to think about it, it was left at that - but I didn't think my lovely new wife to be would be too keen on me leaping off for various training weekends and a fortnight's annual training, no sir! We returned to Sheffield with due ceremony. The train pulled into Midland Station and the CO's silver bugler disembarked and blew for battalion muster. We then formed up as on the square did the appropriate musketry drill and marched back to barracks - headed by the band - who had just about got through their entire repertoire by the time we had trudged to Endcliffe Hall, the latter part of the journey being uphill.

The final weekend training session does stay in my memory for two reasons. The first was that we went to a training ground in Sherwood Forest - which is not far from the Sheffield area incidently. Here it had been decided that we would undergo a mock 'strafing' from the air, by the RAF to simulate one of the hazards encountered from time to time by armoured columns during a real life war. All I can say that I would not wish to be present during the real thing! The jets that did the attack were pretty good at it and it wasn't hard to imagine what it would be like for real. We were camouflaged up for the event but they found us all right and we would have been in a right mess had it been for real. I think we had some Brens positioned for anti-aircraft defence - which would have been useless as the speed of the planes as they dived upon you (and then disappeared) was extraordinary, and only a lucky shot would have hit one. The din was horrendous!

My second memory was of doing my last ever guard duty (or stag.) We did an hour each guarding our vehicles during the night, despite the fact we were miles from anywhere or anything for that matter. Like many ex-servicemen, it is hard to take in the apparent laxity of today where it appears that many camps are guarded by civilian security staff. The word being that squaddies cannot be spared from their training and other duties. Nobody likes doing guard (except perhaps a Gurkha) but let's face it in this day and age it would seem an absolute necessity to me!

So, having done my two years and three and a half in reserve my time was up as a 'musket bearer'. Major Hutton asked me to consider signing up for a further period, but although I had great admiration for him - he did not press the point when I told him I'd had enough, one way and another. So, there it was - without any ceremony I was no longer 22139844 Private Ives but a 'Mr' once again. After this, only one other military engagement was to take place for me. Despite the end of all our military careers we were still technically on reserve for a further period of several years! I subsequently received a summons - and a rail warrant to attend for a medical at a barracks in Pontefract! This was just before the Suez crisis in 1956 - so I had a nasty feeling that I might just be singing "Good Bye Dolly - I Must Leave You" when that particular balloon went up. However I wasn't - but it occurs to me that I was never officially notified when the official reserve period was up! Oh heck! better keep my shoes well bulled up eh!

Some coincidences remain - touching on my time with the Hallamshire Battalion. Attending a social function down here in Devon one evening, years ago, I was chatting to the father of our daughter's school friend - and the army came up in the conversation. Not only had he lived for a time in Sheffield this man had actually held a commission in The Hallamshires in the early sixties! He enjoyed some of my stories particularly the one about a whole platoon of us - in uniform, being marched into the George Hotel in Hathersage (a very posh watering hole indeed) to be served with a pint of best bitter on the platoon commander who had something to celebrate. Strangely enough I was to live not far from this famous hostelry three years later - but at the time was quite unaware of this of course. He, in turn was able to tell me that Major Hutton eventually became Commanding Officer of the battalion!

Another coincidence came about by reading a very good novel based on The Somme battle of WW1 - in which is described the story of a City Battalion being trained up from raw recruits to one of the finest fighting units ever produced by the town. It took a year to build and mould this battalion, and it was wiped out in just a few terrible minutes by machine guns. The main coincidence for me was that - one of the book's heroes is a trainee reporter from *The Sheffield Telegraph* newspaper. He volunteers for this local outfit and it is through his eyes that the story unfolds. When I read this I found it very strange because my Uncle Frederick really was a trainee reporter on this very newspaper

- and he also volunteered to serve in the army. The difference being that my uncle was commissioned into The Royal Engineers - was gassed at the battle of Cambrai and was then transferred to The Royal Flying Corps! In WW2 this kindly man became a Major in what I believe was a Hallamshire Battalion Home Guard. In 1945 as a youth of fourteen I had proudly watched him leading his company during the Victory Parade at the end of hostilities in Europe!

One final coincidence if you will bear with me. Like many other people I enjoy 'The Antiques Road Show' T/V programme. A few weeks ago it came from Yorkshire and lo! and behold, one of the items brought in was a Hallamshire Battalion (infantry pattern) helmet from the late 1800's, which had been in the present owners family for many years. The expert gave the history of the unit at the time the helmet would have been worn. I was completely knocked out by the fact that apparently they were mobilised after some terrible defeats to the British in South Africa - and sent out to fight in the Boer War thousands of miles away! Just imagine the scene in a few hundred homes of the period when dad (or son) came back from a training weekend and saying to his loved ones "sorry about this folks - but we're off to South Africa to fight the Boers!" "Be back as soon as I can!" Couple or so years later they came back! Please remember - this was a reserve unit of weekend soldiers! Made our moaning about three quiet years in the T/A seem like a Sunday School picnic.

So my personal war with Chairman Mau and 'Uncle' Joe Stalin was over, as was a completely undistinguished military career. Strange to relate but when things were gloomy some wag was bound to pronounce a constantly recurring line of soldier-speak i.e 'Stalin for King - and home for Christmas!' In view of the newly revealed history of the Russian Communist Party - this would most certainly not have been a good idea on reflection!

The struggle to beat the communists in Malaya went on for many years - and is well documented. However it was as late as 1968 before the final 'comrade' came down from the hills with his hands metaphorically 'up'. This gives some idea of the tenacity of our opponents and many epic encounters took place before the red menace could be considered over. It was a splendid victory - but somewhat played down at the end many felt. The Brits did what others significantly failed to do in South East Asia and that was achieved only by a long drawn out but determined struggle. The end could not have been achieved without the help and co-operation of the local population - and in the end democracy triumphed!

As mentioned earlier, terrorist incidents in Malaya peaked (so I read) in 1952 - co-inciding with the arrival of the then General Templar (who was hand picked by Winston Churchill recently re-elected as British Prime Minister) - and from then on slowly but surely, the security forces gained the upper hand. But this is not to say that anyone had it 'easy' - the terrorists saw to that. Every book on the subject indicates that the conflict had found the right leader - and it was he who 'dynamised' the campaigning!

Independence came to Malaya in 1957 and the communists then became the enemy of all the Malayan peoples - and so the 'Emergency' was considered over in 1960! However diehard members of terrorist groups were still in jungle hideaways and began surrendering slowly at first - but the trickle became a flood as financial incentives were offered plus guarantees of safe conduct and future citizenship. On the subject of financial inducements, I have been amazed to read that at the height of the 'Emergency' large sums of money were offered to any terrorists who would desert the cause and surrender to the authorities. Many did take up the offer and deserted. Although the rewards were large, they were a good investment from a government point of view, as the surrendered terrorists (S.E.P's) - happily led patrols back to the camps they themselves had recently deserted!

There was an 'undercover war' running parallel to the one we knew as footsloggers or 'ulu bashers', This was a secret war of intelligence operations against communist supporters and associates as well as mainstream operations. If the famous 'Q' - of James Bond fame had been around then - he could have cut his teeth on some of the gadgetry that was employed against the communists with considerable success! Much of this is illustrated in the excellent book by Noel Barber - entitled *The War of the Running Dogs* - and published by Arrow books. Contrary to what we believed it seems that arms and ammunition were getting through to the terrorists from over the border with Thailand! I mentioned earlier that we believed that only the arms left over from WW2 were ranged against us.

I read also that some thirty eight famous British county regiments were involved in the Malayan campaign - plus various Guards, Artillery and Armoured Regiments with of course Gurkhas from various brigades, and surprisingly enough some units from the Commonwealth. Also later on, various formations recruited from the Malay peninsula played an increasing role. From my native heath of Yorkshire, not only were The East and West Yorkshires involved but also the K.O.Y.L.I (Kings Own Yorks. Light Infantry.)

Possibly a humorous vignette about The K.O.Y.L.I was told to me by 'Jungle Joe' - my best mate in Malaya. When he came to do his TA reserve training - he found himself posted to them. Now the light infantry do everything at the double - and their marching pace is much quicker than the normal infantry. Joe was amazed to find that on the command 'get on parade', they were all fallen in before he'd started off!

Our regiment, The Green Howards, were pretty early in the field in the Malayan conflict and learned the hard way the secrets of jungle lore. They earned their corn all right, and had a respectable scoreboard of terrorists eliminated and captured before leaving Malaya in 1953. I was pleased to read in Major Oldfield's excellent book *The Green Howards in Malaya* (published by Gale & Polden) that 'D' company - my alma mater, came second in the battalion's scoreboard of terrorists eliminated and captured. This was not achieved without a downside, including the loss of the 'D' company commander, Major Chadwick, following an ambush in 1952.

In 1953 the battalion left Malaya - marking a further chapter in a distinguished fighting history. No one who was with the regiment - however 'un-regimental' in outlook can fail to be impressed by the fine record of The Green Howards. Wherever the action was, over the centuries, they seemed to be there making a distinguished contribution!

As long as I live I'm sure I shall never forget my time with the regiment and service in Malaya. Three things take me back to those days in a flash. Newly turned earth in the garden, particularly when moving a shrub for instance. Digging seems to produce a similar odour to what can only be described as a jungle 'smell'. The call of monkeys from the tall trees frequently heard in nature programmes - (often heard but rarely seen in our case,) is another. The third - not often played now, is a very old song called I think 'The Rose of San Antone' - this number was constantly on the lips of one Danny Kemp - so much so that we all began to sing the thing till it became engraved almost on our vocal cords. Where are you now Danny boy?

I would certainly like to return to Malaya some day and do a tour around the areas and places that are still so familiar in my mind. A couple of years ago I was a guest at the annual reunion of 'The Somersets' a light infantry regiment who went to Malaya around 1954. During the evening a slide show was presented by an ex-squaddie from the their ranks who had recently returned from a nostalgia tour of Malaysia. 'Twas something of a revelation for us - as the small townships we had all known in our convoy escort days (and sometimes bases) were now large flourishing cities. Bentong - our first H/Q as new arrivals, is now seemingly a University town! It is pretty well known too now, that Kuala Lumpur currently boasts the worlds tallest building! It also boasts the worlds most ornate railway station - which most certainly was there in our day.

A postcript to my visit to the reunion was seeing a familiar face coming towards me during the evening. Amazingly enough he was a work colleague of my wife's from Tavistock. Needless to say our opening words were "what are you doing here!" Roy attends this reunion every year, although he himself was a regular - many if not most of those present were National Servicemen! I see Roy on many occasions now at social functions and we always have a natter about 'the old days!' He told me about one of their areas set midst dire swampland and how compass bearings were of necessity the order of the day - with men calling out the number of paces taken lest they plunge into the morass. All this being part and parcel of their normal patrolling. The reason they had to do this and be in there, was that the enemy (probably feeling safe) were in there too.

On the subject of great changes in Malaysia, I had been told of some of these some years before - but it was seeing the slide programme that brought it all home to me. Back in the eighties I worked for a large organisation that had an export department. Within this department worked a very attractive oriental lassie - who from time to time I had some dealings with. On one occasion I asked where she came from and was amazed to hear her birthplace and home town was Ipoh. I was able to tell her that I had been to Ipoh many times - 'before she was but a twinkle in her daddy's eye' - as the old saying goes! She was impressed! (I think.) Anyway having heard that I hoped to go back one day she remarked on the huge explosion of the towns and cities, and cited as an example some of her fathers experiences. Seemingly he had been Chief of Police in Ipoh - but the place had grown so much - what with flyovers and underpasses etc - that whenever he got the car out he frequently found himself lost in his own city!

Talking of acquaintances - on holiday recently I met a man from Bolton who had been in Malaya at the same time as me. Apparently he had been a 'Medical Corps' man and had spent his entire service out there on permanent train duty, ferrying sick and wounded squaddies to hospitals up and down the peninsula. The trains, he told me, had been shot up on many occasions!

During 1997, the world heard much about the huge pall of smoke that had spread and hung across Malaysia from the tremendous forest fires burning out of control. Perhaps some of the rain forest we stalked and sometimes hacked our way through has now disappeared? However one thing is for sure, and that is that it wouldn't have happened in our day the ceaseless daily and nightly rain would have stopped it dead in its tracks!

Since coming to live down in deepest Devon (the girl from the shoe polish counter and I) - we are a pretty long way from Richmond - and any connection with the old regiment really. However, many coincidences abound. We now live just a couple of hours drive from Dunster Castle - where The Green Howards were originally raised in 1688! We shop regularly in Exeter (about 45 mins away) where the regiment had its first 'posting' upon the arrival of the Prince of Orange! Our 'new' neighbours, when we arrived here a quarter century ago were also Northerners. Ron and Norah were lovely people and were devoted to the Scout movement. Norah had Green Howard connections as her father had been a senior NCO with the Regiment in WW1. She was able to proudly show me some crested silverware he had won at shooting!

Like my father he had been gassed and wounded but unlike Dad was later captured. One of the last to be repatriated - he married still in his hospital 'blues'. He then devoted much of his life to the training of Army Cadets. Many of 'his' boys served in WW2, and the family remembers survivors of Dunkirk visiting him - and thanking him for the training that had helped them survive! A picture of this formidable warrior and a press cutting about his life are reproduced in this volume.

Very recently an acquaintance down here said to me (we were discussing rivers at the time) - and he had no idea that I'd ever heard of Richmond - did I know that Tavistock and Richmond in Yorkshire had the unique distinction of having the fastest rising rivers in Britain! As Michael Caine would say 'not a lot of people know that!' Yet another coincidence. My other neighbour was a career soldier in intelligence. He said to me some months ago - your old mob are actually in the Telegraph today and passed me the cutting. Seemingly King Harald V of Norway (Honorary Colonel in Chief of the regiment) and Field Marshal Sir Peter Inge CIGS - the country's leading soldier and formerly a Green Howard, were to receive Honorary Degrees at Lancaster University. The report said in conclusion that 'the University organist is currently rehearsing the Green Howards regimental march'. It occurred to me that I had not heard this march since 1951 - so I wrote to Lancaster University to ask if the organist would very kindly grant me an audio tape perhaps of one of his rehearsals.

Surprisingly enough they had not seen the press cutting and were very chuffed about the write up! So much so that they did much better than an audio tape by sending a video of the whole event plus the official programme. The whole thing was very moving and to hear the old regimental march again after so many years was nostalgic to say the least! I shared the viewing (by sending the tape) with Jim, who was best man at our wedding also many years ago now. Jim was the guy who married Marjorie the little cigarette girl from the earlier part of this story. Wouldn't you know it - he was also a Green Howard. Rather a different one though as he had been a commando at the end of WW2 - and one of the youngest warrant officers yet in the regiment I believe.

As I reach the end of this narrative about the trials and tribulations of National Service I can hear the slightly sceptical reader saying "why after almost 50 years is this man going on about his old regiment, when quite plainly it wasn't all beer and skittles by a long chalk." It could also be said that he (and many others - were very pleased when the two years were up!) I don't really know the answer to this one. I suppose the regiment was the 'university' of our era - not that we of that time had a cat in hell's chance of going to such a place. However, those that have, will never ever I feel sure, forget their time at Bristol, Liverpool, Leicester Sheffield or wherever. Neither will they forget the scrapes they got into, their tutor's - and above all the friends they made there.

Thus I suppose it is with most us! Our campuses (to quote the University analogy) were spread far and wide and were international in their flavour. National Servicemen served and fought in many locations from Malaya, Korea, Aden, Africa (following the Mau Mau uprising) Cyprus, to Suez - and I'm sure there were others to test their mettle!

Mind you it wasn't all horror stories. An acquaintance of mine was due to go to Korea - not the most pleasant of locations. Suddenly, and with no explanation he found himself switched to a draft to Bermuda - where he spent a glorious two years of colonial splendour!

Just a word in conclusion about modern youth. A very maligned species it would seem. At the moment press reports keep surfacing about the lack of fitness of to-days typical young man and his general 'softness' and unsuitability in many cases for service life. Trainers are held responsible for a downgrading of many a foot, and central heating supposedly has weakened our ability to cope with adverse temperatures. Recently, down here in the West Country an apparent recruiting drive by The Royal Marines has concentrated on getting back former marines - whose physical prowess has already been tested!

My own view is that if and when the chips are down for us all again - the nation's young men will respond just as countless young men have responded before. My generation - some of whom wore boots to work, and who had never heard of central heating still found service life tough. Our feet still blistered on route marches - and we still froze in ice cold barrack rooms. Each generation supposes its successors are weaker and less determined than they, I guess.

An example of this came from my father, a WW1 veteran. I was 'reunited' with the majority of my family who resided in the London area - when we moved down from Sheffield to live in Reading in 1962. My father it emerged had joined the regular army in 1910 and had some fascinating tales to tell. All my brothers saw service as either National Servicemen or regulars and when one or two of us were together we might have moaned about some aspects of service life, possibly about punishments we saw or may have received. "Field punishment" - said our Dad, grimly, "in those days they tied you to a wagon wheel - flogged you - and left you hanging to the wheel in the sun to reflect on your crime - and expected you to be back on duty the next day!" There is no answer to that one.

I'm glad The Green Howards remain still an independent regiment - unmerged as far as I know with any other. When I was with them all those years ago, they had a battle-cry. From whence it came I know not - but it was 'Geronimo - and up The Green Howards'.

THEREFORE,
"GERONIMO- AND UP THE GREEN HOWARDS."

The End

POSTSCRIPT

To paraphrase President Kennedy at his inaugural address - it could well be asked - "what did you do for your country during National Service?"

It is a difficult question to answer, but I suppose after training we were completely, utterly and entirely available to go where and whence our government decided there was a need. In my own case - having volunteered for service in Malaya I was partly responsible for what followed.

All of us who served out there were defenders of an outpost of the Raj as it then was, and our bodies were offered up to a sometimes almost troglodyte existence in the dark rain forests of the Malay Peninsula - where we were the target of every biting stinging insect known to man - carrying unbelievable weights upon our backs and loaded with weaponry and marching for weeks on end sometimes. As well as the unforgiving conditions of the terrain there was also a determined politically motivated adversary - wiser perhaps than we in the arts of jungle lore and survival!

In the case of Malaya we conscripts, together with our regular army associates - were the finger in the dyke against a flood of far eastern Communism, which history records as a significant victory for the Brits. Many gave their lives and their health in achieving this. So this I can say - I played a very small part in preserving the freedom of a state in the making - for very soon after my time out there Malaya gained her independence!

Malaysia itself is now a prosperous, amalgam of nations - well able to take care of its own affairs and the defence of its shores

Here in Britain many call for the return of National Service as a means of finding a role for difficult, unemployed - and perhaps rootless, young men. The discipline would do them good they say. Perhaps it might - but a huge army of conscripts with no empire to police and very few (if any) garrisons overseas would be a recipe for large scale boredom. You cannot go on whitewashing coal for ever!

In our day there were many places to go and many small wars to fight and we went where we were sent without complaint because that was how it was. Our fathers, uncles and perhaps older brothers had just emerged from a world conflict of enormous magnitude - what was two years in comparison with that?.

So times have changed - today's young men do not have their employment prospects blunted any more as were ours by the onset of National Service - but sadly such is the irony of history, for many, there are just no jobs at all!

The other question is of course - what did National Service do for you?

Jokingly, at one time I would have said "learned me how to light a fag - at 60 miles per hour on the back of a 15cwt Dodge truck" - which indeed it did. (I'm still fag lighter by appointment to the Memsahib - when conditions dictate - even though I gave up years ago!)

However there was far more to it than that needless to say. From being a slightly scruffy individual I emerged fully into the camp of well pressed clothes and clean shiny shoes. Appearance really mattered in the army at that time - and it was very hard to break the habit. I could also take care of myself in the catering department. Jungle cooking - such as it was, ensured that the basics were understood well enough - and added to this of course was the ability to wash clothes, iron them and put them away straight! Darning and button sewing were essential skills for us all as well - for in the services nobody, but nobody does it for you!

Getting on with people from all walks of life was another attribute and being able to accept the discipline of the workplace another. Many of the lessons we learned free of charge, are being duplicated now on expensive 'team building' courses - the concept being fully understood currently in the world of commerce and big business!

Running parallel to this was of course the comradeship bit. Difficult to define comradeship when you haven't experienced it in the true sense. These days it would have to be classed as 'teamwork' probably - but as I have stated earlier, men who had served in some of the war's hot spots were coming back into the services because civilian life could not replace this vital ingredient in their lives!

Whether the ability to spot a leader at five miles range is an asset or not I'm not sure - but most of us could and undoubtedly still can. Sadly it is an art form rarely found these days - particularly in the field of politics! We all came across leaders who we would have followed anywhere - others we would have to follow as discipline and rank demanded - but we might not have been so close behind if you know what I mean!

You could also say by contrast that you undoubtedly knew your own leadership potential. I for one, never felt that I had what it took to be a leader - and was very happy at that time to be led! Technical competence is a good thing - but it doesn't necessarily make you a good leader.

Whether things might have developed for me had I stayed on is a matter for conjecture. Natural leadership is an inborn thing. It is often a force transcending both background and education - although these in themselves can be half way to getting there. Most leaders have strong personalities but all true leaders have that indefinable something.

So, all in all perhaps National Service for most of us was a fifty-fifty thing. Some people hated it - and went to great lengths to 'escape' - but most endured it. All from time to time had moments of pride, and looking back, now, it was the making of many of us. The phrase 'standing on your own two feet' comes to mind - for very few who emerged after two years couldn't!

Was it a waste of time? Today's young man might think so. So many jobs today demand youth and all that goes with it. Young traders in the City would be a good example of this. At the time of which I write things didn't move as fast - and most senior people - or bosses if you like - were generally much older and more mature than today's. What National Service did do for many was to alter their perception of the job they had been doing before call up - so that a fair number changed their tack and decided to do something else afterwards.

Similarly with personal relations. The girl you left behind often changed considerably in the two years you were away - as indeed did you. No one knows the percentage of failed romances after National Service - but I'll bet it was quite high.

What more can I say? Looking back I have to say that the whole thing changed my life - as it undoubtedly did thousands of others. Our lives had been turned upside down and we looked at things totally differently on our return to civvy-street. The same no doubt as young people of today have their perceptions challenged at University or College. Nothing is quite the same afterwards. We have seen a different life and in many ways it was what we made of our experiences afterwards that was the important thing.

One thing is for sure - we could never be the same again.